ETHICAL INTERSECTIONS

Ethical Intersections

Health research, methods and researcher responsibility

EDITED BY JEANNE DALY

WestviewPress

A Division of HarperCollins*Publishers*

First published in Sydney, Australia, 1996 by
Allen & Unwin Pty Ltd
9 Atchison Street, St Leonards, NSW 2065 Australia
Phone:(61 2) 9901 4088
Fax:(61 2) 9906 2218
E-mail: 100252.103@compuserv.com

Published in 1996 in the United States of America by
Westview Press, Inc.,
5500 Central Avenue,
Boulder, Colorado 80301–2877

Library of Congress Cataloguing-in-Publication
Data available upon request

Set in 10/12pt Goudy Old Style by DOCUPRO, Sydney
Printed by KHL Printing Co Pte Limited, Singapore

10 9 8 7 6 5 4 3 2 1

CONTENTS

*F*IGURES AND TABLES

FIGURES

TABLES

ACKNOWLEDGMENTS

These papers were written for a conference on research ethics funded by St Vincent's Hospital, the Australian Institute for Health and Welfare, and the Research and Development Grants Advisory Committee of the Australian Federal Department of Human Services and Health. Ian McDonald and Evan Willis made an invaluable contribution to the organisation of the conference and to developing the ideas for this volume.

CONTRIBUTORS

Ian Anderson is Chief Executive Officer of the Victorian Aboriginal Health Service in Melbourne. He is a medical practitioner and doing postgraduate research in sociology. He is the author of *Koorie Health in Koorie Hands* (Koorie Health Unit, Health Department, Victoria, 1988).

Max Charlesworth is Emeritus Professor, formerly Professor of Philosophy and Dean of the School of Humanities at Deakin University, Melbourne. In 1990 he was made an officer of the Order of Australia (AO) for his contribution to philosophy and bioethics. He is the author of *Life, Death, Genes and Ethics* (ABC Books, 1989) and *Bioethics in a Liberal Society* (Cambridge University Press, 1993).

Jeanne Daly holds a PhD in sociology, and also holds degrees in environmental science and chemistry. She teaches medical sociology and research method in the School of Sociology and Anthropology at La Trobe University. She is co-editor of *Researching Health Care: designs, dilemmas and disciplines* (Routledge, 1992), *Technologies in Health Care: Policies and politics* (Australian Government Publishing Service, 1987) and *The Social Sciences and Health Research* (Public Health Association, 1990).

Alvan R. Feinstein is Sterling Professor of Medicine and Epidemiology in the School of Medicine, Yale University, New Haven. He pioneered the field of clinical epidemiology and has received many international awards for his work. He is editor of the *Journal of Clinical Epidemiology* and the author of a large number of books and articles. His books include the landmark publication *Clinical Judgment* (Williams & Wilkins, 1967), as well as *Clinical Biostatistics* (C.V. Mosby, 1977), *Clinical Epidemiology: the archi-*

tecture of clinical research (W.B. Saunders, 1985) and *Clinimetrics* (Yale University Press, 1987).

Rhonda Galbally is director of the Victorian Health Promotion Foundation, a funding body which supports health research and health promotion programs through a tax on tobacco sales. She has a long history of activism in the health and social services fields.

Gordon Guyatt is a Professor of Medicine and Clinical Epidemiology and Biostatistics at McMaster University, Canada. He has a distinguished publishing career in the fields of clinical trials methodology, quality of life measurement, and technology assessment. He has contributed extensively to the evidence-based medicine movement in medical education and practice and is editor of a series of papers in Journal of the American Medical Association entitled 'User's Guides to the Medical Literature'.

Terri Jackson is senior research fellow in the Monash University Health Economics Unit of the Centre for Health Program Evaluation, Melbourne. She has had a long association with the consumer health movement. Her research interests are in costing and utilisation management of hospital services and resource allocation in health care. She is a member of the Australian Health Ethics Committee.

Allan Kellehear is senior lecturer in the School of Sociology and Anthropology, La Trobe University, Melbourne. He has published widely and is the author of a number of books, including *The Unobtrusive Researcher: a guide to methods* (Allen & Unwin, 1993) and co-editor of *Health Research in Practice* Vol. 1 (Chapman and Hall, 1993) and Vol. 2 (Chapman and Hall, 1996).

Hal Kendig conducts and teaches applied research as director of the Lincoln Gerontology Centre in the Faculty of Health Sciences at La Trobe University. He is a Fellow of the Academy of Social Sciences in Australia, a Life Member of the Australian Council on the Ageing, and a member of the Australian Health Ethics Committee.

Paul Komesaroff is active in the areas of clinical endocrinology, medical research and the philosophy of medicine. He is executive director of the Eleanor Shaw Centre for the Study of Medicine, Society and Law at the Baker Medical Research Institute, Melbourne. He is the author of *Objectivity, Science and Society* (Routledge & Kegan Paul, 1986), editor of *Troubled Bodies: critical perspectives on postmodernism, medical ethics and the body* (Duke, 1995) and co-editor of *Reinterpreting Menopause* (Routledge, forthcoming).

Richard Larkins is the James Stewart Professor of Medicine at the University of Melbourne.

Pranee Liamputtong Rice was born in a small town in the south of Thailand. She is senior lecturer in the School of Sociology and Anthropology, La Trobe University, Melbourne, and Research Fellow at the Centre for Mothers' and Children's Health. Her research into the experience of migrant women during childbirth has been published in *My Forty Days* (The Vietnamese Antenatal/Postnatal Support Project, 1993) and *Asian Mothers, Australian Birth* (Ausmed, 1994).

Judith Lumley was director of the Centre for Mothers' and Children's Health at Monash University, Melbourne. She is now director of the National Perinatal Epidemiology Unit at Oxford University. Her books include *Birth Rites, Birth Rights* (Penguin, 1980) and *Missing Voices* (Oxford University Press, 1994).

Ian McDonald is director of the Centre for the Study of Clinical Practice, St Vincent's Hospital, Melbourne. He is the author of *Introduction to Echocardiography* (Thomas, 1976) and many medical articles. He was given the award of Pioneer in Echocardiography by the World Federation of Ultrasound in Medicine and Biology.

Paul M. McNeill is Associate Professor of Law and Ethics in the Faculty of Medicine, University of New South Wales, Sydney. He has published *The Ethics and Politics of Human Experimentation* (Cambridge University Press, 1993) and papers in international journals reporting his studies of research ethics committees.

Peter Mudge is Clinical Dean of the North Queensland Clinical School of the University of Queensland. He has published widely in the field of general practice, has had a long commitment to rural health and is renowned for his pioneering work on Ross River fever.

William Noble is Associate Professor in the Department of Psychology, University of New England, Armidale. He has a long-time research interest in the social dimension of behaviour with a special emphasis on hearing impairment.

Terry Nolan is Associate Professor in the University of Melbourne's Department of Paediatrics, and head of its Clinical Epidemiology and Biostatistics Unit. His research focuses include vaccine safety and efficacy, and the causes and prevention of child injury.

Howard Waitzkin is Professor of Internal Medicine and Social Sciences, University of California, Irvine, and Attending Physician at the North Orange County Community Clinic in Anaheim, California. His research addresses the overlap between clinical care and medical sociology and he has published widely in this field. His books include *The Politics of Medical Encounters: how patients and doctors deal with social problems* (Yale University

Press, 1991) and *The Second Sickness: contradictions of capitalist health care* (Free Press, 1983).

Johanna Wyn is director of the Youth Research Centre at The University of Melbourne. She is the author of many monographs, reports and articles on young people. Recently completed work includes studies of the educational and policy implications of sexually transmitted diseases for young women, and of the continuing significance of early school leaving for Australian education and training policy. She is co-author of *Shaping Futures: youth action for livelihood* (Allen & Unwin).

INTRODUCTION

ETHICS, RESPONSIBILITY AND HEALTH RESEARCH

Jeanne Daly and Ian McDonald

The rise of bioethics as a discipline has been rapid (Fox, 1990: 203–4), and has been accompanied by changes in its focus, with the expansion first of biomedical research, then of health services research. Our experience as health researchers has persuaded us that bioethics has not been of as much benefit to the researcher as it might have been. Of particular concern has been the tendency of institutional ethics committees to judge research proposals according to abstract ethical principles which researchers have found to be simplistic, inappropriate or irrelevant. Researchers, we believe, have their own local knowledges about how best to conduct responsible ethical research, but these are fluid, tentative and dependent on specific contexts and discourses. The justification for this book is to take stock of developments in the ethics of health research over the past 30 years from the perspective of the researcher in the field.

The essays presented here do not encompass all current debates in bioethics. Rather, it is our intention to give the stage to researchers some of whom have never before formally considered the ethics of research practice. Papers have been selected to demonstrate the care which many researchers in various local contexts bring to the task of ensuring that their research is ethically sound, an issue easily overlooked in a simplistic regulatory process.

ETHICS AND HEALTH RESEARCH

Medical science and public health as an arm of the welfare state, both products of the last century, have had only a short time to reflect upon and to evolve their ethical positions. Clinical ethics, on the other hand, codified by Hippocrates and modified by Judaeo-Christian beliefs and values, has evolved over thousands of years in intimate relation to medical practice (Temkin, 1991). During the rise of medicine as a profession, traditional medical ethics became conflated with etiquette, with customs related to dealing with patients, and with the behaviour of one doctor towards another, aimed at the protection of medical self-interest (Rothman, 1990: 185). Prominent features of this tendency were a paternalistic attitude towards revealing information about illness and treatment (Katz, 1984), and a reluctance among doctors to criticise one another.

The Hippocratic clinical tradition was not immediately relevant to laboratory-based biomedical research. The growth of modern bioethics as a discipline owes more to the soul searching which followed gross abuse of medical research in Nazi concentration camps (Pence, 1995: 184–9). Following the Nuremberg trials of 1946, the judges enunciated ethical principles for human experimentation which became known as the Nuremberg Code (Pence, 1995:188). This was subsequently incorporated into the World Medical Association's much-quoted Helsinki Declaration of 1964. In the 1960s, in the United States, attention was focused on human experimentation more generally by the revelation of examples of abuses which threatened the life and well-being of subjects (Shenkin, 1991:232–3). A case which provoked much concern was the Tuskaloosa experiment, in which treatment was withheld from black patients with syphilis in order to study the disease (Pence, 1995:189–204). Another key event, however, was the publication by Henry Beecher (1966), a respected figure in the U.S. research establishment, of specific instances of serious abuse of trust by health researchers (Rothman, 1990:189–90).

Disclosures such as these led to the perception that some researchers were breaching not only ethical standards but basic tenets of human decency. It aroused the fear that such abuses might be widespread. The political reaction in the U.S. was manifest as pressure on the National Institutes of Health to promulgate guidelines for human experimentation (Barber, 1981: 327–8). In the background, argues Rothman (1990: 190–6), was additional concern about the ethics of science provoked by issues arising from the Second World War, especially the use of nuclear weapons. There was also an atmosphere of declining public trust in authority; the public appeared less willing to accept that self-regulation according to the Hippocratic code would necessarily be sufficient to counterbalance medical motivations of status, personal gain and scientific interest.

Ethical concerns about medical research therefore arose for historical reasons and because medical ethical traditions pertained only to clinical practice and education, not to research. The growth of bioethics can be seen as a reaction to the shortcomings of the traditional Hippocratic code in the face of biomedical and technological advances. It can also be seen as a manifestation of an increasingly technocratic society, of the cult of the expert who increasingly sought to apply professional skills to the solution of community problems. This tendency in turn articulated with the extension of complex medical technology into sensitive areas of public concern seen also as the province of philosophy.

The focus of bioethics has been largely on 'matters of life and death', including the scrutiny of medical decisions made at the beginning and ending of life. Issues raised by technological change included 'futile' resuscitation in intensive care, the definition of brain death, and a host of problems surrounding organ transplantation, in-vitro fertilisation and embryo experimentation, and euthanasia (Kuhse and Singer, 1992: iii). Bioethics has emerged as a field of study with its own journal, *Bioethics*; the inaugural congress of the International Association of Bioethics was held in 1992.

The initial concern about bioethics emerged in the U.S. where analytical philosophy was in the ascendancy. Its approach was to apply broad and abstract philosophical principles to specific problems. A widely used set of such principles, applicable to clinical practice and research, comprises beneficence and non-maleficence on the part of the doctor, autonomy of the individual, and justice. The major guiding principle which came to be applied to research ethics was autonomy of the subject (Fox, 1990: 210). In general, autonomy was seen to have been respected if informed consent had been freely given.

THE TASK OF THE INSTITUTIONAL ETHICS COMMITTEE

In the late 1960s and '70s many institutions undertaking health research set up institutional ethics committees to act as ethical watchdogs over their research. Funding bodies now commonly make it a condition of funding that such a committee approve a research proposal. On these committees, ethical concern has remained centred on questions of exposure to potentially harmful interventions, informed consent, and ensuring the confidentiality of data on study participants (Pettit, 1992: 94). These are important issues for the community in general and for the research community in particular and, certainly, no responsible researcher would deny the importance of taking these issues into account in the planning and conducting of research.

The task of institutional ethics committees has, however, been greatly complicated by the rapid growth and diversification of health research. The focus of concern of clinical research has shifted from organs and tissues to include seeing the patient in a social context. This shift has been accompanied by an increase in the involvement of non-medical disciplines such as sociology, anthropology and economics in both clinical and public health research, and a dramatic increase in the range of research methods used. Projects in health services research, health promotion in the community and nursing research have also contributed to the use of non-experimental procedures such as survey and interviewing which have been seen as being as much in need of ethical scrutiny as those more obvious cases in which participants are required to submit to experimental interventions such as the administration of a drug. To encompass the myriad of pressing health questions, researchers have had to exploit the entire range of available research methods, and this has sometimes involved multidisciplinary team research. There has been a growing perception that such broad-ranging research projects can impinge on the interests of communities and other social groups and this, in turn, has led to an emphasis on the involvement of community groups even in the planning and conduct of research. Such considerations take the activities of committees into new and sensitive areas, and the ethical issues raised range far beyond that of informed consent to a simple intervention (Albury, 1994).

The multiplication of ethical issues, explosion of protocols and emergence of unfamiliar research designs have been a major challenge to ethics committees dominated by what one commentator termed 'doctors, lawyers and representatives of God' (Swan, quoted in Pettit, 1992: 106). Uncertainty has become the order of the day. The range of research approaches is bewildering to medical members of such committees who are accustomed to the biomedical model of laboratory research involving objective scientist and passive object. Other members of ethics committees—the lay, legal and religious representatives—have often had little or no training in research method, let alone in the diversity of research methods now employed in health research. Even the traditional principles of ethics which they might have called upon to guide them have come under attack. Singer (1994) argues that traditional ethical doctrines such as the sanctity of life have displayed fatal weaknesses in dealing with problems of modern medical practice even with respect to relatively familiar issues of life and death. Thus a new ethic is needed:

> I am not interested in continuing to patch and adjust the traditional approach so that we can pretend that it works when it plainly does not. The failures of the traditional ethic have become so glaring that these strategies can only offer short-term solutions to its problems, solutions that, like the policy of the American Medical Association on patients in irreversible coma, need to be reformulated almost as soon as they are pronounced. (Singer, 1994: 4–5)

THE PROBLEM FACING RESEARCHERS

With ethics committees facing difficulties in making informed decisions about the research proposals submitted, there has been a move to develop guidelines for what is to count as ethical scientific research. Within these guidelines, there is commonly a complex interweaving of issues of methodological rigour with issues to do with the protection of the subjects of research. In the case of qualitative methods, methodological issues predominate. The Australian 'guidelines', for example, are largely concerned with justifying the use of qualitative methods and explaining how such studies may be conducted, while issues of ethics are limited to discussion of the traditional areas of informed consent, confidentiality and restriction of covert or deceptive research (National Health and Medical Research Council, 1994). There is at least the implication that members of ethics committees can use this information (including a bibliography of methodological texts) to acquire a useful understanding of the subtleties of this research method.

The assumption underlying the move to research guidelines is that the problem of adjustment to an expanding range of research methods is merely one of applying traditional criteria for scientific validity and ethical standards to various research approaches. Nothing could be further from the truth. Ethically we do need to be assured that research will produce scientifically valid results using ethically acceptable methods of data collection and analysis. While the need for a scientifically rigorous research method is beyond dispute, there is likely to be confusion about the various ways in which different disciplines go about achieving rigour. There is also uncertainty about the ultimate goal of research. Is it sufficient to be contributing to the store of scientific knowledge about health, or should research also be assessed in terms of its potential for making a direct contribution to community health? Within this context, the need to minimise potential risks to participants in health research may not be as straightforward an issue as previously believed.

When the wide variety of research methods in use today, applied to a broad range of health issues, is not fully understood, there is a twofold danger. Methodologically rigorous studies may be rejected because the methods proposed are not understood and the ethical implications of unfamiliar methods may not be appreciated.

In addition, from the perspective of the researchers, ethics committees have been seen as regulatory bureaucracies, developed in response to research scandals (Pettit, 1992) and having little to contribute to the everyday life of the responsible researcher. These committees have an inbuilt need to 'play safe'. There are few rewards for making correct decisions, small penalties for turning down a good proposal and large penalties for accepting a dubious one. The drive to over-cautious decisions could exclude proposed research which carries any risk of harm, however small, and any breach of confidentiality. Thus the process of ethical review may be endangering valuable research. More seriously, as Pettit argues, it may be endangering 'the very ethic that is needed to govern research' by developing a 'culture of resistance' among researchers. If researchers feel that ethics committees are ignorant of the basic assumptions and procedures of research carefully designed to address ethical issues, resistance can only intensify. Perhaps a more troubling problem is that researchers may be encouraged to think that issues of research ethics are resolved once their proposals are passed by a committee, so that ethical issues which arise in the process of conducting that research are overlooked.

BEYOND GUIDELINES: GIVING VOICE TO THE RESEARCHERS

There is, we would argue, a long tradition of health research in which ethical considerations have played an explicit or implicit role. In each health research setting, responsible researchers have gone about their research task in a thoughtful manner, and the basic ethical principles of conducting research have been taught to students in various health disciplines in both formal and informal ways. We would like to suggest that the following points would be acceptable to most researchers when evaluating the implications of their own work for study participants, for the scientific community, for funding bodies and for the wider community.

The problem which the research addresses should be a significant problem in terms of its potential **impact on community health**. The pursuit of topics which do not fulfil this need may be fascinating to the individual researcher but may be a wasteful use of health resources. We also need to be assured that the problem has not yet been resolved in one of the many disciplines which are now active in the health field.

The **most appropriate research method** should be used, that is, that research method which is most likely to address the research problem in the most scientific manner, given the constraints in the field (see Daly, McDonald and Willis, 1992). Failure to skilfully match research method to scientific question can result from the methodological ignorance of the researcher or the prejudice of the researcher, peer groups or granting bodies. An inappropriate method may lead to misleading results or systematic distortion of the research agenda. To ensure that important questions concerning psychological and social variables in clinical practice are addressed, some research must involve relatively unusual research procedures such as observation of clinical events and interviewing of doctors and patients. Methodological prejudice acting against the use of such methods is unethical.

The methods of data collection should **intrude as little as possible** into the lives of participants in the research. To collect new data without fully analysing equivalent data previously collected, even that collected by other researchers, can be wasteful of resources, hence unethical.

Research should be carefully planned to avoid the possibility of inflicting harm or, where this is impossible, any potential harm should be carefully explained and justified. This may involve, for example, minimising the dose of a drug, or more subtle considerations such as minimising insensitive interrogation in the course of a survey on, say, sexual health.

Data collection and analysis should be **as rigorous as possible**. In addition to using established, systematic forms of analysis, we should avoid biasing our analysis by making unjustifiable, even unwitting, assumptions. This problem will present in different ways in different research settings. So, for example, mathematical economic models may have subtly incorporated assumptions of the economic worth of the elderly, or of women, which is detrimental to these groups. One way of identifying this problem is to have the research conclusions scrutinised by the community most concerned.

Once data are analysed, researchers have a responsibility for the appropriate **dissemination of results**. A researcher can be asked to take some responsibility for misinterpretation or misapplication of research results as a result of careless reporting. Results should be presented in such a way that the research contributes to the improvement of health of the community most affected, especially those who have participated in the research. Failure to publish the results of research with negative findings is a further problem. Non-reporting of negative trials, for example, seriously distorts the medical literature and has come to be seen as scientific malpractice.

This overview of the types of considerations which responsible researchers might bring to the research task cannot be used to evaluate the ethical impact of any or all research proposals. Nor should this be our aim. In a postmodern world, the claim to grand narratives, including grand narratives of ethics, is open to question. The promise of grand narratives in research ethics is that they may be applied across the broad range of health research, enabling those with little detailed understanding of the everyday activities of health research to cast a watchful eye over the activities of health researchers. These expectations have not been fulfilled and there are questions about whether, in the contemporary world, we can expect to find a single universal principle which will provide a test for ethical validity. Instead, Komesaroff (1992:169) argues, ethical principles are generated through social discourse:

> . . . individuals both constitute and are constituted by society. The interaction and communication in which they participate are themselves shaped by the historically derived social structures. Ethical discourse and action arise from the same source; they flow from interactions between individual subjects in

relation to social demands and constraints and in the context of dynamic cultural traditions.

These conclusions are no less relevant to the conduct of health research. The starting point for this collection of essays is therefore to make public the social discourse on ethics used by responsible, practising researchers in order to demonstrate the detailed and fine consideration given to the ethics of the research task. This will vary from discipline to discipline and even within disciplines as the research context changes. Thus the focus is on a research ethic which is 'highly differentiated and richly heterogeneous, albeit firmly grounded—grounded, that is, not in some gratuitous theoretical principle but in the fact of human interchange' (Komesaroff, 1992: 173). This interchange should involve a dialogue between health researchers from various disciplines, clinical practitioners, consumers and members of research ethics committees. This book is an attempt to facilitate just such a debate.

There is, we would argue, a long tradition of health research in which ethical considerations have played an explicit or implicit role. Before placing what may be seen by researchers as being unjustifiable but well-intentioned constraints on health research, we need to develop a better understanding of the ways in which methodologists working in various disciplines go about ensuring that their research is ethically responsible. This would ensure that principles of research ethics in the health field emerge gradually from both abstract philosophical principles and health research methodology interacting in a continual dialogue. Only then will the decisions of research committees reflect both philosophical wisdom and the concrete realities of experience in health research.

REFERENCES

Albury, R., 1994, 'Towards a culture of ethical research', paper presented at the annual conference of The Australian Sociological Association, Geelong, December.

Barber, B., 1976, 'The ethics of experimentation with human subjects'. In T.A. Shannon (ed.), Bioethics: basic writings on the key ethical questions that surround the major, modern biological possibilities and problems, Ramsey: Paulist Press.

Beecher, H.E., 1966, 'Ethics and clinical research', The New England Journal of Medicine, 274: 1354–60.

Daly, J., McDonald, I., and Willis, E. (eds), 1992, Researching Health Care: designs, dilemmas and disciplines, London: Routledge.

Fox, R.C., 1990, 'The evolution of American bioethics: A sociological perspective'. In G. Wemasz (ed.), Social Science Perspectives on Medical Ethics, Dordrecht: Kluwer.

Katz, J., 1984, The Silent World of Doctor and Patient, New York: Free Press.

Komesaroff, P., 1992, 'Review essay: Medical ethics', Bioethics, 6, 2, 166–73.

Kuhse, H. and Singer, P., 1992, 'From the editors', Bioethics, 6, 2, iii–iv.

National Health and Medical Research Council, 1994, *Ethical Aspects of Qualitative Methods in Health Research: an information paper for institutional ethics committees*, report of the Australian Health Ethics Committee, Canberra: National Health and Medical Research Council.

Pence, G.E., 1995, *Classic Cases in Medical Ethics*, New York: McGraw-Hill.

Pettit, P., 1992, 'Instituting a research ethic: Chilling and cautionary tales', *Bioethics*, 6, 2, 89–112.

Rothman, D.J., 1990, 'Human experimentation and the origins of bioethics in the United States'. In G. Wemasz (ed.), *Social Science Perspectives on Medical Ethics*, Dordrecht: Kluwer.

Shenkin, H.A., 1991, *Medical Ethics: evolution, rights and the physician*, Dordrecht: Kluwer.

Singer, P., 1994, *Rethinking Life and Death*, Melbourne: The Text Publishing Company.

Temkin, O., 1991, *Hippocrates in a World of Pagans and Christians*, Baltimore: Johns Hopkins University Press.

PART I

ETHICS, ETHICS COMMITTEES AND THE RESEARCHER

This section sets out the sometimes troubled relationship between ethics, ethics committees and the researcher. The intention here is not to argue against ethical review of health research. Any responsible researcher would agree that there is always benefit in having external scrutiny of the way in which we go about the research task. Rather, the purpose is to show that the present institutional framework and its methods of proceeding are not adequate for this important task.

Max Charlesworth starts by outlining the development of bioethics. Radical changes in medical technology, in the social dimension of medicine and in views of the patient–doctor relationship have brought about new developments in medical ethics including the emergence of bioethics and health-care ethics. New institutions and structures—such as the various national bodies concerned with medical ethics and bioethics—have come into being. Simplistic views about ethical reflection encourage the view that bioethical problems can be definitively 'solved', but a plea is made for a more modest and realistic view of what is possible in this area.

Paul McNeill focuses on the institutional ethics committees which have been set up to monitor the activities of health researchers. He argues that the review of research requires a balancing of two major interests: those of researchers and those of subjects. The interests of researchers and subjects should be more independently represented to overcome a bias in favour of vested research interests. In addition, ethical review should be more concerned with issues of value than with scientific validity. He suggests that the appropriate research standards to be applied by a review committee are those of the relevant scientific discipline and that committees should have fewer members and rely more on relevant outside expertise for a broad overview of research methods.

Judith Lumley's account of the exigencies of dealing with ethics committees during a number of epidemiological studies demonstrates the problems which the researcher, however responsible, faces in having research projects cleared by ethics committees. The essay also gives us a clear picture of the problems faced by members of ethics committees who are required to evaluate proposals when they are perhaps not fully informed of the context of a research proposal covering a number of sites. The delays and obstructions which occurred seriously compromised the research task.

Paul Komesaroff proposes a fundamental change to the way in which we would see ethics in a postmodern world. He locates the problem in a narrow, positivist approach to science, and ethics, which has dominated discourse since the Enlightenment. These traditional accounts of ethics do not adequately engage with what practitioners do in the course of medical practice. Similarly, they fail to reflect adequately on the research task. Practitioners and researchers are better served by the emerging postmodern approach to ethics in which various voices engage in a debate about what is to count as ethical. Komesaroff's account is complex, making evident the difficulties which members of ethics committees must face if they go about their task with the assumption that it is to be based on detailed knowledge of contemporary debates in health ethics.

What's the Use of Bioethics?

Max Charlesworth

A celebrated English philosopher was once asked the question 'Does God exist?' After some pondering and much sucking on his pipe the great thinker replied: 'It all depends on what you mean by "does" and what you mean by "God" and what you mean by "exists".' Faced with the question 'What's the use of bioethics?' I am tempted to make much the same reply: 'It all depends what you mean by "use" and what you mean by "bioethics".'

Unfortunately, despite its popular acceptance, the term 'bioethics' is not well defined in the sense that it refers to a distinct set of issues and to the use of a distinct method. In fact, I want to suggest that it covers a very wide and heterogeneous range of problems and issues and topics, and further that there is no one distinct method of inquiry and discussion that it employs. Rather, it makes use of a diffuse set of approaches.

In particular I wish to demystify the idea of ethics in general and bioethics in particular. Ethical reflection about how we ought to live (Socrates, one of the Greek founders of the discipline of ethics, once said that the central ethical question was simply 'How should I live?') is not a matter of special expertise that only educated or trained people have. It would be paradoxical if knowing how one ought to live and act in a properly human way were beyond the ken of ordinary people and accessible only to an elite of moral sages. Ethical reflection must be something that I have to do for myself, since no one else can be moral or ethical for me. The same is true of reflection in medical ethics and bioethics: it is something that patients and physicians and health-care professionals and medical research scientists and subjects must do for themselves. No doubt the professional moralist or ethicist can often help by clarifying issues and suggesting different ways of seeing things and criticising fashionable ideas. But ultimately we each have to be our own bioethicist.

The term 'bioethics' was invented in the 1970s to refer to a cluster of new and unprecedented ethical or moral issues thrown up by the new forms of biotechnology, particularly in the fields of reproductive technology (*in vitro* fertilisation and its variants) and genetic manipulation. David Suzuki (Suzuki and Knudtson, 1988) proposed the term 'genethics' for the study of the ethical implications of genetic manipulation, but happily that neologism has not caught on. Subsequently the term 'bioethics' was used in a general way to refer to the whole range of ethical issues brought up by medical science and practice.

It is worthwhile looking briefly at the historical development of medical ethics or bioethics (in its wider sense), since this gives a good idea of the large and heterogeneous range of issues and problems that the discipline, if you can call it that, covers. In general terms, then, one can distinguish between (1) traditional medical ethics in what one might call the Hippocratic tradition; (2) medical research ethics, which came into being with the revolution in medical research after the Second World War; (3) bioethics, which was primarily concerned with the ethical aspects of the new biotechnologies of the 1970s and 1980s, and (4) health-care ethics, which has been occupied with the ethical dimensions of the new public health movement of the 1980s and '90s (in particular with the ethics of health-care resource allocation). Let me say something about each of these developments.

Traditional medical ethics was mainly concerned with the relationship between the physician and patient. In the Hippocratic code and its variants this relationship was seen as a paternalistic one: physician was to patient as parent was to child. In this view the professional expertise of the physician places her in a privileged position vis-à-vis the patient. In a quite obvious sense the patient often does not know what is good for her, medically speaking, and she has to trust the physician. But with the development of the liberal ideal of personal autonomy (the right of each person to control and determine his or her own life), the patient's right to control her own medical treatment has come to the fore. Indeed, some have claimed that the role of the physician is that of a mere ancillary or servant to the patient.

Clearly, we need some kind of middle way between these two extremes. But it is not easy to find the appropriate model. The well-known American health ethicist Daniel Callahan has this to say:

> If we want to have good doctor–patient relationships, we can't reduce that relationship exclusively to the language of rights, particularly the language of patient rights. A consequence is to jeopardise the doctor's important role as a moral agent. At one extreme the doctor is turned into nothing but a plumber. The challenge is to recognise that when doctors and patients enter into a relationship they begin to create a community, or at least a profound relation-

ship which the language of rights does not adequately describe. In one sense each has to help the other. The doctor has to educate the patient, help the patient understand what might serve his or her welfare. And the patient has to find a way to tell the physician what he or she is trying to live for. It ought to be a richer language than is captured in the language of autonomy and rights. (Callahan, 1988: 60)

There is, no doubt, a good deal to be said for Callahan's view; but far from demonstrating the need to go beyond the language of autonomy and rights it reinforces the centrality of that language, in that the physician–patient relationship involves a mutual respect for the autonomy of each other. The physician must respect patients' autonomous right to control their own health and to refuse treatment (even if death ensues) and to demand the right to exercise informed consent; patients must respect the physician's right as a professional to insist upon professional standards and to exercise some degree of justified paternalism where patients cannot, or are unwilling to, take responsibility for their own health-care decisions.

There is an analogy between the patient–physician relationship and the relationship between learner and teacher, since in both cases the physician and teacher are (ideally) *enabling* the patient and student to assume responsibility for their own health and learning. One cannot *cause* or determine another to be an autonomous or self-determining agent—that would be a contradiction in terms—but one can nevertheless create conditions which enable others to awaken to the meaning of their autonomy and the realisation that they are masters of their fate and captains of their own souls. Knowing is an autonomous act which people must do for themselves, but the teacher can, like a Socratic midwife, help students no longer to be faithful parrots but to know for themselves. In the same way the physician must always, so far as is possible, help patients to exercise some degree of autonomous control over their health. That means that patients, like student learners, must have genuine choices and alternatives available to them.

Finding an appropriate model for the physician–patient relationship is extremely important because without such a model the much-used terms of 'informed consent' and 'informed decision-making', and the weight given to personal autonomy in contemporary positions about the right of patients to refuse medical treatment, all remain unclear. In my view this is a fundamental medical ethical issue (though it is not often seen by bioethicists as such) which involves a careful analysis of the relationship of trust and of the mutual respect of each other's autonomy by patient and physician. (For further discussion see Charlesworth, 1993.) Some recent thinkers have spoken of the need for 'micro-ethics', which involves finely detailed (or 'phenomenological') descriptions of the subtle but important ethical implications of the physician–health-care professional 'encounter' with the patient or health-care consumer. As in any such interaction there are all kinds of opportunities for exploitation and manipulation and 'bad faith' on both sides, and it is difficult to maintain that mutual respect for each other's autonomy that is of the essence of the patient–physician relationship.

It is worthwhile remarking that there has been a large and developing legal interest in this whole area whose focus has been on patient autonomy as against the older emphasis on medical paternalism. The recent report on informed consent by the Australian Law Reform Commission (Australian Law Reform Commission, 1989) and cases such as the recent Rogers versus Whitaker case in the Australian High Court (see Chalmers and Schwartz, 1993) stress the stringent obligations of medical practitioners to provide relevant information to patients. This represents a move away from traditional paternalistic 'doctors may be presumed to know best' attitudes. Despite medical practitioners' distrust of lawyers, a good deal of medical ethics is now emerging through the work of law reform commissions and the judgments of the courts. Certainly in the United States, and to some extent in the United Kingdom, some of the most original and interesting discussions of bioethical and medical issues are to be found in the law journals (see, for example, Robertson, 1986; Ikemoto, 1988).

From the 1940s, with the immense increase in medical research, the ethical implications of medical *research* on human subjects became an important part of medical ethics, and the relationship between researchers and their subjects and the safeguarding of the rights of subjects became a central issue. The Nuremburg Code, the Helsinki Declaration and the Australian National Health and Medical Research Council's guidelines on human experimentation were concerned with those rights and with drawing limits to medical research and experimentation (see McNeill, 1993).

Other ethical issues came to the fore in the 1970s and 1980s with the new biotechnologies. The issues that were the focus of 'bioethics' were very dramatic ones: the moral and legal status of the human embryo brought into being outside the body of its mother, human embryo donation, human embryo experimentation, IVF-assisted surrogacy arrangements, genetic manipulation of the human embryo and so on. They were, as it has been put, 'neon issues' which raised both hope and fear in both the public mind and the media mind. The extraordinary number of official inquiries in Australia and elsewhere into the ethical and legal and social implications of the new biotechnologies is evidence of the 'brave new world' fears that those technologies excited. In Australia, the former National Bioethics Consultative Committee was set up in 1987 to advise the federal and state ministers of health mainly on issues arising from the new reproductive technologies.

The older Hippocratic tradition of medical ethics saw medicine largely in individualistic, asocial, terms. But since the 1940s medicine has been seen more and more as a social phenomenon, with the state taking a direct interest in providing health care to its citizens and with the emergence, through bodies such as the World Health Organisation, of the idea that we all have an ethical and quasi-legal *right* of access to basic health care. In liberal democratic societies, health care, like education, is seen as a necessary condition for the exercise of personal autonomy and the development of a fully human life. In other words, health care is now seen as a 'public good' which the state has a duty to provide to its citizens and not just as a 'private good' which individuals must buy for themselves on the open market. We now take this for granted, apart from some free market ideologues, but it is really a relatively new social development. In the U.S. the idea of having a strict right to basic health care is still controversial. As Hall and Haas have put it, in the U.S., access to goods and services such as health care is seen as a 'reward for individual effort': for the undeserving poor it is seen as a 'handout' (Hall and Haas, 1992: 438).

An important area of this new concern for the social dimensions of medicine and health care is the allocation of health-care resources. With the realisation that such resources are finite and limited and that demands on the health care system are rapidly increasing in both numbers and costs, we now accept that there must be some kind of rationing of health resources. We cannot give all the people all the health-care resources they want, but we can give all the people *some* of the basic health resources they want. In discussions about the best ways of rationing health resources, there has been an enormous emphasis on cost–benefit efficiency in providing the greatest health-care gains or outcomes for the least amount of money. This has involved quantifying health outcomes so that they are measurable and comparable with each other so that, in turn, we can make choices between them. Thus, for example, it is claimed that we can measure the health outcomes provided by major organ transplants and hip replacements and schizophrenia treatment and then compare them against each other and rank them as better or best 'buys'. The idea of Quality Adjusted Life Years (QALYs) has played a major part in this, and the elaborate system for ranking health care procedures and rationing health care resources established in the U.S. state of Oregon has been seen as a model of 'rational' planning (i.e. planning based upon quasi-quantitative calculation) in this field.

As I have said, the emphasis so far has been on quantifiable and measurable 'outcomes' and on cost–benefit efficiency, and ethical considerations of justice and equity and respect for personal autonomy have been neglected. The assumption seems to have been that if you get the efficiency and economics of health-care resource rationing right, the ethics will take care of themselves, just as so-called economic rationalists believe that if you focus on fundamental economic issues, the 'vision thing', as President George Bush called it, will take care of itself. However, it is obvious that a system of health-care allocation can be quite *efficient* but at the same time quite *unjust* or *unfair* and also quite *paternalistic* in that it overrides the personal autonomy both of patients or health-care consumers and of health-care professionals. (In many health-care rationing schemes, bureaucratic paternalism takes the place of the older medical paternalism.)

In Australia, the National Bioethics Consultative Committee and the Medical Research Ethics Committee were both in 1991 absorbed into a new body called the Australian Health Ethics Committee. One of the main interests of AHEC so far has been in the ethical aspects of health-care resource allocation. After a conference on this issue in 1992, AHEC issued a set of ethical guidelines for health-care resource allocation (Australian Health Ethics Committee, 1992). They are very general in scope but their intention is to force people in the allocation business to realise that utilitarian considerations of efficiency are, while necessary, not enough. Justice and respect for patient and health professional autonomy are also needed.

What I have been trying to do so far is to show how varied and disparate are the issues that come up within medical ethics or bioethics or health-care ethics. As I have indicated, those issues are changing all the time. Whereas the issues raised by the new reproductive technologies and the new genetics were very much in the centre of things in the 1980s, the issues raised by the provision of health-care and access to health-care and the allocation of health-care resources are of primary importance at the present time. The change of titles from the National Bioethics Consultative Committee to the Australian Health Ethics Committee is significant in this respect.

Finally, there are the socio-ethical-legal questions that come up about the kind of society in which we live and within which our discussions about bioethics and health-care ethics take place. We live in a liberal society and our discussions of the ethical implications of medicine, medical research, biotechnology and health-care resource distribution have to take account of the values that are the foundation of the liberal society. In a liberal society personal autonomy is the central value, that is, the right of all people to determine and live out their own ethical values and to engage in what John Stuart Mill (1946: 8) calls their own 'experiments in living'. It follows from this that the state and the law must not intervene in the area of personal morality so long as an individual's exercise of personal autonomy does not directly harm other people. In a liberal society there is a sharp disjunction between the sphere of law and the sphere of personal morality, and the law may not be invoked to 'enforce morality'. Again, in a liberal society governed by the value of personal autonomy there is a toleration of ethical and religious diversity or pluralism, and we 'agree to disagree' about quite basic ethical and religious positions. In such a society there is then a severe limit to social consensus, or agreement on a set of fundamental ethical values by the members of society.

If one teases out these values, which are of the essence of the liberal society, very radical conclusions follow in the medical ethical–bioethical area. Take, for example, the idea of IVF-assisted surrogacy arrangements of the kind used some years ago by the Kirkman sisters in Victoria (Kirkman, 1988). If the formation of a family is a matter of personal morality, an exercise of personal autonomy, then one ought to be free to form a family in whatever way one chooses, so long as others are not harmed. Some have, in this sense, spoken of a 'right to procreative liberty'. When one sees IVF-assisted surrogacy arrangements in this light it is difficult, so I think at any rate, to argue that the law should intervene to prohibit and criminalise such surrogacy arrangements.

I have been arguing that there is not one distinct set of issues that medical ethics or bioethics is concerned with but that we are confronted with a very diffuse and heterogeneous set of issues and problems. I now want to argue that there is not a single method of discussing those issues and problems. In my view, the only 'use' of medical ethics or bioethics is to reflect on and clarify issues, to put them into context and to see things in a new light. Many people expect medical ethics and bioethics to produce final and definitive 'solutions' to the problems that come up, but in my view that is possible only very rarely.

There are two misleading views of ethics which need to be exorcised if we are to get a clear view of what is possible in medical ethics or bioethics and of what 'use' bioethics may have. The first is that ethics consists of a set of universal and absolute 'principles', something like the Ten Commandments, which can be 'applied' deductively to particular problems so that the problems are 'solved'. For example, it is morally wrong to take the life of a human being. But a human embryo is a human being; therefore it is morally wrong to take the life of a human embryo in, for example, non-therapeutic experimentation. There are, of course, general ethical or moral principles or rules but they always need to be interpreted in the light of the circumstances in which we have to act. It is not always morally wrong to take the life of a human being, for example in self-defence or in a just war or in a situation where the saving of one person's life means the leaving of another person to die, or where a biologically human being (e.g. an anencephalic foetus) is not really a human person. Thus, instead of saying in an unqualified way that it is morally wrong to take another human being's life, we have to say that it is morally wrong to take the life of a human being who is a real human being, who is not an aggressor threatening another's life, who is not a combatant on the other side in a war, etc., etc. Again, we have to make distinctions about directly killing another person and deliberately allowing a person to die. If my saving A means leaving B to die, I cannot be said to be 'taking' the life of B even though B dies directly because of my act.

Then, when we have qualified the moral rule about not taking human beings' lives, we have to interpret the particular case to which we are applying the rule: In what sense is a human embryo a human being? Is it 'human' merely in the biological sense or is it human in the sense of being a person or autonomous moral agent with its own individual identity? What moral status does it have and what degree of moral respect should we give to it?

Further, there may well be a conflict between moral rules or principles. In the case of abortion there is a conflict between the woman's right to control her own reproductive processes and the right of the foetus to continue its development into a human being, and it is not clear in the abstract which right should prevail. Again, if the right to privacy of research subjects is absolute and if no information about them can be made available without their express consent, then most epidemiological research will be impossible and society will lose the benefits of such research. These kinds of ethical conflicts or dilemmas are not rare or exceptional: they are the very stuff of the ethical life.

The model of medical ethics which sees it as a deductive process of applying general principles or rules to particular cases is, then, wholly simplistic. We do not, and cannot, live our moral lives in that way and we cannot engage in medical ethics or bioethics in that way.

The other misleading view of ethics is what might be called the consequentialist or utilitarian view, which claims that the morality of any act is determined by its measurable consequences or 'outcomes' and which sees ethical problems as quasi-engineering problems. It is this view which lies behind the outcomes approach in the rationing of health-care resources and which assumes that we can measure and weigh all health outcomes by a common measure. Even the quality of a person's life can be quantified! As a result, all those factors which are not easily amenable to quantitative measurement tend to be screened out as being unimportant. As Leeder and Grossman put it:

> Most people in our society now recognise that imposing health outcomes should not just be a matter of locating disease and eliminating it at all costs. They realise that there are things in life which matter and which may conflict with seemingly straightforward medical judgments in the pursuit of cure or standard care. But, even having recognised this, it is still tempting to measure what is easily measurable and ignore the rest. (Leeder and Grossman, 1992: 292)

Again, the utilitarian emphasis on outcomes conveys the impression that we are never really confronted with genuinely 'hard choices'. In principle at least, if we calculate the outcomes carefully and long enough we will always get an answer. This fosters what might be called false ethical optimism, the attitude that all ethical problems can be 'rationally' and finally and definitively solved. Finally, the utilitarian outcomes model fixes our attention on the *product* of any action we take and de-emphasises the *process*. Thus in the allocation of health care resources what counts is that 'health gain' is maximised and not whether patients are given the opportunity and the wherewithal to exercise some degree of autonomous control over their health care.

The therapeutic criticism and exorcism of these misleading models of ethical discussion is an important part of medical ethics and bioethics and health-care ethics. Once we have got them out of the way we can see that ethical inquiry makes use of quite obvious and ordinary and commonsense methods of reflection: asking ourselves, for example, what a morally mature person would do in a given set of circumstances (for Aristotle the ultimate test is, What would a *phronimos*—a morally experienced person skilled in making ethical decisions—do in this situation?); analysing what is meant by concepts and terms like 'human life', health 'outcomes', the 'quality of life' and so on; interpreting the meaning of rules in given circumstances ('Is this a case of killing or of letting someone die'); putting things into context—for example, seeing surrogacy arrangements as one way of family formation and as falling under the 'right to procreative freedom'; seeing things in a new light—for example, seeing the physician–patient relationship as involving mutual respect for each other's autonomy and as akin to the teacher–student relationship. In ethical reflection it is not rationality in the sense of deductive and calculative reasoning that is of central importance but rationality in the sense of empathy and imagination—being able to put oneself in another's situation, to see things from another and unfamiliar vantage point, to escape from one's own self-centred and self-interested point of view.

In this sense, then, ethics is not a special discipline with its own special method: it is simply a business of reflecting imaginatively and carefully on what we are doing (I sometimes think that we ought to do away with the term 'ethics' altogether, since it has so many misleading connotations). I have been trying to show that all aspects of medical research and practice and biotechnology and health care raise ethical questions of one kind or another. It is because health is a necessary condition of a fully human life that ethical questions are inescapable. And insofar as medical ethics or bioethics or health-care ethics reminds us of this, it goes without saying that bioethics is indispensably 'useful'. But if we think that medical ethics or bioethics can provide us with clear-cut and final solutions to the kinds of problems we have been considering, by applying ethical principles to particular cases in a deductive way or by doing simple-minded utilitarian calculations, we are doomed to disappointment. It is because people often have mistaken views of what is involved in ethical reflection that they have unreal expectations about what is possible in ethics and bioethics, and that they are then inclined to say that bioethics is 'useless'. Such people need reminding that ethical and bioethical reflection is a quite ordinary and humdrum—though fundamentally important—business of the kind described before.

REFERENCES

Australian Health Ethics Committee, 1992, *The Place of Ethics in Health Care Resource Allocation: where to now?*, Canberra: National Health and Medical Research Council.

Australian Law Reform Commission, 1989, *Informed Decisions about Medical Procedures*, Canberra: Australian Law Reform Commission.

Callahan, D., 1988, 'Beyond individualism: Bioethics and the common good', *Second Opinion: Health, Faith and Ethics*, 9: 52–69.

Chalmers, D. and Schwartz, R., 1993, 'Rogers v Whitaker and informed consent in Australia: A fair dinkum duty of disclosure', *Medical Law Review*, 1: 139–59.

Charlesworth, M., 1993, *Bioethics in a Liberal Society*, Cambridge: Cambridge University Press.

Hall, J. and Haas, M., 1992, 'The rationing of health care: Should Oregon be transported to Australia', *Australian Journal of Public Health*, 16: 435–40.

Ikemoto, L.C., 1988, 'Providing protection for collaborative, non-coital reproduction: Surrogate motherhood and other new reproductive technologies and the right to intimate association', *Rutgers Law Review*, 40: 1273–309.

Kirkman, M. and L., 1988, *My Sister's Child*, Ringwood: Penguin Books.

Leeder, S. and Grossman, J., 'Targets matter, but so does archery', *Medical Journal of Australia*, 157: 291–2.

McNeill, P., 1993, *The Ethics and Politics of Human Experimentation*, Melbourne: Cambridge University Press.

Mill, J.S., 1946, *On Liberty*, R.B. McCallum (ed.), Oxford: Blackwell.

Robertson, J.A., 1986, 'Embryos, families and procreative liberty: The legal structures of the new reproduction', *Southern California Law Review*, 59: 939–1041.

Suzuki, D. and Knudtson, P., 1988, *Genethics: The ethics of engineering life*, Sydney: Allen & Unwin.

2

RESEARCH ETHICS COMMITTEES: IS THE TAIL WAGGING THE DOG?

Paul M. McNeill

In this essay I maintain that review of experimentation on human subjects by a research ethics committee is a political process as much as it is an ethical process. This is politics in the broadest sense. It is about balancing one set of interests in the community against other sets of interests: the interests of research and researchers on the one hand and the interests of the human subjects of research on the other. Although there are differences from one country to another, I maintain that this is the underlying task of review committees wherever they are found.

Research ethics committees around the world grew out of a concern to protect human research participants who are vulnerable to exploitation by researchers. The committees were first used in a national and consistent manner in the United States, where they are known as institutional review boards (IRBs) (McNeill, 1993). Given the different names in different countries, however, I refer to them by the more generic term 'research ethics committees' or 'review committees'. Implicit in the subtitle of this chapter is a concern that protection of subjects may not be the predominant function of committees. If we take committees to be the dog (put in the yard to protect research subjects) and the tail of the dog to be vested interests in research, the concern is that research interests may predominate on review committees.

A BIAS TOWARD RESEARCH INTERESTS

Research ethics committees typically comprise members of staff from a research institution together with a few members from the community. For example, the Australian guidelines for research ethics committees (known as 'institutional ethics committees' or IECs) are contained in the National

Health and Medical Research Council (NHMRC) 'Statement on Human Experimentation'. This statement requires that committees include (as a minimum): a minister of religion, a lawyer, a lay man and woman, and a medical graduate with research experience (National Health and Medical Research Council Statement, 1992). Similarly, the federal regulations for IRBs in the U.S. and guidelines for the formation of research ethics committees in Canada and Britain require at least one community member (McNeill, 1993).

Our studies have shown that committees typically include those required members and several additional staff members from the research institution. We found that Australian research ethics committees had eleven members on average, including: four medical graduates; an administrator; two or three other professionals (including nurses, psychologists, non-medical researchers); and the required lay members, lawyer, and minister of religion (McNeill, Berglund and Webster, 1990). The question is whether this composition is appropriate for the functions of these committees. I am particularly concerned with the adequacy of the representation of the subjects and the adequacy of the representation of research.

The members with research expertise, by their training and investment in the scientific process, have a unique commitment to research. Their priorities and values are not necessarily shared by the rest of the community or by subjects of experiments. Even with the best intentions, therefore, committees with a majority of members who are staff members of the institution have an inherent bias toward supporting research. Although the NHMRC statement requires that priority be given to protecting human subjects of experiments, the system may operate as if the priority is on getting research approved.

It is my view that the 'non-research' members of the committee are not easily able to overcome this bias. They are in the minority. Secondly, they do not have the same pre-established working relationships and they do not have the same opportunities for consulting with each other outside of meetings. More importantly, they depend on the 'expert' members of the committee to help them understand research proposals and to grasp clearly the implications for human subjects.

Given this bias, I argue that there is a need to change the basis of membership of research ethics committees to more adequately represent the interests of subjects.

REPRESENTATION OF SUBJECTS

The people on whom research is conducted, the 'subjects of research', are not represented on research ethics committees as they are presently constituted. These are the people who are most affected by research—especially if something untoward occurs. Patients (in particular) are trusting of medical researchers and will volunteer for experiments, drug trials, and innovative treatment without understanding the possible impact of a study on their lives. They need the protection of people who have no investment in the research. For this reason I argue that subjects should be directly represented. Representation of their interests conforms to the democratic principle that we should all have some means for influencing decisions that affect our lives, but many of the national guidelines on review committees specifically rule out choosing members on the basis of representation (McNeill, 1993). This exclusion acts unfairly against the interests of subjects in that theirs is the only interest which is not already represented.

Numerically, at least, the interests of research and the research institution are in the majority on research ethics committees as presently constituted. While research members are chosen on the basis of their expertise and positions, they function effectively as representatives of research and of their institutions. For example, they are almost invariably people with professional affiliations and positions of responsibility in research institutes, and they have the support of those institutions. Furthermore, they are accountable, at least informally, to their colleagues. Research representatives can expect to be challenged outside of committee when colleagues disagree with a decision taken by the committee.

Lay members, ministers of religion, and lawyers are not accountable in this manner. Often they are elected to committees because they are known to another committee member or person within the institution. Their primary allegiance is to other members of the committee rather than to research subjects. Nor are they given any explicit indication that their role is to represent the interests of subjects.

While it is probably true that most lay members are concerned about the welfare of those who participate in research, they are in a difficult position in weighing that concern against persuasive arguments in favour of research. In this situation the non-research members (other than the lawyers) tend to sit back and leave it to the experts. This is supported by our findings that lay members and ministers of religion on research ethics committees are less active than other members and are seen as being less important, both to themselves and to other committee members, in reaching decisions (McNeill, Berglund and Webster, 1994).

This brings us back to the difficulty already discussed, that most of the influential members have a commitment to research either because they are researchers themselves or because they are staff members of the institution and committed to furthering the institution's goals (which include research). The effect is that committees are balanced in favour of the interests of research. Research concerns and interests predominate. The tail is wagging the dog.

OTHER CONCERNS

ADEQUACY OF REPRESENTATION OF RESEARCHERS

It is my observation that researchers in one discipline are not always able to appreciate the research methods of another. As a non-participant observer of research ethics committees, both in the U.S. and in Australia, I have been present when studies have been rejected by research ethics committees which included predominantly medical-graduate members. On two occasions the reasons for rejection arose from an expressed dislike of accepted methodology in psychology rather than from the shortcomings of the particular proposal under review. One was a proposed study, at a hospital in Boston, on the recovery of grieving parents after the death of a child. The concern was that the study would itself be traumatic for parents even though the research team was competent to handle these interactions sensitively. There was evidence that parents welcomed the opportunity to discuss their loss. I believe a committee of social scientists would have been more accepting of this proposal.

Another instance of concern was the rejection of a study which included a questionnaire. Committee members considered that people responding to a questionnaire would not give answers that were well thought out and that this would lead to invalid results. This is contrary to a body of evidence attesting to the validity and usefulness of properly constructed question-naires.

Others have raised a concern about the dominance of a biological and reductionist view of science in ethics committee evaluations. Australian researchers have complained to me that research ethics committees (composed of a majority of medical-graduate members) have rejected proposals on methodological grounds when they were not equipped to make these methodological assessments. The complaint was that the committees had not understood well-accepted research practices in other disciplines: in one case, for example, it was an economic study and in another case it was a sociological study.

For this reason, researchers' representatives should present the concerns of researchers from within the relevant discipline. If a proposal being reviewed is from one of the 'social sciences', for example, ethics committee members from other disciplines, such as medicine or the biological sciences, should be careful not to discredit the study because the science does not seem adequate from a biological or medical point of view. The proposition is equally true in reverse. The appropriate criteria are to be established within the relevant science. It is the research representative's responsibility to consider the methodology from an appropriate perspective.

On most committees, members will require the assistance of outside reviewers to do justice to this task. The committee must be empowered to draw on expertise beyond that of its own members to assist in understanding a study, the methodology, its value and its likely impact on subjects. This is already allowed for in the guidelines and regulations of various countries. In the U.S., for example, an institutional review board has the discretion to invite individuals with special expertise to assist the committee, although those individuals may not vote.[1]

VALUE AND VALIDITY OF SCIENCE

One of the major ethical concerns, particularly of researchers on ethics committees, is whether proposed research is properly designed. The issue, as it is usually put, is that risk to subjects is not justified if a study is incapable of reaching a conclusion. This issue, however, raises two quite separate questions to do with the validity and value of research. The issue of design deals with validity of research and the issue of risk and justification deals with the value of research.

In my view it is not appropriate for both issues to be the responsibility of a research ethics committees. My concern is that an emphasis on validity has the effect of making technical and scientific issues fundamental in deciding the ethical merit of proposed studies. I maintain that scientific validity is not the primary ethical issue. It is primarily a technical issue. The important ethical issue is not whether studies are scientifically well grounded but whether there is a risk of physical or psychological harm, or risk of loss (economic or some other loss) to subjects. The difficult ethical issue is balancing the relative *value* of the research against the interests of subjects. Obviously to be valuable a study needs to be valid. In other words, it needs to be capable of establishing what it sets out to establish. But the issue of validity is a 'threshold condition' which precedes the question of relative value (Freedman, 1987). There is an advantage in considering separately questions of validity and value. Not all members of ethics review committees have the relevant expertise to resolve issues of validity. Expecting ethics committees to resolve the issue leaves those without the necessary expertise being (and feeling) superfluous. For these reasons, I argue that validity of studies ought to be established prior to a research ethics committee consideration.

AN ALTERNATIVE MODEL

I propose an alternative model for committee review. It is based on a recognition that research ethics committees are endeavouring to reconcile different values. These are:

1. the values of research, both to the researchers and to other possible beneficiaries in the community, and
2. the value that should be given to protecting the interests of the subjects.

I argue first, that both of these perspectives need adequate representation; and second, that the representatives for each perspective need to be people with equal support and influence. This is the basis of the suggestion that research ethics committees be composed of equal numbers of representatives of subjects and representatives of researchers. Representatives of both perspectives need to be on an equal footing in terms of their relative strength and influence within committees and on national and international committees that consider research ethics.

Just as the research perspective is presented by appropriately qualified researchers who have the support of professional affiliations, I argue that representatives of subjects should also be properly qualified for their role and that they too need adequate support. Subject representatives can gain this support with the backing of an appropriate community group. There is a distinction between lay members and properly accountable 'consumer representatives'. The way in which this distinction applies to research ethics committees is that lay members are included on committees as individuals from the community whereas subject representatives would be nominated by an appropriate community group with an interest in the welfare of subjects of human experimentation. Subject representatives are then able to represent subjects' interests from an independent and informed position. Furthermore, subject representatives can be accountable to the community through the relevant organisation.

It is acknowledged that there are practical difficulties in putting these suggestions for representation of subjects into practice. Namely, there is no readily identifiable group to represent all subjects of research nor is there one view that is representative of them. However, finding adequate representation is a problem common to all community groups. In my view, the practical difficulties in finding adequate representation should not mean retreating from the principle of representation. In Australia, groups such as the Consumers' Health Forum, or one of their member bodies, could be asked to nominate representatives of research subjects. Alternatively the Australian Council of Social Services and its various State branches might be appropriate. These bodies are skilled in inviting representatives, giving those representatives support and training in their roles, and creating structures for consultation between the representatives and their constituency.

ROLE OF SUBJECT AND RESEARCH REPRESENTATIVES

It follows from the above that the role of research representatives and subject representatives is different. Representatives need to be capable of fulfilling their function. I have developed these ideas more fully elsewhere but the following is a brief description (McNeill, 1993).

SUBJECT REPRESENTATIVES' ROLES

The main function of representatives of subjects is to understand the likely impact of the proposed research on subjects. Their primary question is 'Should this study go ahead?' and this should be addressed particularly from the perspective of the interests of potential subjects. As necessary, subject representatives could consult with members from the proposed subject population to understand the issues from their point of view. Answering the question will also require working cooperatively with the research representatives to predict, as closely as possible, the experience and outcome for subjects. Representatives should be particularly alert to any possibility of unforeseen consequences of entering a study, such as: a loss of options in treatment; the possibility that the study might drag on beyond the nominated completion date; the impact on subjects' privacy; any likely pain, suffering or other discomfort; and potential for loss of earnings. If subject representatives are satisfied that it is not unreasonable to ask subjects to participate, then a number of subsidiary issues arise. The study needs to be understandable to potential subjects. Subject representatives need to ensure that subjects are provided with information on their rights, such as the right to withdraw at any time, and that participation in the study is optional and will not affect subjects' treatment in any other respect.

Consistent with the ideas of accountability already advanced, subject representatives have a responsibility to report back and consult with their nominating organisation. This does not imply that every decision to be taken by a subject representative needs to be ratified by the nominating organisation. There is obviously a practical need for representatives to be able to make decisions independently. However, a responsibility to report back and consult provides an information channel and allows the community group to develop relevant policy. It also provides an additional channel for subjects to make their views known to their representatives.

RESEARCH REPRESENTATIVES' ROLES

Appropriate research representatives will be drawn from a group of people with experience in research on human subjects that is relevant to the research considered by the committee. Although they will be concerned with *all* ethical issues that arise, the research representatives would have particular responsibility for considering issues of: scientific validity; techniques employed by the researchers; the likely impact of the research on the subjects; the adequacy of arrangements for attending to subjects in the event of something untoward happening; the appropriateness of the researchers' predictions and expectations in relation to international literature on the topic; and interpreting and explaining the technical and scientific aspects of the study for the subject representatives. They should also be prepared to discuss the value of the research in relation to the risk of harm.

Although I have argued that the issue of validity is one that should have been adequately dealt with by a specialist committee or assessors prior to the research ethics committee review, the research representatives would nevertheless need to ensure that this prior assessment was adequate. Research representatives would therefore be responsible for marshalling the technical information necessary for an adequate assessment and calling for additional help as necessary.

SIZE OF COMMITTEES

Research ethics committees should be much smaller than the average committee we looked at in our survey. One committee we surveyed had 23 members. This is too large and wasteful of time. There could be a maximum of eight members with two or three representatives of researchers and two or three representatives of subjects. Along with the representatives of researchers and subjects, I suggest including the committee administrator and a lawyer (or someone with a training in philosophy or ethics) who has no other affiliation to the institution.

SUMMARY

The balance of power on research ethics committees needs to be more evenly distributed. This would be achieved by selecting the majority of members to represent the two major interests: the interests of researchers and the interests of subjects. The representatives need a clear definition of their role and the ability to represent their constituency. Research proposals need to be considered by standards of scientific rigour and methodology appropriate to the nature of the research. The issues and concerns of subjects of research need adequate and informed representation. Given this composition and clarity of function, we could be more confident that research ethics committees would fulfil their function of balancing the interests of research with the need to give priority to protecting research subjects. We would then have a dog that was independent and free to wag its own tail.

NOTE

1 Federal Policy for the Protection of Human Subjects, 1991; British Department of Health, Guidelines, 1991: 8, make a similar provision.

REFERENCES

Freedman, B., 1987, 'Scientific value and validity as ethical requirements for research: A proposed explication', *IRB: A Review of Human Subjects Research*, 9, 6: 7–10.

McNeill, P.M., Berglund, C.A., Webster, I.W., 1990, 'Reviewing the reviewers: A survey of institutional ethics committees in Australia', *Medical Journal of Australia*, 152, 6: 289–96.

McNeill, P.M., 1993, *The Ethics and Politics of Human Experimentation*, Sydney and London: Cambridge University Press.

McNeill, P.M., Berglund, C.A., Webster, I.W., 1994, 'How much influence do various members have within research ethics committees?', *Cambridge Quarterly of Healthcare Ethics: The International Journal for Healthcare Ethics Committees*, Special Section: Research Ethics, 3: 522–32.

National Health and Medical Research Council, 1992, *NHMRC Statement on Human Experimentation and Supplementary Notes*, Canberra: National Health and Medical Research Council.

3

ETHICS AND EPIDEMIOLOGY: PROBLEMS FOR THE RESEARCHER

Judith Lumley

Because this account of some recent experiences with institutional ethics committees (IECs) will have a critical flavour, I feel the need to begin by reassuring you, or perhaps myself, that I regard ethical issues as an integral aspect of life and work. My concerns about research and ethics go back to 1968, when I wrote a chapter in my PhD thesis reflecting on ethical aspects of the clinical physiology experiments which formed the basis of the research project—something which, in retrospect, probably accelerated my shift to a different research methodology. Since then I have been a member of the Advisory Board of the Centre for Human Bioethics at Monash University, a member of the Queen Victoria Medical Centre Research Committee and a member of the Monash Medical Centre Ethics Committee.

The common themes in what follows are the frequent lack of due process, the need to distinguish technical from ethical issues and lack of agreement among IECs on the interpretation of the National Health and Medical Research Council (NHMRC) supplementary notes on epidemiological research. I will return to these themes at the end with some practical suggestions for researchers.

The chapter presents two case studies.

THE USE OF DIAGNOSTIC ULTRASOUND IN PREGNANCY AND ITS EFFECTIVENESS IN DETECTING FOETAL MALFORMATIONS BEFORE 20 WEEKS

BACKGROUND

Diagnostic ultrasound is used for a range of purposes in pregnancy: to see whether there is a developing foetus in early pregnancy, and to look for the presence of a foetal heartbeat if there are complications in the first months; to assess foetal growth and gestational age; to identify twins; to describe the location of the placenta; and to facilitate investigative procedures such as amniocentesis and chorion villus sampling. In recent years, an increasingly important role has been the identification of major malformations at a stage of pregnancy when recognition of the problem might well alter the management of the pregnancy. Choices such as giving birth in a teaching hospital, planning for assessment or surgery immediately after birth, testing the foetus for a chromosomal anomaly, making decisions about caesarean delivery, or deciding to terminate the pregnancy at that stage may result from such a diagnosis.

There was, and is, no available information in Australia about the extent and timing of obstetric ultrasound and the research project planned to collect that information very inexpensively across Victoria and combine it with an evaluation of *one* component of diagnostic ultrasound, its effectiveness in identifying major malformations before twenty weeks. The many randomised trials of ultrasound use in Europe and the U.S. have not been large enough to address this question.

Information on the number and timing of scans was planned to be obtained by adding three questions to the information collected routinely for every birth in Victoria. This was to be followed by a review of the scan reports and some additional information from the mother's and infant's medical record for all cases where there was a diagnosable major malformation—estimated to be 300–400 in a year, and for an equivalent sized random sample of infants with no reported malformations.

PROBLEMS

There are 140 to 150 hospitals in Victoria with maternity beds, all of which had to be approached for permission to ask the additional three questions. The Victorian Department of Health and Community Services has an IEC one of whose roles is to facilitate permission for research at multiple hospitals. Unfortunately an earlier research project (described below) had shown that being approved by this IEC—a process which took eight months—did not prevent any Victorian hospitals from requiring approval by their own IEC.

Examples of the experience of approaching hospitals included:

- The research committee of Hospital Z recommending to its ethics committee that the project be rejected on ethical grounds; the ethics committee deciding that these 'ethical concerns' were not ethical issues but research issues and referring it back to the research committee for review. These meetings took place over four months and members of the research team were interviewed by the committees on three separate occasions.
- A letter from the medical director of Hospital Y giving final approval and adding that we should know that many members of the medical staff 'thought there was a hidden agenda' to the project. He added that he did not, personally, share this view.
- A telephone call from the medical director of Hospital W telling me, reluctantly, that the hospital was about to refuse participation since a senior member of its medical staff—who was also on the staff of Teaching Hospital V—had informed him that Teaching Hospital V had rejected our application. This was completely untrue and I was almost too startled to respond. I did say that his senior colleague was misinformed, which, as he pointed out, did not seem likely. When I got my wits together I rang back to suggest that, with the permission of Teaching Hospital V, I would fax him a copy of its letter of approval. Hospital W then agreed to take part. I have described elsewhere a similar experience with IEC members misreporting decisions made by other institutions (Lumley, 1993).

Hospitals had marked differences in interpretation of the NHMRC's supplementary notes on epidemiological research when it came to the phase of the study requiring access to medical records, more than 1400 of them. Eleven private and two country hospitals required written patient consent for access to their medical records though this was not required for private patients in public hospitals. Some private hospitals also required permission from the woman's obstetrician. One required permission from the radiologist or ultrasonologist who had performed the scan as well. The impact of these factors on record access was substantial. Several women took the opportunity to ring a member of the research group to discuss the study in more detail. At least one of these women was in need of a counselling referral over the birth, and recent death, of her baby. All the women who telephoned were happy to permit access to their records. There was only one refusal among all the women whose written consent was sought. The main problem was non-return of the consent form by 76 women. A relatively large proportion of families move in the year after birth and there was no opportunity for the researchers to update the addresses or to send reminders, which would be the standard ways of improving the response rate.

I must, in fairness, add that the experiences described above were not universal. A majority of hospitals dealt with us in a courteous and professional way. All but three hospitals in Victoria—a large suburban private hospital, a suburban community hospital and a very small country hospital—finally took part.

The IEC and other internal hospital committee approval processes took nine months, or 30 per cent of the time funded for the project's completion.

SURVEY OF RECENT MOTHERS, 1989 AND 1994

BACKGROUND

The first of these surveys was carried out in conjunction with the Ministerial Review of Birthing Services as a way of providing information on the views of a large, representative sample of women who had recently given birth, about their satisfaction with care, their birth experiences and their preferences. The project involved a questionnaire mailed to all the women in Victoria who gave birth in a selected week. So that it would be both anonymous and confidential, hospitals were to mail it out and the recipient was to return it to the researchers in the enclosed stamped, addressed envelope. A letter from the researchers was also enclosed, giving telephone numbers for anyone who wished to ask any questions or make any comments, and also a brief account of the project in six community languages. Women were told that they were free not to reply but were requested to return the material anyway. Full details of the methodology have been published (Brown and Lumley, 1993).

The second survey, mailed out in March, 1994, was partly aimed at detecting changes in maternity services and satisfaction with care since the completion of the ministerial review, but it also took further some issues which had been identified as important in 1989 and in a follow-up interview study: women's physical health after childbirth, continuity of care, depression after birth and the special problems of women at high risk of complications.

In approaching IECs this time around, we were able to say that in 1989 the response rate had been over 71 per cent; that more than 30 per cent of women had written extensive comments at the end of the questionnaire and that more than half had given their telephone numbers, expressing willingness to take part in further research. The acceptability of the process had already been demonstrated, as had its usefulness in identifying common problems and setting reasonable priorities during the Birthing Services Review.

PROBLEMS

The 1989 survey took fifteen months to be approved by all maternity hospitals with IECs, including eight months by the IEC at the Department of Health and Community Services: the project was funded for only twelve months. The 1994 survey took fourteen months to complete the process, 33 per cent of the funded project duration.

- Each of the 26 IECs had a different proforma and different, highly specific, requirements for information. Many required ten or twelve copies of all the information. The material for the IECs required 47 reams of paper.
- In 1993, Hospital U lost all the documentation it was sent: only a follow-up phone call to ask how the IEC process was going brought this to light.
- In 1989, Hospitals S and T objected to a question asking whether the woman had been using birth control at the time she became pregnant. This question had to be deleted—we could not afford to print two versions of the questionnaire.
- In 1989, Hospital T also objected to a question about the woman's reaction to finding out she was pregnant—we pasted a white label over this question for all women who gave birth at Hospital T.
- In 1993, Hospital R wrote to say that it would not be taking part as some of the questions were biased. We wrote again at the end of the process to say that all other hospitals with IECs had approved and asked Hospital R to reconsider. We also asked which questions were causing problems so that they could be reviewed by the study's reference group, or possibly deleted for this hospital. The final response was that the questionnaire was 'constructed in a way which would condition the respondent towards consideration of negative outcomes, and would sub-sequent (sic) therefore bias the results in this respect'. The hospital saw no point in being more specific, as all the other major hospitals had approved, and they declined to participate.
- In 1989, there were several discussions about the mode of administration. We were told we should be handing out a single sheet of questions in the postnatal ward to be completed before the woman left hospital. The arguments for the timing and mode of administration are in fact technical ones, but the issue seemed to be perceived as a matter of 'common-sense'. Another 'common sense' issue was the length of the questionnaire. In 1993, an IEC member at Hospital Q stated: 'Beyond three pages what you'll be getting won't be worthwhile, I can assure you. Why don't you

limit it to the essentials?' The length had been subject to testing in the UK and found not to be a factor in acceptability or completion rates.

- The same member had concerns about biased questions. His example was: 'Were you given anything to speed up your labour?' We replied that any specific problems with questions would be referred back to the study's reference group. The hospital eventually decided to take part without requesting any changes.

- In 1993, Hospital P wanted us to add a question on women's knowledge of the risks of amniocentesis and chorion villus sampling. Despite a lengthy discussion about the very small numbers of women likely to have had either procedure in the sample, and the fact that the questionnaire did not deal with women's knowledge of any other procedures or her perception of their risks, the IEC continued to request the inclusion of this item in its subsequent letter to us but stopped short of requiring it as a condition of participation.

- IEC members at Hospital O doubted whether women would be able to recall the events of pregnancy and labour.

- Hospital N decided to implement an 'opting-out' procedure, which it did not inform us about until after it had done this. All the women who were to receive the questionnaire were sent a letter asking if they had any objections to receiving it. Those who objected within a given time were excluded from the study. Luckily, no one did object.

COMMON THEMES

THE PROCESS

Examples of lack of due process include cancellation of meetings, inability of institutions to give dates of meetings followed by requests to attend at two days' notice for an out-of-hours meeting, refusal to meet with the researchers to discuss perceived problems with the project, refusal to give specific reasons for rejecting a proposal, and lack of any appeal process.

TECHNICAL ISSUES

In a case-control study it may seem convenient to interview the people with the disorder (alias the cases) in hospital while they are still 'captive', and the people without the disorder (alias the controls) at home, but there are overwhelming technical reasons for approaching and interviewing both in exactly the same way. Similarly, it may seem convenient to give women a form about their satisfaction with care to fill out before they leave hospital after the birth rather than send them something later when they will be busy and distracted or they might have moved. Yet there is evidence that women have a different view of their birth and hospital experience several months later, when they are more willing to voice criticisms. Also, responding to an in-house survey while still a patient may make people reluctant to comment adversely.

The length of a questionnaire, the language, the timing of its administration, and the mode of administration are technical questions. Its acceptability to the group for whom it was designed, the burden its completion would place on them, the time required for completion, its comprehensibility are matters to be resolved in development and piloting. The 'best guess' of an IEC member on such issues is just that—a guess.

ACCESS TO MEDICAL RECORDS

In a current study, carried out in conjunction with the clinicians who provided the original care, we are following up 12 000 women who sought assisted conception between 1979 and 1992 in order to assess their risk of later breast and ovarian cancer. No contact is being made with women themselves. The hospitals involved and the IEC of the Anti-Cancer Council accepted the urgent need for the study and the impossibility of seeking consent from the 12 000 women before looking for cases of cancer in state cancer registries. Given that the reproductive technology programs and their former patients are not, and may not even wish to be, in continuing contact, the quality of the study and even its validity would likely be compromised by restricting it to those who could be found to give written consent. Other clinicians, researchers, counsellors and former patients have been certain that their own hospitals would never have agreed to the proposal and would have required written permission from the former patients. How do IECs weigh up the competing principles? Do they take account of logistic and feasibility issues? There is no doubt that the research question is an important one and that Australia is the best place, perhaps the only place, where it can be answered.

WORDS AND DEEDS

IEC members are intelligent, educated and articulate. Words are very important to them and they are especially sensitive to the ways in which language can be harmful or—as they themselves might put it—*intrusive*. Thus they ask to see the full text of questionnaires and survey instruments. They have a general duty of care with respect to animals which they take very seriously but they do not insist on examining the individual sheep or rats. Nor do they require applicants to come along to IEC meetings with instruments, probes and needles, though many of these are quite frightening. Thus we have the almost farcical situation of an IEC which approved all sorts of research in the development of reproductive technology refusing permission to follow up children born from assisted conception and their parents on the grounds that follow-up would be 'too intrusive'—unlike the procedures they had already undergone, presumably.

Similarly, women's experiences of pregnancy, birth and life with a new baby are very diverse and they often have negative and physically intrusive aspects; far more intrusive and negative than a question about the best and worst aspects of antenatal care or about how a woman felt when she discovered she was pregnant.

The reality is that people feel free to refuse to answer questions they do not like (classically, questions about family income); they have no compunction about throwing questionnaires in the rubbish bin. They annotate survey forms with apologies for the jam or the two-year-old's drawings and, most pertinent of all, they provide their own critique of the questions, and the gaps (Brown *et al*, 1994).

STRATEGIES FOR SURVIVING THE IEC PROCESS

SET UP A REFERENCE GROUP

Setting up a reference group at the beginning of a project has many benefits, but one of them is that the representation of stakeholders and interested parties will ensure that the project is not threatened by coming up against unrecognised professional interests and rivalries. The ultrasound project, for example, was widely perceived as being 'really about' questions such as which professional group—radiologists or obstetricians—should carry out obstetric ultrasound; whether ultrasonographers could interpret scans; or the (substantial) costs of routine scanning. No wonder we were seen as having a hidden agenda when in fact we were merely naive, and no wonder specific professionals had an effective veto over the project's approval. Professional groups within an institution may have an explicit power of veto as well as a more subtle influence over proceedings. Paul McNeill's critique of IECs and mine come together at this point.

In approaching IECs for the 1993 survey of satisfaction with maternity care, reference group members who were also members of the senior medical staff came to the IEC meetings with the research team, which demonstrated their understanding of and support for the project.

RECOGNISE THE TIME AND RESOURCE IMPLICATIONS

A major epidemiological project involving several institutions will take at least six to nine months to achieve IEC approval. If different committees request different changes to the protocols, the process can take a year. Quite apart from staff time, the costs in terms of paper, photocopying and postage can be substantial. It is wise to be prepared for this in advance and to plan to be doing something else at the same time. Unfortunately, full-time research groups wholly dependent on research grants do not yet have a way of supporting staff during these time periods.

A realistic understanding of the time involved is essential for students contemplating an honours or masters project as it is most unlikely they will be able to do anything which is not part of an already approved project.

TAKE ETHICAL ISSUES SERIOUSLY

One IEC requested a one-page attachment, among the papers to be submitted, describing the ethical considerations. We found this a helpful way to summarise our thinking for IECs and made this sheet a standard inclusion to other institutions.

BE POLITELY PERSISTENT

It is very easy to get depressed by the process and to stop pursuing approval. A better strategy is polite persistence; offering to attend the IEC meeting to clarify any points, always replying to any questions in writing, not giving up because it is taking too long, always asking for written reasons if there is a rejection, asking them to reconsider if there is the slightest chance they might be swayed by extraneous considerations such as all the teaching hospitals, or indeed all the other hospitals in the state, agreeing to take part.

FIND AN HONEST BROKER

Occasionally, when there are major disagreements between IECs, it may be possible to resolve them with the assistance of an 'honest broker', someone non-partisan, respected by all parties, who is also accepted as being knowledgeable about ethical issues. In the absence of an appeals process there may be no formal process available and therefore little to lose (Lumley, 1993). It was not necessary in either of the two case studies described above and it is indeed a strategy of last resort.

CONCLUSION

Given the responsibility of IECs and the uneven nature of the rewards and penalties they face (Pettit, 1992), I do not foresee any quick and easy solutions. Some form of cross-accreditation between hospital IECs is urgently needed but it is difficult to see who might take the responsibility for this, given the lack of success the Department of Health and Community Services has had in getting hospitals to allow the departmental IEC to approve projects on its behalf. One simple suggestion would be for the

Australian Health Ethics Committee to develop a standard form for submissions to IECs and for this to be tested by a variety of institutions for the range of research proposals they usually receive. Another is for researchers to document the process and its costs so that, if the present situation continues, it may be possible for these costs to become part of the research budget. A third is for the documentation of differing decisions about the same proposal, and for a forum for discussion of the ethical principles involved. A fourth is for the establishment of an appeals process through which, once again, attention can be given to the ethical principles involved. Finally, as the case studies make clear, many of the problems researchers encounter have very little to do with the ethics of epidemiological research.

ACKNOWLEDGMENTS

To the co-investigators in the projects mentioned in this chapter—Stephanie Brown, Robin Bell, Alison Venn, Judith Yates—who have borne the brunt of these experiences, my heartfelt thanks for permission to share the stories.

REFERENCES

Brown, S., Lumley, J., 1993, 'Antenatal care: A case of the inverse care law?', *Australian Journal of Public Health*, 17: 95–102.

Brown, S., Lumley, J., Small, R. and Astbury, J., 1994, 'Researching pregnancy, birth, motherhood and depression', S. Brown, J. Lumley, R. Small and J. Astbury (eds.), *Missing Voices: the experience of motherhood*, Melbourne: Oxford University Press.

Lumley J., 1993, 'Gate keeping by ethics committees'. In V. Brown and G. Preston (eds), *Choice and Change: ethics, economics and policy in public health*, Canberra: Public Health Association of Australia.

Pettit P., 1992, 'Instituting a research ethic: Chilling and cautionary tales', *Bioethics News*, 11, 4: 3–21.

4

MEDICINE AND THE ETHICAL CONDITIONS OF MODERNITY

Paul Komesaroff

Two major recent discussions have raised important questions about our understanding of the moral content of the medical sciences: the discussion concerning what used to be called 'practical philosophy' and that focusing on the nature of modernity and its status in the contemporary world. In this essay, I should like to set out some of the themes of these discussions and to consider their implications for medicine. Although my emphasis will be primarily on medical practice rather than on research, the results are broadly applicable to both areas, and in any case, I believe that the questions concerning the latter cannot be settled until those concerning the former are adequately clarified.

Discussions about ethics within medicine, like the classical discussions about ethics, depart from the question which anyone seeking to accomplish a practical task must answer: how should I proceed, what should I do? Within medical practice, this question is ever-present; furthermore, as is well recognised, depending on the circumstances, it may admit of a 'technical' as well as an 'ethical' interpretation. All cases, however, involve an appeal to a set of philosophical assumptions and a reliance on a historical tradition. In general, medical practitioners have understood the technical, or scientific, aspect of their work in conventional, positivistic terms, and in ethical debates they have tended to draw on the three classical sources of Kantian moral theory, utilitarianism and Aristotelian ethics. The basis for a questioning of these traditional assumptions arose from a number of theoretical developments out of which the contemporary debates have emerged.

These developments, which form the background for the discussions here, include the advent of the post-empiricist philosophy of science, which scrutinised the process of object formation within scientific theories and emphasised the dependence of the latter on normative considerations and social and cultural variables. They also include the development in sociology, psychology and philosophy of a variety of approaches purporting to offer alternatives to the erstwhile positivistic epistemologies, the most important of which were phenomenology, structuralism and the so-called 'post-structuralist' theories. And they include the enhanced appreciation that has developed of the heterogeneity and complexity of contemporary societies which in part derives from these theories. Against these tendencies, it should be acknowledged, within the biological sciences themselves there has also occurred in recent years a revival of old mechanistic and reductionist ideas, in the form of sociobiology and the biological reductionism of modern molecular genetics; this is an interesting and important phenomenon in its own right, but will not be considered further here.

THE MANY FACETS OF ETHICS IN MEDICINE

In the past 25 years or so, the ethical content of medicine has come to be understood in terms of the formulations arising from a cluster of theories known as 'bioethics' or 'biomedical ethics'. Although there is some heterogeneity amongst these theories they share certain common features—in particular, their commitment to a rational, universalistic ethical theory based on abstract principles. In spite of a superficial plausibility and a wide audience, however, bioethics has proved itself seriously limited, partly because medicine serves a wider variety of ethical goals than can be accommodated in these theories and partly because the assumptions on the basis of which they are constructed are themselves open to question.

Some of the ethical dimensions of medicine are obvious. Medicine can contribute directly to the relief of suffering and pain. By overcoming or mitigating the effects of disease and physical disability that have hitherto been limiting and have compromised the range of available choices, it can help to release us from the limitations imposed by our biological facticity. In individual instances, moreover, conflicts may arise which demand decisions regarding issues involving traditional moral values such as justice or the sanctity of human life. On the other hand, it is well recognised that the practical applications of medicine are limited and distorted by social conditions—by the facts of poverty and wealth, of impotence and power—and that the outcomes of medical knowledge and know-how are not unambiguously beneficent. Indeed, it has been argued trenchantly that the development of modern medicine has been associated with some profoundly malign social consequences (Illich, 1976), including the degradation of intimate and meaning-endowing human experiences into mere technical events (Illich, 1976: 26) and the loss of personal autonomy (Ehrenreich, 1978). In any case, it is clear that ethics is not merely adventitious with respect to medicine, affixed to it after the fact by philosophical experts. Ethics and medicine are intertwined; medicine, as Edmund Pellegrino once put it, is 'a practice of ethics'.

There is another sense in which medicine reveals itself as a practice of ethics. Every clinical relationship consists of a continuous series of ethical events each of infinitesimal dimension and often inconspicuous to the participants. The doctor within the clinical interaction is constantly faced with the ethical question, 'What should I do?' How, for example, should I ask this difficult or potentially intrusive question? How should I palpate the abdomen of this man in pain? How should I express the diagnosis of lung cancer to this elderly woman? Of course, there is nothing remarkable about questions of this kind, which are familiar to every clinician. In the flow of the clinical interaction they occur frequently, arising momentarily and being responded to in the ongoing process of communication. They demand ethical decisions, even if those decisions may be made in an intuitive manner. The character of the response may take many forms: it may involve a particular choice of words or manner of delivering those words, or it may be embodied in the pitch of the voice, the length of the pause or the softness of the touch. It will, of course, in turn evoke a response in the patient, to which a further adjustment by the doctor will be made. I admit that this pattern of response and counter-response is a long way from the more familiar processes of ethical argumentation; however, its irreducible ethical content is undeniable and, what is more, it is of crucial importance with respect to the clinical outcomes.

This constant process by which ethical issues arise, are dealt with in the course of the interaction and subsequently pass away, I call the 'microethical structure' of medicine. It is important to recognise the microethical domain because it allows us to describe what doctors and patients actually do, from an ethical perspective. It shifts the focus of ethical discourse about medicine to an analysis of the processes of moral decision-making in the clinical encounter and it makes it possible for us to undertake an anatomy of the ethical interaction in broader terms. It brings into visibility many issues that are inaccessible to the conventional viewpoints of biomedical ethics. Finally—and, of particular importance—it can provide a powerful tool for analysing the complexity of the clinical process and contributing to its further development.

Despite its central importance, the microethical aspect of medicine—and indeed, what might be called the 'sociology of moral action' in medicine—has been very much neglected from the theoretical point of view. The reasons for this are complex: they include the influence of the cultural tradition and the absence of adequate tools to deal with the phenomena that arise. Indeed, despite its straightforward appearance, the concept of microethics involves some very radical claims which entail a fundamental departure from many of the assumptions on which philosophical ethics has been built. For the perspective of microethics to be accepted, these claims need to be stated and justified in full; and, in addition, the overall utility of the theoretical approach needs to be demonstrated.

Microethics is an important component of both clinical medicine and research. This does not, however, imply that it exhausts the entire ethical content of the clinical relationship. It must be understood in the wider context mentioned above—of the social and cultural structures within which the ethical interactions occur and of the philosophical tradition which may be brought to bear in reflecting on ethical and even epistemological issues at a higher level of abstraction. The ethical dimension of medicine is heterogeneous and multi-faceted. To understand it we must have access to a theory that can accommodate this diversity and respond to contemporary cultural developments.

ETHICS AND THE ENLIGHTENMENT

Modern reflections on ethics in medicine derive in large part from the project in ethics which had its origins in the European Enlightenment around the mid-seventeenth century. The basic conviction that has guided this project has been the belief, inspired by science, that, in an unlimited, universal and inexorable way, progress will occur towards greater knowledge and social and moral improvement; inherent in this vision, furthermore, is the confidence that this progress will be generated and protected by the application of reason.

The Enlightenment provided the nascent project of the Galilean theory of nature with a definitive, systematic elaboration. The goals of science were articulated clearly and succinctly. Science was understood to be a critical part of a social project of universal scope and unlimited application; its *telos* was nothing less than the liberation of mankind through the complete mastery and domination of both external and internal nature. For almost 200 years this expansive—and perhaps somewhat immodest—objective provided the goal that guided the aspirations of scientists, philosophers, social theorists and political activists.

Ethical thinking and its self-interpretation were brought under the same project. Despite their formal differences, both the overall goals of philosophical ethics and its theoretical objectives—as expressed through its methods of argument and analysis—became continuous with those of science. Ethics and freedom were now coterminous, for, as Diderot put it, 'if man is not free . . . there can be no rational goodness or wickedness'. The goal of ethical thought, then, like that of science, was human liberation; accordingly, its standards were similarly anthropocentric. In addition, its theoretical objectives, again like those of science, included the abolition of doubt and the establishment of reliable locations for phenomena within systematic unities subject to irrefragable laws. To realise the goal of human liberation both the achievements and the methods of science were to be applied universally for the development of society. This objective was as important for moral sceptics like La Mettre as it was for utilitarians like Helvetius, materialists like Diderot or 'idealists' like Kant. For ethics, this meant that a single system of thought had to be sought which was capable of embracing all ethical values or, at least, of providing a method for the resolution of ethical problems.

As a result, in ethics, as in science and art, there was a powerful tendency to systematisation and unification (Taylor, 1989: 76–7); in the case of ethics and morality, the task was defined as the search for a rational justification of rules for good conduct. Indeed, morality itself became understood as a process of following rules, usually of universal application. This search for a single principle to guide action became a key feature of modern moral philosophy. Older approaches to ethics and morality, which had previously commanded wide acceptance, such as the foundational role of the virtues, or the recognition that there is a number of quasi-autonomous goods, were discounted. In the same way, the role of the philosopher was defined very narrowly. As with the great philosophical theorists of ethics, the philosopher's job was now to identify a procedure or set of procedures that would generate good actions or propositions.

The implications of these assumptions for contemporary ethical theory can be clearly seen in the two major schools of bioethical thought: utilitarian and deontological ethics. Both of these are firmly located in the Enlightenment tradition of philosophical ethics. They share the key assumptions mentioned above; in particular, they share a commitment to the elaboration of universally valid principles through the application of reason and they share an assumption of an objectivistic conception of values. These features constitute the basis both for the ongoing appeal of these theories and, as we shall see, of their main shortcomings.

CRITIQUES OF THE ENLIGHTENMENT PROJECT

The modern tradition of ethics has attracted vehement criticism almost from the beginning. The philosophical interrogations of Hegel, Kierkegaard, Nietzsche, Heidegger and others raised doubts about the ethical project of modernity, although they failed to supplant it. In modern ethics, and in medical ethics in particular, various approaches have come to exist outside the utilitarian and Kantian mainstreams of normative ethics; some of these draw on phenomenology, some on the Marxian tradition, some on a revival of the ideas of Aristotelian ethics. I would like to argue that these critical tendencies in fact are profoundly important for our understanding of clinical medicine and research because they both highlight the deficiencies of bioethics and suggest the possibility of alternative theoretical strategies.

A useful way to approach the modern critiques of ethical theory is to consider Hegel's critique of Kant's moral philosophy. This is because the work of the latter contains the most rigorous and complete embodiment of the Enlightenment project and that of the former its most telling interrogation. Hegel made three particularly potent criticisms of Kant: he charged that Kant's morality amounts to little more than an 'empty formalism', that it issues in an 'abstract universalism' and that, as a result, it is condemned to impotence.

Hegel argued that the formalistic approach taken by Kant prevented any concrete content being given to duties and maxims. As a result, he claimed, Kant's conclusions are either tautologous or, worse, they may actually sanction conduct that is clearly unconscionable. In the Kantian context, the moral viewpoint in general admits of normative statements—that is, statements which prescribe rules of conduct at a high level of generality—which arise in rational debate; however, it excludes evaluative statements about the good life and the chance of realising it in the existing culture. Hegel argues that 'the real bond of moral duty depends on the way in which duties bear on people's social roles and relationships in the ethical life of a rational social order' (Wood, 1990: 132). In other words, moral philosophy remains limited to a formal theoretical standpoint and cannot make contact with the deeper, underlying substrata of social interactions which constitute what Hegel refers to as 'ethical life' (Hegel, 1952: 89–90).

Related to this, Hegel argues that Kantian ethics is dependent on a commitment to an 'abstract universalism'. As a matter of general principle, it ignores the particular context, including the social and emotional contexts, in which problems arise. The concept of duty becomes not just the 'empty thought of universality' but moves to exclude or dominate all other relations (Hegel, 1971: 212). As a consequence of these commitments to empty formalism and abstract universalism, Hegel concludes, morality is impotent with respect to the accomplishment of the good. Because moral acts are restricted to those which are in accordance with 'the law', the good is left 'only in the idea, in representation'. Morality dichotomises reason and experience: it is incapable of making the transition from the pure 'ought' to the 'is' (Hegel, 1971).

These three criticisms by Hegel against Kant are telling ones for contemporary bioethical thought. In all its major variants, bioethics is committed to the distinction between the normative and the evaluative. The whole purpose of ethics, as conceived by the bioethical thinkers, is to provide a machinery for analysing and resolving conflicts and dilemmas through the application of rational modes of thought. Rational argument is the exclusive medium within which conflict resolution takes place. In one sense this approach is unobjectionable: rational discourse is, for example, clearly preferable to violence. However, its main problem is its omission—previously referred to—of the level of ethical life. For Hegel, ethical life—which he calls *Sittlichkeit*—is an essential part of the social world. It is the stratum of social life which is organised into institutions and experienced by individuals in their daily interactions. It is the 'living shape of organic totality' of a community (Hegel, 1975: 108). It thus has a double aspect: it is both a differentiated and structured social order and a subjective disposition within that order; or, put differently, it is both a 'relation between many individuals' and the 'form of the concrete subject' (Wood, 1990: 196).

Bioethics is also vulnerable in relation to the second criticism—that of abstract universalism. The emphasis on normative ethics limits the ability of bioethical theories to consider not just the contexts within which norms are applied but the intersubjective processes through which moral actions are effected in general. What is omitted here is not merely analyses of individual cases, but also the performative aspects of moral interchanges— that is, the manner in which they are located and oriented. Finally, there is also a strong case that bioethics is in practical terms impotent—that is, that it is incapable of effecting the transition from theory to action. This is a more controversial point; here, we shall say no more than that, despite all the debate it has generated about public policies, there appears to be no evidence that biomedical ethics has beneficially affected medical practice at the level of the clinic (Komesaroff, 1995).

Hegel's identification of key problems within Kant's practical philosophy facilitated the development of a variety of alternative approaches to moral theory. In the contemporary context, two of the most important of these are the so-called neo-Aristotelian theories and the discourse ethics of Jurgen Habermas, to which we advert only briefly here.

Habermas seeks to continue the tradition of Kantian ethics, albeit with modifications to overcome the difficulties revealed by Hegel. Like Kant, he is committed to the possibility of universal moral principles, and he continues the search for a method for establishing normative rules through rational argumentation. He departs from the latter—and, for that matter, from the rest of the philosophical tradition—however, by shifting the emphasis decisively towards 'communicative action'—that is, social action directed towards communicative, rather than primarily technical or strategic, ends. For Habermas, communicative action and, specifically, linguistically mediated interactions, constitutes the basic motor of the social processes. In accordance with this basic perspective, his ethical theory is intended precisely to reformulate the Kantian project in inter-subjective terms, as an analysis of moral argumentation. This approach leads to some very strong conclusions, such as his statement of a 'universal principle' of moral action which, he claims, has binding force with respect to communicative interactions in general. In addition, it succeeds in shifting the focus of the traditional moral discourse to the moral 'lifeworld', to use a terms of Husserl's employed frequently by Habermas—that is, to the interactive context within which moral decisions are made, a context which, in the medical context, ought to include the microethical domain.

Unfortunately, however, the moral lifeworld for Habermas is curiously partial and attenuated. His commitment to the search for universal normative principles and his decision to restrict moral phenomena to conflicts in linguistically mediated discursive contexts prevents his theory from gaining access to the interactive contexts within which the great bulk of our ethical experiences occur. Indeed, it is precisely one of Habermas's defining criteria of moral phenomena that they are disengaged from, and therefore cannot be contaminated by, the local conventions of particular forms of life. Accordingly, his theory ultimately prescinds from the real (linguistic and non-linguistic) context of interaction. This condemns it to a very limited field of application—and certainly excludes it from making a contribution at the level of the clinical interchange. As a result, Habermas's discursive reconstruction of Kantian ethics itself ultimately results in a disappointing impotence.

A quite different approach is taken by the so-called 'neo-Aristotelian' philosophers. Like Habermas, they set out to provide an ethics appropriate to the modern age that circumvents the abstractions and formalism in the extant tradition that Hegel exposed so powerfully. Whereas Habermas attempts to develop a procedural approach to morality by radically separating the right and the good, they seek to resurrect a universalistic ethics of the good that appeals to supreme goods transcending all particular forms of life. For them, although ethical judgments are understood to be dependent on specific contexts and circumstances, they are nonetheless not guided by the classical moral question 'What ought I to do?' but by the more encompassing question 'What is the good life?'. Thus Charles Taylor seeks to identify 'constitutive goods', which are underlying moral sources on the basis of which not only individual goods but the motivation to do and be good arises (Taylor, 1989: Chapter 4); similarly, Alasdair MacIntyre, in a classical Aristotelian fashion, outlines a range of 'virtues' the possession of which enables us to achieve specific goods (MacIntyre, 1987: Chapter 14).

This perspective, like that of discourse ethics, offers a trenchant critique of the dominant traditions of moral thought. Further, it emphasises the need for an exploration of 'the order in which we are set as a locus of moral sources', an order 'that is only accessible through personal, hence "subjective" resonance' (Taylor, 1989: 510). On the other hand, as Habermas has argued, it is subject to major problems, which include its alleged commitment to ahistoricism and methodological individualism

(Habermas, 1993: Chapter 3), and its inability to deal with the pluralism of modern societies.

From the point of view of medicine, neo-Aristotelianism undoubtedly has much to offer. However, in view of the variety of the cultural perspectives of individual doctors and patients and the multiplicity of purposes that medicine can serve, serious questions are raised about the claim that competing ways of life can be arranged hierarchically. Further, at the local or microethical level, it is rare that values guiding decision-making can be directly linked to constitutive goods, and attempts to do so tend to be not only theoretically implausible but also often practically restrictive.

THE POSTMODERNIST CHALLENGE TO THE PROJECT OF MODERNITY

While the 'Enlightenment project of ethics' was being subjected to a barrage of criticisms and alternatives, important cultural changes were occurring in the society as a whole—changes with the capacity to produce a profound, direct effect on both the theory of morality and the practice of medicine. The integrity of the project of modernity itself was being thrown into question and its most fundamental assumptions subjected to a searing critique. For some, these changes amount to an epochal transition: from modernity to postmodernity. Now, it is important to note that the nature of 'postmodernism' and its status as a concept remain controversial (Lyotard, 1986; Baudrillard, 1983; Heller and Feher, 1988; Jameson, 1984). Nonetheless, there are certain novel features of the contemporary cultural configurations of developed Western societies which demand to be acknowledged. These include a rejection of the commitment to certain knowledge and the search for an irrefutable foundation for truth. They include a particular emphasis on the need for an ongoing reflection on, and awareness of, the process of the generation of cultural products, including, in particular, of knowledge itself. And they include a rejection of the 'grand narrative' as historically obsolete—especially the great cultural constructions of 'humanity', of 'the proletariat', of 'womankind', of 'beauty', of 'truth' and of the project of universal 'liberation' (Lyotard, 1986: 31). The central subject from which truth and knowledge have flowed for 300 years is abolished; and the notion of a single totalising reason as the organon, guarantor and guardian of knowledge is abandoned (Lyotard, 1986; Derrida, 1982).

From the point of view of postmodernity, in the place of knowledge (in the singular) are now discourses (in the plural) (Murphy, 1991: 118), which can proliferate, and may be incommensurable, but nonetheless are not excluded from the demands of rigour and complexity. In the place of reason there are only 'reasons' (van Reijen and Veerman, 1988: 278). In the place of the central, potent subject is the 'decentered' subject, no longer structurally disengaged from the social processes which constituted it, but implicated within them and constantly being generated by them. The postmodern world, then, is a place of infinite variety and diversity. In it there are no fixed, unchallengeable criteria for judgment. Instead, contending perspectives are fostered and encouraged. This world is a place of radical freedom, in which the existential choices extend not just to the external circumstances of one's life but to the nature of one's subjectivity itself. The postmodern person is thus *contingent*; this is, so it is claimed, the shared experience of the contemporary world (Heller, 1989–90).

While postmodern theory has been applied to art and art criticism and to other aspects of culture in the computer age, it must be observed that it has been applied to a much more limited extent to ethical theory, and almost not at all to medical ethics in respect of either clinical practice or research. Nonetheless, the overall arguments are as compelling here as they are with respect to aesthetics. The dissolution of aesthetic norms has meant a transformation in the nature of artistic creation. No longer is art subject to the category of beauty—which, as the principle guiding the production of artistic works, itself only came into existence with the Renaissance (Heller, 1981: 252–3). Instead, art can now subserve a wide variety of aesthetic interests, 'an infinity of purposes', as Husserl said in another context. It can now challenge many of the distinctions formerly assumed to be inviolable—the distinction between art and everyday life, and between the high and the popular cultures, for example—and it can discover new tasks and experiment with new methods of creation. Similarly, in postmodern society ethics is concerned with a wide range of issues regarding values, the nature of the good life and how one should behave in relation to other people both in general and in specific circumstances. Here too, there has been a growing recognition that society is a battleground for contending value systems. As Max Weber—one of the great theorists of modernity—put it: 'forty years ago there existed a view that of the various possible points of view one was correct. Today, this is no longer the case; there is a patchwork of cultural values' (Weber, 1949: 3–4).

Just as in the field of aesthetics there is no single category of beauty that can provide a universally applicable aesthetic norm, so also in ethics there is no longer a single, universally valid, category of the good. There is not one good but an infinity of goods; there is not one method but a multiplicity of discursive frameworks within which ethical analysis and debate can occur (Lyotard, 1985: 50–9). Once again, great systems are opposed rather than sought, and diversity is promoted and celebrated. The task of ethics is no longer to define the nature of the good, or duty, or 'the ends of man', and much less to derive irrefragable principles for correct action. Rather, it is to uncover the nature of ethical values and the process of value creation; it is to examine existing concepts and to expose their hidden assumptions; and it is to challenge the hegemony of existing value systems and so to expand the possibilities for ethical action.

AN ANATOMY OF THE ETHICAL INTERCHANGE WITHIN MEDICINE

From this brief survey of the deficiencies of the contemporary bioethical constructions and the cultural changes that have characterised late modernity, some proposals regarding the understanding of medicine and its ethical content can be put forward. These proposals must recognise several important facts. First, given the diversification and differentiation of the project of ethics in the 'postmodern' world, it must be accepted that the field of ethical phenomena can be limited neither by the search for universal norms nor by the pursuit of the good life. Rather, evaluative activities that are not specifically orientated towards the good have become equally valid components of the ethical domain. Second, not all interactive behaviour with ethical content occurs in the context of theoretical discourse aimed at generating universally valid norms. While moral action may always carry *some* normative content, this may be only 'local', in the sense of being restricted to the immediate context of interaction rather than extending to the social group or the society as a whole. Third, the importance of this local aspect of ethical interactions—that is, the microethical aspect—needs to be recognised and its nature examined. It is apparent that, in addition to providing the actual site at which moral interactions occur and at which new practical interventions are introduced and tested, the microethical domain has a substantive content and structure of its own. And fourth, the relationship between the microethical structures and the larger-scale structures of ethical organisation in the society need to be elaborated and their dynamics described; in other words, we need to study the interchanges between the ethical structures of the lifeworld (to use Husserl's term again) and those of the social and cultural system as a whole. In particular, medicine must be understood as a complex set of value-laden practices embedded in the social and cultural structures of an evolving society.

Medical practice, and its ethical dimensions in particular, are therefore complex and heterogeneous, but they nonetheless have a definite structure. There are at least three strata. Viewed from the broadest perspective, there are *global* structures which are common to every interaction with ethical content. These have the status of conditions of possibility of ethical discourse; they include procedural principles of universal application, such as Habermas's discursive reformulation of the categorical imperative (with the understanding that the ethical field be expanded to include non-linguistically mediated phenomena). I have said that these principles are 'universal', on the basis of their putative transcendental status, although this should be qualified with the possibility that they may be culturally specific and therefore subject to variation between societies with widely different cultures and traditions. In a functional sense, these principles may be regarded as *constitutive* of the ethical interaction *per se* and are not different for medicine than for any other interactive context.

At the next level, there are the ethical forms that derive from the social groups to which the participating individuals belong. In terms of the interaction, these can be characterised in relation to the specific discursive forms that are deployed in the exchange. In any particular case, there may be several discourses acting simultaneously. Furthermore, the possibility exists of at least some of these having the capacity to reflect on the others—to act, that is, as a 'metadiscourse'; this is precisely the case with the medical discourse. Imperatives can be derived at this level, but they are *regional* rather than universal; their applicability is restricted to the discursive frameworks in which they are embedded. Functionally, these regional imperatives, therefore, are of a *regulative* kind. In the medical context, the regional level refers to the particular discourses that are employed in clinical interactions—the 'biological', the 'social', the 'psychological', the 'therapeutic' and so on—and to the specific requirements that emerge from the structures of the particular relationships that are established. Here it is important to recognise that each discourse may be associated with a set of moral imperatives of its own, and that these may not all be consistent; at this level, therefore, there is a proliferation of moral values, each with a purely regional sphere of applicability.

Finally, at the *local* level, there are the interactive practices that occur within the constraints of the lifeworld. This is the level of microethics—in functional terms, the *substantive* level of the ethical relationship. Here, the interchange proceeds incrementally, with constant reference and responsiveness to its specific circumstances and the changing local context. It is subject to the contingencies of individual interchanges, and because there are many degrees of freedom, the processes may be highly unpredictable. The constitutive principles and the regulative imperatives of the global and the regional structures continue to operate here; however, at this level, there are no endogenous rules to guide conduct along a predetermined path and there are no ultimate criteria by which actions can be retrospectively judged. Any 'ethic' here can be no more than a local procedural one—for example along the lines of an 'ethic of responsibility'; but it must be remembered that even this will be devoid of teleological content.

The microethical domain, despite its unavoidable presence in any ethical interaction, has been remarkably neglected in theoretical discussions about ethics. Because of this lack of study, at this stage a limited amount can be said about its structures. Nonetheless, it is apparent that the microethical domain does have structures of its own; these are substantially the structures of interpersonal interaction in the lifeworld. Some of the characteristic features of the microethical domain have already been described. Its phenomena are continuous, in the sense of constituting an infinite array of infinitesimal events. Each of these is contingent on the current state of the interactive context; because the latter is itself subject to a great many degrees of freedom this makes microethical phenomena inherently unpredictable, and subject to extreme variations with respect to initial conditions. Within the microethical domain, each subject may speak with different voices at different times; this adds further to its heterogeneity and complexity.

The three domains that constitute the ethical structure of medicine are of course interdependent. The global domain is logically prior, in the sense of constituting conditions of possibility for any ethical relationship. On the other hand, the microethical domain is factually and practically prior, since all ethical behaviour passes through this realm and is therefore subject to its structural constraints, including its uncertainties: it is the interface between interpersonal interactions and the remainder of the ethical appa-ratus; it functions as the domain within which values arise and are tested, and ethical pathologies manifest themselves.

ISSUES IN RESEARCH

The theses advanced above apply not only to medical practice but also, equally, to clinical research, where, I believe, they have important practical implications. In both cases, ethical considerations at the global, regional and local levels frequently arise, often closely intertwined.

It is beyond the limits of this essay to pursue an analysis of individual cases (cf. Komesaroff, 1995). However, it may be noted, by way of example, that in any research project, it is obviously important that certain truth claims, such as those supporting the scientific value of the project, can be relied upon and that the information that is given to potential subjects is valid in every detail; these are issues that arise at the global level of ethical discourse. At the regional level, it is important to distinguish the roles of the physician and those of the scientist. Clearly, these are not the same: indeed, their internal goals not only may diverge but at times may actually conflict. It need not be doubted that *as doctors* clinicians want the best for their patients; however, at the same time, *as scientists*, they also want to discover new knowledge for the benefit of other patients, to achieve personal recognition, to advance their careers and so on. It is important to recognise the different discourses in operation and to identify their specific internal imperatives. On occasions, a lack of clarity about the obligations entailed by concurrent roles can cause confusion and uncer-tainty.

At the local level, it is often assumed that the researcher is obliged merely to present the facts to the patient and to allow him or her, as an 'autonomous' subject, to make decisions. This, however, ignores the obvious fact that people with serious diseases are often frightened and vulnerable, bewildered and disoriented, as a result of which they may lack precisely the conditions necessary for autonomous decision-making; indeed, in an obvious sense, that is why they came to a doctor in the first place. Under these circumstances, it is very easy for an investigator to rely on his or her position of trust as a physician to influence the decisions of a patient. The microethical complexity, however, extends still further than this: in any given situation there may be a multiplicity of relationships and ethical responsibilities at stake, involving other health-care workers, relatives or members of the general community, and each of these may contribute important ethical issues which add to the intricate network of values that has to be negotiated. It is part of the special interest and poignancy of both clinical medicine and clinical research that all such questions must be dealt with simultaneously in the various extant dimensions of ethical communication.

CONCLUSION

Departing from contemporary debates about the nature of ethics and society, this essay has examined some aspects of the ethical structure of medicine. In broad formulations, it has suggested that in the light of these debates some fundamental assumptions about morality and morally moti-vated actions must be reassessed. In particular, the possibility of an ethical theory that is not only structurally committed to heterogeneity and diver-sity but also radically disengaged from any unitary notion of the good, must be seriously considered.

Although for some this conclusion may appear somewhat disquieting, it would seem unavoidable if the achievements of modernity are to be taken seriously and the rich, multi-faceted nature of the medicine to which it has given rise is to be recognised. In addition, it provides a much-needed tool for analysing in detail the moral content of both clinical medicine and medical research and thereby for deepening our appreciation of the nature of medicine.

REFERENCES

Baudrillard, J., 1983, *Simulations*, New York: Semiotext(e).

Derrida, J., 1982, 'The ends of man'. In *Margins of Philosophy*, London: Harvester Press.

Ehrenreich, J. (ed.), 1978, *The Cultural Crisis of Modern Medicine*, London: Monthly Review Press.

Habermas J., 1990, *Moral Consciousness and Communicative Action*, Cambridge MA: MIT Press.

——1993, *Justification and Application*, Cambridge MA: MIT Press.

Hegel, G.W.F., 1952, *Philosophy of Right*, Oxford: Oxford University Press.

——1971, *Early Theological Writings*, tr T.M. Knox, Philadelphia: University of Pennsylvania Press.

——1975, *Natural Law*, tr T.M. Knox, Philadelphia: University of Pennsylvania Press.

Heller, A., 1981, *Renaissance Man*, New York; Schocken Books.

——1989–1990, 'The contingent person and the existential choice', *The Philosophical Forum* xxi (1–2).

Heller, A. and Feher, F., 1988, *The Postmodern Political Condition*, London: Polity.

Illich, I., 1976, *Limits to Medicine*, London: Marion Boyars.

Jameson, F., 1984, 'Postmodernism, or the cultural logic of late capitalism', *New Left Review*, 146, 53–93.

Komesaroff, P.A., 1995, 'From bioethics to microethics: The need to return medical ethics to the clinic'. In P.A. Komesaroff (ed.), *Troubled Bodies: critical perspectives on postmodernism, medical ethics and the body*, Durham: Duke University Press and Melbourne: Melbourne University Press.

Lyotard, J-F., 1986, *The Postmodern Condition: a report on knowledge*, Manchester: Manchester University Press.

Lyotard, J-F., 1985, *Postmodern Condition* and *Just Gaming*, Minneapolis: University of Minneapolis Press.

MacIntyre, A., 1987, *After Virtue*, London: Duckworth.

Murphy, P., 1991, 'Postmodern perspectives and justice', *Thesis 11*, 30: 118.

Reijen, W. van and Veerman, D., 1988, 'Interview with Jean-François Lyotard', *Theory, Culture and Society* 5, 2–3: 277–311.

Taylor, C., 1989, *Sources of the Self*, Cambridge MA: Harvard University Press.

Weber, M., 1949, 'The meaning of "ethical neutrality" in sociology and economics'. In *The Methodology of the Social Sciences*, New York: The Free Press.

Wood, A.M., 1990, *Hegel's Ethical Thought*, Cambridge: Cambridge University Press.

PART II

Basic research and experimental designs

The biomedical disciplines dominate decision-making on many health research ethics committees. From the perspective of other disciplines it is therefore of particular interest to understand how such researchers go about the task of defining ethical research within their own sphere. In laboratory research the focus may be on tissues or human effluent which, once collected, are seen as having little continuing interest for the people who donated the specimens. Study participants are presumed to benefit indirectly via benefits to medical science. With experimental studies conducted in the field, issues become more complex since more may be asked of whole, living study participants. The emphasis therefore shifts towards offering them access to direct benefits from the study. In both basic research and experimental studies, it is rare for study participants to be informed directly of the results of the research. The audience is biomedical science itself. This scenario shifts when clinicians do research involving their own patients.

If the participation of 'subjects' in laboratory research is justified in terms of benefit to science, presumably translating into eventual improvement in community health, the high level of health-research funding allocated to the biomedical sciences has ethical implications for the funding of other areas of health research which also have the potential to contribute. Richard Larkins mounts an ethical defence of this funding. He draws on a pragmatic interpretation of ethics, emphasising the capacity of biomedical science to benefit the community through a direct contribution to knowledge and understanding about health and illness, indirectly providing long-term economic benefits, humanitarian gains and better health care.

Terry Nolan emphasises the contribution to health care from clinical research. The scientific benchmark for experimental research conducted with living human subjects is the randomised controlled trial, in which participants are randomly allocated to an experimental group and a control group, allowing comparison of results. In conducting trials, however, scientific interest in the results of the trial must be balanced with questions about potential harm to participants—including delays in access to a new development until it has been tested. He argues that the generally acceptable principles for conducting a randomised controlled trial need to be reassessed in particular contexts, with particular groups of people, including children and adolescents.

Gordon Guyatt addresses the problem of applying the randomised controlled trial to the individual patient in order to optimise the clinical management of that patient: the N-of-1 trial. Ethics committees, in Guyatt's experience, insist that N-of-1 RCTs be treated as research. The implicit policy is that physicians can prescribe medication without careful monitoring of the results and avoid scrutiny, but if they rigorously ensure that patients are benefiting by using a research design, ethical scrutiny is required. He argues that ethics committee review should be required only if clinicians intend to publish their work; when the procedures, tests, interventions, or questionnaires completed by the patient go beyond the requirements of optimal clinical care; or when individual patients might be publicly identified.

Ian McDonald sums up the section, arguing that traditional ethical considerations in biomedical research have been replaced with complex, technical issues to do with the design of randomised controlled trails. Central to these problems is the relationship between clinicians and patients whom they have to enrol in trials if the scientific requirements of trial design are to be met. He suggests that participation in experimental research should be the subject of community debate and that there be a balanced allocation of funds on the basis of the potential contributions of the various disciplines involved in health research.

5

Basic research and the ethics of resource allocation

Richard Larkins

In these days of financial constraints, it is tempting to use all the funds available for health care for the prevention of disease and the treatment of sick patients. The long-term benefits of basic medical research often appear to be an unaffordable luxury. However, a very small proportion of the huge sums required for acute health-care services allows good support for basic research and there is compelling evidence that it is a wise and sound investment.

The following are some of the arguments for allocating adequate resources for basic medical research.

ECONOMIC

Although we should not think of economics as the major principle under-lying allocation of resources, there ceases to be any logical argument against funding basic medical research if it can be demonstrated that the economic returns justify it. Two pieces of evidence from the past suggest that there is a very large potential for economic returns from investing in basic medical research.

The amount of money saved in direct health costs from the prevention of polio by the introduction of the Salk and then the Sabin vaccine is greater than the entire global expenditure on medical research. Thus, it could be argued that any future economic dividend is in the way of a bonus, the investment having already justified itself. The second example relates to increasing income rather than cutting expenditure as a result of medical research. It is claimed that the earnings from marketing a single drug (cimetidine) have been greater than the income from the entire wool clip of Australia.

Thus, history tells us that the findings that can flow from basic medical research have the potential both to save huge amounts of money and to produce a large income. In response to those who might say that such savings or income are from the past, and that there is little potential for similar returns in the future, one need only point out that the development of effective anti-viral treatments for influenza and HIV infection, effective treatment of solid tumours and the effective prevention or treatment of diabetes would have huge financial implications both in terms of savings and in terms of income for marketing the drug(s). This year's medical research allocation in Australia is approximately equivalent to the cost to Medicare of an influenza outbreak, demonstrating the relative triviality of expenditure on research in relation to the potential savings and income.

HUMANITARIAN

Most of us would regard this as a more significant argument for basic medical research. Again, history demonstrates the effectiveness of medical research in delivering new drugs and technology that have enabled effective treatment for tuberculosis, made leukaemia and lymphomas curable diseases, produced effective anti-bacterial treatment and allowed precise diagnosis of those conditions.

The argument has been put forward that in an overpopulated world, developing cures for the scourges of mankind will only worsen the problem. However, it should be borne in mind that it is medical research that has provided the detailed knowledge of the physiological regulation of reproduction which has enabled the development of effective methods of birth control (both pharmacological and 'natural'), which is surely the only humanitarian way of regulating population growth. Many challenges lie ahead, but again the record justifies expenditure on basic research because of the proven contribution of advances derived from basic research toward the health and welfare of mankind. For the future, the relief of suffering which will come from the development of effective vaccines against malaria and HIV infection is almost unimaginable.

BASIC MEDICAL RESEARCH PROVIDES TOOLS WHICH CAN INFORM EPIDEMIOLOGY, PUBLIC HEALTH AND PREVENTIVE MEDICINE

Some argue that it is better to spend money on public health and disease prevention than on basic medical research. However, the two are complementary, and indeed diagnostic techniques derived from basic research have been essential in planning effective public health programs dependent on charting the spread of disease and devising methods of disease prevention.

The demonstration that the human immunodeficiency virus is the cause of AIDS, and the ability to identify infected individuals; the identification of the several different viruses causing hepatitis and the ability to trace their spread in the community and identify infected individuals are instances in which sound public health measures could not be devised without the knowledge derived from basic medical research. The ability to make prenatal diagnosis of disease at a stage when many find therapeutic abortion safe and acceptable, will allow the prevention of many cases of cystic fibrosis, Huntington's disease, Down's syndrome and many other genetically determined conditions. Of course, this ability also raises ethical issues, but it does enable individuals to make informed decisions. The development of a range of vaccines to prevent diseases such as measles, diphtheria and polio has depended on the ability to identify and culture viruses and bacteria.

Rather than arguing that resources should go to either basic medical research or to public health and preventive medicine, we should recognise that the two work together to advance the health of our community.

TECHNOLOGY TRANSFER

It has also been argued that, as Australia has a relatively small population base and a correspondingly small gross domestic product, it is hard for it to develop a critical mass in basic medical research and that it would be more rewarding to rely on advances developed in other countries. Apart from the history of major contributions by Australian scientists to the pool of world knowledge and the moral responsibility for Australia to play its part in furthering scientific knowledge underpinning medical practice, the involvement of Australians in basic medical research in their own country facilitates introduction of new technology that may have been developed overseas. For example, widespread introduction of molecular techniques for diagnosis of disease, in particular genetic disease, is dependent on Australia having a pool of medical scientists working in the areas of molecular biology and able to understand the significance of the new techniques and introduce them into clinical practice. Many new diagnostic and therapeutic tests and procedures are introduced in essentially research environments before becoming part of a routine laboratory. For this technology transfer to be effective, it is important that there be a close interface between clinicians and scientists. For this reason, it is very important that clinical academic departments have a blend of basic scientists working on clinically relevant topics and clinicians with sufficient scientific understanding and training to be able to contribute to the basic research and also to interpret the findings of that research in terms of their relevance to clinical medicine.

PURSUIT OF KNOWLEDGE AND UNDERSTANDING

Quite apart from any pragmatic justification for basic medical research, there is a more abstract justification: namely that it is part of the pursuit of knowledge and contributes to our understanding of the human condition. Much of human activity has been based on the desire to expand knowledge of the physical and biological environment in which we live, and virtually all of modern life is dependent on curiosity-driven research and investigation of one form or another. There is a parallel between our desire to understand the basis of biological existence and our desire to understand the nature of matter and the nature of our planet and our universe.

The alternative to continually trying to expand our knowledge is stasis, apathy, lack of curiosity, susceptibility to dogma and an inability to respond to new challenges. Having argued, perhaps defensively, for the allocation of some of our precious resources to basic medical research, I believe it is important to qualify some of my arguments by emphasising the need for balance and responsibility on the part of the researchers. For example, although curiosity-driven research has in general terms proven to be cost effective, those receiving public funds have a continuing responsibility to use these funds in an accountable manner. Part of this responsibility involves using money only to fund projects of high quality, and being able to justify research by demonstrating its potential relevance. Thus, the pursuit of knowledge for its own sake cannot be taken to such extremes that the study of fascinating phenomena with no potential impact on health, and little generalisability to other situations, receives public funding. It is therefore important that processes be set in place to ensure accountability and the allocation of resources to projects which have potential to provide useful information—albeit often at a basic level. The National Health and Medical Research Council (NHMRC) has developed a system whereby the final grading of research applications is done by a multidisciplinary committee after scrutinising reports from experts in the field of the application. Applicants are therefore required to demonstrate not only the scientific merit of their proposal but also its potential relevance to health. It must be borne in mind, however, that since the potential relevance may not be entirely apparent at the time of the initial investigation, a fine balance must be struck.

A corollary of much of the above is that attempting to target spending at specific diseases (such as breast cancer) may not be the most effective way to produce major advances in the management of the particular condition. For example, money specifically spent on breast cancer research may lead to marginal improvements in survival rates using different balances of currently available treatments, but the next quantum leap forward in our management will come from much more basic research areas, such as the regulation of the cell cycle, the regulation of oncogene expression in the cell, retroviral research, more knowledge about the nature and regulation of growth factors, and other basic research.

In most developed countries, at least 2 per cent of the health-care budget is allocated to government-funded research. The current allocation in Australia is considerably smaller than this, and it is logical from every point of view to increase it to this level. Basic medical research justifies the expenditure of this small amount of the total health-care budget because it is cost effective, because it has and will continue to produce results in terms of the health and well-being of our community, and because it provides information essential for preventive medicine and public health, aids technology transfer and helps us to better understand the human condition.

CONCLUSION

Basic medical research has proven itself to be cost effective. Major benefits to humanity have come from its application, and there remain important problems whose solution can only come from basic medical research. Epidemiology and public health policy both use the tools and knowledge that basic medical research provides; this illustrates their complementary relationship. Effective transfer of advances in basic medical research achieved in other countries to clinical practice in Australia requires an active coterie of scientists and clinicians involved in basic research in that country. Finally, basic medical research, like other forms of research, involves the pursuit of a better understanding of the nature of life and existence. To fail to support it is to favour intellectual stagnation, susceptibility to dogma and an inability to respond to new challenges.

6

TRADITIONAL SCIENTIFIC
DESIGNS AND ETHICS

Terry Nolan

This section focuses on some ethical issues associated with the use of human experimentation to determine the risks and benefits of therapeutic and preventive interventions. It is, however, misleading to dichotomise clinical care and clinical research, an argument made by Gordon Guyatt in his essay on N-of-1 trials. In effect, he argues that the view from the laboratory bench should be no different from the view from the bedside when we consider the role of participants in health research.

What are traditional scientific designs anyway? In the context of human experimentation, traditional designs are probably uncontrolled case series and historical comparisons (Figure 1). While the idea of a controlled evaluation is ancient, it is only in the past 40 years that we have witnessed the incarnation of the modern randomised clinical trial. In this short time, it has struggled to achieve popular benchmark status. To be sure, its rigour and uncompromising standards have been held up by some as the shining gold standard of medical science (Silverman, 1985; Feinstein, 1985; Sackett, Haynes and Tugwell, 1985), but its tight constraints have frustrated others, who have called for modifications (Zelen, 1979) or even replacement by some as yet unspecified, equally solid but logistically easier tool (Royall, 1991; Hellman and Hellman, 1991). Worse still, some have continued medicine's ancient tradition of not bothering to undertake rigorous evaluation at all.

Figure 1 outlines the principal research designs used for the evaluation of therapies in humans. Comparative studies are inherently stronger in evidential quality, principally because they permit discounting of maturational (natural history) effects of the condition under study. Designs with internal controls—those in which controls are sampled from the same pool as that from which the cases are drawn—are not subject to serious concerns

Figure 1   An outline of experimental evaluation designs used for human therapies

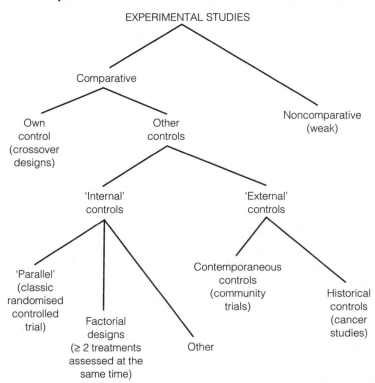

about comparability (that is, fairness), which externally controlled studies almost always experience.

Now, some might regard themselves as honest, hard-working, by now somewhat paranoid coalface researchers. A good number feel they have been mauled by ethics committees while pursuing defensible, indeed laudable objectives to improve the health of the population. Others feel similarly ravaged by clinicians and health service consumers desperate for access to new remedies for tragic diseases. They cannot wait for the slow, measured pace of learning about safety and efficacy through the randomised trial while they, their patients, or their loved ones perish in the interim. Regrettably, no escape is imminent because the science and the ethics cannot be separated easily.

ETHICAL CONCERNS ABOUT RANDOMISED CLINICAL TRIALS

As Alvan Feinstein (1985) and others have pointed out, virtually every aspect of the conduct of randomised clinical trials has been subject to ethical scrutiny. The first crucial and contentious aspect of the randomised clinical trial is that chance decides which intervention the person receives. The second is that the comparison intervention, be it the best currently available treatment or prevention, a placebo, or nothing, may or may not benefit the subject.

In 1974, Fried enunciated the 'personal care principle', namely that the doctor's main commitment is one of unqualified fidelity to the patient's health, to do what is best for that patient. Royall (1991) observed that 'this principle does not mean that the doctor does whatever he thinks is best for the patient, regardless of the patient's preferences: the role of the doctor is to advise and propose, not to impose judgment. The right to decide what is truly in the patient's best interests belongs to the patient.'

Now this all seems fine, until we have to consider the premise under which a randomised clinical trial is established, namely equipoise. Equipoise refers to the state of genuine uncertainty about the value of a therapeutic or preventive innovation. After considering the weight of all the available evidence, equipoise exists if the clinician cannot *reasonably* determine the efficacy and safety of the innovation. Note that this does not mean *absolutely*. Wald (1993) points out the common, and incorrect, belief that the aim of clinical trialists is to dot the i's and cross the t's.

Royall believes that the dilemma arises under the personal care principal in what he calls 'demonstration', rather than 'experimental', trials, namely those trials which are carried out where the clinicians are confident that the innovation is superior to its comparison, even though this confidence is not based on evidence from randomised clinical trials. In this situation, he argues that the personal care principle cannot be upheld, because it specifically forbids giving a patient what the doctor believes to be an inferior treatment in order to demonstrate its inferiority for the benefit of other patients. He therefore concludes that the personal care principle prohibits demonstration trials.

Even in an experimental randomised clinical trial, the problem arises as evidence accumulates to favour one or other therapy. The trial then metamorphoses, in Royall's thinking, into a demonstration trial. Royall's solution to this problem is to use adaptive randomisation techniques whereby the probability of being assigned to the treatment arm which is doing better as the trial progresses is increased.

The proposed solution to the personal care dilemma is to offer subjects the opportunity, as part of the consent process, to give up their right to personal care. Most would argue that the consent for any randomised clinical trial involves two separate consents anyway—first, consent to be randomised, and second, consent to be treated under the conditions of the trial.

Figure 2 The randomised consent design of Zelen (1979)

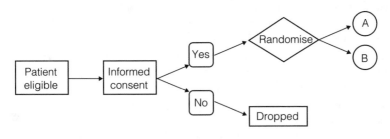

CONVENTIONAL: compare A with B

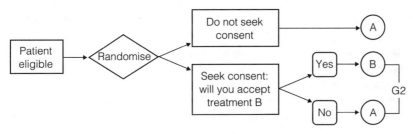

RANDOMISED CONSENT: compare A with G2 (A or B)

Note: A = standard therapy, B = innovation
Source: Zelen, 1979

Zelen proposed to randomise eligible subjects without their knowledge (Zelen, 1979) and to offer the innovation treatment to (and seek informed consent from) only those randomised to receive it (Figure 2). Those randomised to the comparison group would not be offered the innovation at all, nor be required to consent. Regardless of whether subjects subsequently accept the novel treatment or not, the consent group (G2) is analysed as a whole and compared to the no-consent group.

Although this design has been used in trials of neonatal extracorporeal membrane oxygenation (ECMO) for life-threatening lung disease, federal regulations in the United States now require consent to be obtained from all treatment groups (Zelen, 1991). Recently, a Melbourne teaching hospital research ethics committee approved a study using Zelen's randomised consent design to evaluate a potentially life-saving therapy in a situation where it was argued by the investigators that those providing consent would be too distressed to be able to consider and accept randomisation. The alternative, it was argued, was that no trial would be done at all.

It is probably simplistic and possibly dangerous, however, to accept the distinction between demonstration and experimental trials. In fact, this is probably another example of a false dichotomy between clinical care and clinical research. There are all too many cases where clinicians have been convinced about the value and safety of interventions, and have been proven wrong when proper evaluation has been carried out. The classic example was internal mammary artery ligation in subjects with angina, subsequently shown to be completely ineffective after a sham-surgery controlled randomised clinical trial which would not receive ethics-committee approval today (Gilbert, McPeek and Mosteller, 1977). More compelling still are examples of dangerous paediatric interventions formerly believed to be of obvious clinical benefit, such as the uncontrolled use of oxygen therapy in premature newborns who subsequently developed retinopathy of prematurity (Silverman, 1985), or the use of chloramphenicol, resulting in the lethal grey baby syndrome (Silverman, 1985), and sulfa antibiotics, producing kernicterus (brain damage), in jaundiced newborns (Sutherland, 1959). Chloramphenicol and sulfas were both potent antibiotics which were enthusiastically administered to infants without any expectation that metabolic poisoning (the grey baby syndrome) or permanent brain damage (kernicterus) would result from their use. As discussed by Feinstein elsewhere in this volume, the limitation of the randomised clinical trial insofar as it produces a result for the 'average' patient thus needs firmly to be borne in mind when proposing the application of previously evaluated interventions to population subgroups in whom proper evaluation has not been carried out—evaluation of both efficacy and safety.

There is no apparent, easy solution to these dilemmas. The need to respond to consumer demand for rapid access to new treatments must be weighed against consumer demands for safety of licensed therapies. The ethical concerns about human involvement in therapeutic evaluation must be balanced against similar ethical concerns about widespread use of treatments of uncertain value and potential danger (Royall, 1991; Simes, 1991; Byar, 1991; Wald, 1993).

SPECIAL PROBLEMS FOR CHILDREN AND ADOLESCENTS

These last examples illustrate how adult data falsely reassured clinicians about the safety of therapeutic agents in the very young. The ethical problems for research involving children need special mention, particularly in the context of experimental trials. A number of countries have attempted to clarify for the guidance of researchers how trials might proceed ethically (Gidding et al, 1993; Consent Panel Task Force of the National Council on Bioethics in Human Research, Medical Research Council of Canada, 1992; Medical Research Council working party on research on children, 1991). Australia is not yet among these countries.

In Canada, the report on research involving children by the Consent Panel Task Force of the National Council on Bioethics in Human Research (1992) enunciated the most important positive principle to guide research on children: 'The absence of research in children represents an injustice to children as a group, should they be deprived of the possible benefit of paediatric research, a possible benefit available to adults as a group in so far as research involving adults is permissible.'

This examination was prompted by research which was not permitted or not possible under existing Canadian Medical Research Council guidelines including:

1. Normative studies of biological parameters (for example, normal or population reference ranges for neonatal clotting levels, bronchial provocation or asthma challenge testing)
2. Comparison group with no active therapeutic agent
3. Parent consent required for studies of drugs, sexuality, etc. (they won't participate).

Specifically, the task force found that research involving children should be undertaken to:

• protect children from harm
• benefit individual children
• benefit children as a group

They also added that such research should be pursued with justice, implying that it should be pursued only under conditions in which participating children are protected from undue harm, are selected according to a fair process, and are treated with respect. The justice principle also recognised that children ought not to be deprived needlessly of the possible protection and benefit to be derived from their participation in research activity.

With regard to the risk of harm to children involved in health research, the British Medical Research Council tackled this issue by distinguishing therapeutic or preventive (immediately beneficial) from non-therapeutic or non-preventive (no immediate benefit) research (Medical Research Council working party on research on children, 1991).

UK MRC GUIDELINES FOR RESEARCH ON CHILDREN

These guidelines see research on children as justified only if:

1. The relevant knowledge could not be gained by research on adults.
2. It is approved by the appropriate local research ethics committee.
3. Either those included have given consent or consent has been given on

their behalf by a parent or guardian, and those included do not object or appear to object in either words or action.

4. For therapeutic research, the benefits likely to accrue to a child participating outweigh the possible risk of harm.

5. For non-therapeutic research, participation places a child at no more than negligible risk of harm.

Of similar importance are the legal versus ethical issues concerning child participation in research, but space is not available to pursue this matter here. Other countries, including Australia, need formal ethical guidelines similar to those adopted in Canada and the UK to ensure that research on children proceeds to protect these rights.

CONCLUSION

Clinical research is an absolute prerequisite for the best principles of effective, safe and ethical clinical care. Therefore, to dichotomise these activities leads to a set of misleading premises which threaten basic principles of care. The randomised controlled trial has not yet been superseded as the best available guarantee of standards of evidence required to maintain these principles. The need to respond to consumer demand for rapid access to new treatments must be weighed against consumer demands for safety of licensed therapies. The ethical concerns about human involvement in therapeutic evaluation must be balanced against similar ethical concerns about widespread use of treatments of uncertain value and potential danger. The rights of children to benefit from new therapies should not be constrained by their exclusion from medical research. All countries need formal ethical guidelines similar to those adopted in Canada and the UK to ensure that research on children proceeds to protect these rights.

REFERENCES

Byar, D.P., 1991, 'Comment', *Statistical Science*, 6: 65–8.

Feinstein, A.R., 1985, *Clinical Epidemiology: the architecture of clinical research*, Philadelphia: W.B. Saunders.

Fried, C., 1974, *Medical Experimentation: personal integrity and social policy*, Amsterdam: North Holland.

Gidding, S.S., Camp, D., Flanagan, M.H., Kowaiski, J.A., Lingl, L.L., Silverman, B.L., 1993, 'A policy regarding research in healthy children', *Journal of Paediatrics*, 123: 852–5.

Gilbert, J.P., McPeek, B., and Mosteller, F., 1977, 'Progress in surgery and anaesthesia: Costs, risks, and benefits of innovative therapy'. In J.P. Bunker, B.A. Barnes, F. Mosteller (eds.), *Costs, Risks, and Benefits of Surgery*, Oxford: Oxford University Press.

Hellman, S. and Hellman, D.S., 1991, 'Of mice but not men: Problems of the randomised controlled trial', *The New England Journal of Medicine*, 324: 1585–9.

Medical Research Council working party on research on children, 1991, *The Ethical Conduct of Research on Children*, London: Medical Research Council.

Consent Panel Task Force of the National Council on Bioethics in Human Research, 1992, *Report on Research Involving Children*, Ottawa: Medical Research Council of Canada.

Royall, R.M., 1991, 'Ethics and statistics in randomized clinical trials', *Statistical Science*, 6: 52–88.

Sackett, D.L., Haynes, R.B., and Tugwell, P., 1985, *Clinical Epidemiology: a basic science for clinical medicine*, Boston: Little Brown.

Silverman, W.A., 1985, *Human Experimentation: a guided step in the unknown*, Oxford: Oxford Medical Publications.

Simes, R.J., 1991, 'Comment', *Statistical Science*, 6: 78–80.

Sutherland, J.M., 1959, 'Fatal cardiovascular collapse of infants receiving large amounts of chloramphenicol', *American Journal of Diseases of the Child*, 97: 761.

Wald, N., 1993, 'Education and debate: Ethical issues in randomised prevention trials', *British Medical Journal*, 306: 563–5.

Zelen, M., 1979, 'A new design for randomized clinical trials', *The New England Journal of Medicine*, 300: 1242–5.

Zelen, M., 1991, 'Comment', *Statistical Science*, 6: 81–3.

7

CLINICAL CARE AND CLINICAL RESEARCH: A FALSE DICHOTOMY

Gordon Guyatt

The same ethical principles govern clinical care and clinical research. These principles include respect for persons (autonomy), the duty to help others further their interests (beneficence), the duty to avoid doing harm (non-maleficence), and fairness or justice. The principles tend to be applied at a higher standard in research, and their ranking may differ. We tend, for instance, to place a higher ranking on autonomy within the setting of research (Brett and Grodin, 1991). While the different standards applied to the delivery of clinical care and the conduct of research appear to be growing more divergent all the time, the boundary between clinical care and research is not nearly so clear. I will begin my exploration of the nature of the difference between clinical care and research, and the basis for the different standards, with a story that I believe highlights the issues.

N-OF-1 RANDOMISED TRIALS

One of the main challenges in research is to minimise bias, which leads to findings systematically different from the truth. Medical history is littered with once popular but now discarded treatments, previously thought to be effective, now known to be useless. For these treatments, misleading results were a consequence of studies with limited or flawed designs. A dominant source of bias in these studies has been non-comparable groups: treatment and control patients differ with respect to prognostic factors, and these differences typically result in findings of inflated treatment effects. This problem can be solved by randomisation, which, when treatment groups are large enough, virtually ensures comparability. Other biases have resulted from the expectation that treatment is, or desire that it be, effective, and these can be minimised by use of placebos and by double-blinding.

A few years ago, a number of us at McMaster University reflected on the ways in which bias could intrude when a clinician makes treatment decisions in individual patients. They include the placebo effect, the natural history of the illness, the expectations that the clinician and patient have about the treatment effect, and the desire of the patient and the clinician not to disappoint one another. To avoid these pitfalls, trials of therapy would have to be conducted with the same safeguards that we use in large-sample randomised trials to keep both patients and their clinicians 'blind' to the treatment being administered. Our reflections led us to apply the methods of what psychologists have called 'single case' or 'single subject' research to real-life treatment decisions. We called our new methodology 'N-of-1 randomised trials' (N-of-1 RCTs), 'N-of-1' denoting that each randomised trial involved only a single patient.

In general terms, the N-of-1 RCT design is based on pairs of active/placebo, high dose/low dose or first drug/alternative drug combinations, the order of administration within each pair determined by random allocation. In conducting an N-of-1 RCT, we monitor treatment targets (directed specifically at the patient's complaints) in a double-blind fashion on a regular, predetermined schedule. The trial continues as long as the clinician and patient agree that they need more information to get a definite answer regarding the efficacy, superiority or side effects of the treatment, or until the patient or clinician decide for any other reason to end the trial.

The ethical implications of N-of-1 RCTs become evident when one considers the circumstances in which one would consider conducting an N-of-1 RCT, and the alternative ways of handling the problem. The clinician faces a patient suffering from some unpleasant symptoms, and considers prescribing a drug to relieve these symptoms. Hopefully, randomised trials have shown that in a group of similar patients, the drug does more good than harm. This doesn't, however, mean that the drug will do more good than harm in a particular individual. Inevitably, there is considerable heterogeneity of treatment effect, and patients whom the drug doesn't help will still be subject to its adverse effects. In some instances, the clinician may consider prescription of a treatment without randomised trial evidence, and therefore face the even greater possibility that the patient will not benefit.

So the clinician prescribes a treatment which she believes will help some, but not all the patients, to whom it is offered. The patient before her may be one of those who benefit, or one who receives no symptom relief but only treatment side effects. How might she handle the situation? One option would be to prescribe the drug and leave it at that. For treatments that RCTs have shown do more good than harm, the doctor adopting this approach can at least be confident that, overall, her patients will benefit. However, they will not have received the maximum benefit, which would come from prescribing only to those in whom the treatment would significantly ameliorate symptoms.

To try and achieve the goal of treating only those who will benefit, the clinician may conduct the time-honoured 'trial of therapy' by prescribing the drug and monitoring the subsequent clinical course. If the patient reports improvement, the drug is continued; if not, it is stopped. However, many factors may mislead clinicians conducting conventional therapeutic trials. They include the placebo effect, the natural history of the illness (the patient might have improved without treatment), the expectations that the clinician and patient have about the treatment effect, and the desire of the patient and the clinician not to disappoint one another. All of these can bias the results of the trial of therapy, in most instances leading to a false conclusion that the drug is beneficial when it isn't (Molloy *et al*, 1991). The N-of-1 RCT, then, minimises the bias of the conventional therapeutic trial, and makes it far less likely that the final conclusion will be spurious. Indeed, we have demonstrated that N-of-1 RCTs result in changes in treatment decisions about 35 per cent of the time (Guyatt *et al*, 1986).

How should a clinician wishing to take the most rigorous approach to a treatment decision, the N-of-1 RCT, proceed? She must explain the dilemma of the treatment decision to the patient, and the alternative ways of solving the dilemma. If the patient understands the concept of the N-of-1 RCT, and is willing to expend the time and effort involved, the physician and patient, in partnership, can plan and conduct the trial.

Or can they? Should the physician consult an ethics committee before she goes ahead? Being research-oriented folk, my colleagues and I went straight to the McMaster University institutional review board before proceeding with our first N-of-1 RCT. The review board's answer surprised us: This isn't research, they told us, it's optimal clinical care. If you feel compelled to take your proposal before an ethics committee, take it to the institution's clinical ethics committee rather than the research ethics committee.

Subsequent experience with institutional review boards has been closer to our original expectations. Ethics committees at other hospitals considered N-of-1 RCTs to be very much research, and stipulated their requirements for us, including the obtaining of written, informed consent. Eventually, we were encouraged to return to the McMaster ethics committee for another review of our work with N-of-1 RCTs. The personnel on the board, and their attitudes, had changed. Our work was now treated very much as research. Indeed, the committee was reluctant to grant us blanket approval for all our N-of-1 RCTs, and suggested that perhaps we should bring each individual N-of-1 RCT before the institutional review board. The final decision was to provide us with blanket approval, but ethics committees in other institutions have demanded that they review each individual N-of-1 RCT being undertaken in their jurisdiction.

Consider once again the clinician facing the symptomatic patient and contemplating prescribing a drug. Whether or not the drug has been tested in an RCT, the clinician needn't have any particular plan for follow-up or monitoring to prescribe the medication. If she does plan to monitor, she can neglect issues of the placebo effect, the natural history, and the patient's expectations without anyone raising objections. If, however, she wishes to conduct her therapeutic trial in a more rigorous manner that will ensure the patient benefits from the treatment, she must subject herself to scrutiny by an institutional review board.

A primary care physician who, before my meeting him, had never heard of N-of-1 RCTs, recently told me of two mothers in his practice who came complaining of possible milk allergy in their newborn infants. In both cases, both doctor and mother were uncertain whether milk allergy was a problem. The doctor recruited the patients' neighbours, who would deliver a blinded formula, either milk-based or milk-free. In one instance, the patient discovered that the child's problems only occurred on the conventional formula, whereas the other child's distress was independent of which formula was given. The physician was pleased with having sorted out the problem and differentiated the child who had milk allergy from the child who did not. It never occurred to him that he was involved in research, and consulting an institutional review board was the farthest thing from his mind.

The issue of N-of-1 RCTs illustrates the size of the difference between standards we set for clinical care and for research. These enormous differences might not be problematic if there were a clear boundary between clinical and research activities. The N-of-1 RCT example provides one illustration of lack of clarity in the boundary between clinical and research activities, and I shall now consider another example.

CLINICAL CARE OR CLINICAL RESEARCH?

Let us say that a clinician wishes to monitor the extent to which she is successful in achieving full vaccination for all children in her practice. No one is likely to suggest that she is conducting research, or that she had better appear before an institutional review board or risk subsequent censure from her colleagues when her clandestine research activities are brought to light. What if she wishes to conduct her monitoring in collaboration with a number of colleagues with one goal: to ultimately compare how well each of them is doing? What if, as a group, these physicians negotiate with the local public health department for a public health nurse to help them establish registries of their patients with systematic reminders to help achieve full vaccination? What if they now monitor, in a before–after fashion, the extent to which the intervention of the health department improved the vaccination rate? Finally, what if the group decides to publish the results of their experience, in the hopes that they might be beneficial to others?

At what point (if any) do these clinical activities become research? At what point should they be subject to the scrutiny of an institutional review board? Under what circumstances should the clinician be obliged to consult patients about use of their charts, or obtain consent for use of their data?

A SOLUTION

It is evident from these examples that systematic clinical observation, continuous quality improvement, and clinical research are overlapping activities. These activities are on a continuum, and the ethical standards we apply should reflect that continuum. We require a broad definition of clinical research which would include both systematic clinical observation and much of what we have thought of as quality assurance. A definition such as 'the systematic application of rigorous methods to adduce generalisable observations about clinical phenomena' might be suitable. If one uses such a definition, then not all research should be subject to scrutiny by an ethics committee. Under what conditions would it be appropriate to insist that a clinician planning a research project appear before an institutional research board?

1. *The researchers intend to publish the results of the work*
As long as the sole purpose of diagnosis, treatment, or monitoring is improved patient care, the potential for a clinician's conflict of interest is minimal. When clinicians also see themselves as researchers, and when self-interest may affect their attitude toward their research, more detailed scrutiny of their activities is warranted. An investigator, thinking ahead to what might be required to satisfy the criticisms of a reviewer of her manuscript, may be tempted to subject a patient to tests that are not required for optimal clinical care. While such additional testing may be well justified within the context of a research study, independent adjudication of the burden on or risk to the patient is warranted.

2. *The procedures, tests, interventions, or questionnaires completed by the patient go beyond the requirements of optimal clinical care*
Even if there is no intent to publish, clinicians' curiosity may lead them to carry out investigations, or obtain information from patients, that would not be necessary to manage their medical problems. In applying this criterion, we should remember that monitoring one's own health-care delivery is an integral part of providing optimal care. Consequently, mon-

itoring for purposes of continuous quality assurance would not constitute research mandating institutional review.

3. *Patients might be individually identified.*
None of us want our privacy violated. If there is any risk of public identification of research participants, ethics review is necessary.

These criteria are notable for the research which would be exempt from institutional review. N-of-1 RCTs, when conducted strictly to optimise treatment for the individual, would not require independent scrutiny. Chart reviews, or extracting information about clinical encounters from patient records, in which individual patients would not be identified in the results, would require institutional, but not individual patient, consent.

The approach to research ethics which I am suggesting has implications not only for what should fall within the domain of institutional review boards, but for the way those boards should function. Those reviewing research protocols and procedures should bear in mind the standards which we impose, and the freedom we grant, to those engaged in day-to-day clinical practice. In general, when patients are not at increased risk as a result of the conduct of research, the standards and requirements which ethics committees promote should not be far more rigorous than those placed on clinicians and should not impede the conduct of research.

AUTONOMY AND SOCIAL RESPONSIBILITY

Ethics committees have become increasingly attentive to ensuring that investigators respect patient or research-participant autonomy. This attention is a response to carelessness and arrogance on the part of clinician-investigators, who in the past have committed egregious abuses of patients' trust. Clinician-investigators are not able to police themselves, and someone must protect patients.

The attitude toward patient autonomy that sometimes emerges from the appropriate concern about possible abuse of trust, however, represents a pendulum that has swung too far. This attitude plays itself out, for instance, in demands that patients' permission be obtained before information is abstracted from their charts, or before their charts are reviewed to determine if they would be eligible for research studies. One way of looking at this issue is in terms of the balance between individual autonomy and social responsibility. Chart review entails minimal patient risk with the possibility of appreciable societal benefit, and demands that informed consent be required even for chart review imply a balance between individual autonomy and societal responsibility in which the former is given a preponderant weight.

An alternative orientation is to acknowledge the responsibilities of the society to the individual, and the individual to society. One of the latter is the obligation to help in the accumulation of knowledge which will benefit the group. If one accepts this orientation, then capricious or eccentric refusal of permission becomes poorly tolerated, and perhaps unacceptable, behaviour. When a patient will never be identified, and her subsequent care will not be affected, refusing permission to use information from her chart represents capricious or eccentric behaviour. There should, therefore, be no need for consent from individual patients under these circumstances. This argument may be more powerful in societies in which the state assumes major obligations to the individual citizen, and in which the sense of a corporate whole is strong. Even in cultures such as that of the US, where individual autonomy is valued much more highly than corporate well-being, however, an obligation toward the accumulation of knowledge for the corporate good remains.

If one takes this approach, who is to decide what is to the corporate good? That, it seems to me, is part of what ethics committees should be all about. It implies, of course, that they should have the appropriate representation, which would include members from a broad spectrum of the community. This would present challenges of education, but a community better informed about what clinical research is all about would benefit both the medical world and the lay public.

CONCLUSION

Some institutional review boards have adopted misguided approaches. A false dichotomy between clinical care and clinical research has arisen, and the standards of conduct of clinicians whose activities are labelled as research are far more rigid and constraining than standards for clinical care. Ethics committees should recognise the continuum of clinical care and clinical research, and set explicit standards which are consistent with this continuum. In addition, they should strike an appropriate balance between protecting individual autonomy and the benefits that accrue to us all when we assume corporate responsibility for the accumulation of new knowledge.

ACKNOWLEDGMENTS

I am indebted to Dr Harry Pert, who conducted the N-of-1 studies of milk allergy and the study of strategies to improve vaccination rates in primary care that inspired the examples I used in this essay.

REFERENCES

Brett, A. and Grodin, M., 1991, 'Ethical aspects of human experimentation in Health Services Research', *Journal of the American Medical Association*, 265: 1854-7.
Guyatt, G.H., Sackett, D.L., Taylor, D.W., *et al*, 1986, 'Determining optimal

therapy—randomised trials in individual patients', *The New England Journal of Medicine*, 314: 889–92.

Guyatt, G.H., Keller, J.L., Jaeschke, R., et al, 1993 'The N-of-1 randomised trial: Clinical usefulness', *Annals of Internal Medicine*, 112: 293–9.

Molloy, D.W., Guyatt, G.H., Wilson, D.B., *et al*, 1991, 'Effect of tetrahydroaminoacridine on cognition, function and behaviour in Alzheimer's disease', *Canadian Medical Association Journal*, 144: 29–34.

8

BASIC RESEARCH AND EXPERIMENT: A SUMMING UP

Ian McDonald

During the present period of mounting interest in the ethics of human research, there has arisen a politically potent movement which challenged the ethics of animal experimentation (Shenkin, 1991: 243–59). A hard-line minority has taken the stand that it is unethical to undertake any research on animals and that all such research must stop; extremists have even resorted to sabotage to make their point (Shenkin, 1991: 244). Those willing to compromise accept animal research provided that it is confined to a necessary minimum and that there is adherence to the rules governing care of animals. We will not discuss these debates further. Experimentation on the intact human subject is an even more sensitive issue, fraught with such ethical difficulties that it is seldom seen as feasible. Instead laboratory research has concentrated on disease mechanism, involving analysis of human tissue often as a by-product of routine diagnosis; this rarely provokes ethical debate.

Of recent years, the focus of scrutiny has shifted away from the study of disease mechanism in human subjects and in animals. In the wake of a surge of interest in health services research, there has been increased interest in experimentation conducted in the field with living human subjects. These experiments are randomised controlled trials, in which participants are allocated by chance to a conventional treatment or to one of as yet unproven effectiveness and safety. Such trials were proposed as the linchpin for testing medical interventions (Cochrane, 1971). However, despite widespread adoption of this proposal, their use has remained per-sistently controversial on the grounds of possible abrogation of the rights of the individual patient and compromise of the doctor's contract with the patient.

THE DOCTOR'S DILEMMAS

At the centre of the ethical debate is the issue of the extent to which a patient should be seen as under some obligation to cooperate with medical research in the interests of the society at large and of future generations. A strong view opposes human experimentation on the basis that it is unethical to use the individual patient as a means towards the end of better treatment for the community (Cocking and Oakley, 1983). A pragmatic utilitarian argument is that, in the light of past errors, there is an urgent need to use trials to make treatment more certainly effective and safer (Passamani, 1991). A commonly held view at present would allow doctors to negotiate patients' entry into a trial, provided that they genuinely had no reason to prefer the treatment under test to that already established, and assuming 'adequate' informed consent (Passamani, 1991). However, even if we accept the utilitarian point of view, some thorny ethical issues remain with respect to the role of the doctor managing the patient.

There is a school of thought which sees the role of the clinician as fundamentally ambiguous in the setting of a randomised trial (Hellman and Hellman, 1991). The nature of the clinical contract rules out the possibility that the doctor could simultaneously offer best judgments on individual care and, at the same time, act in the interests of medical science (Burkhardt and Kienle, 1978). In the case of the randomised trial, a key issue is whether the clinician can truly be in a state of 'equipoise' with respect to conventional and test treatments. If clinicians were to exercise their best judgment, that is to honour the clinical contract, the crucial issue is that they must believe that the likelihood of therapeutic success without ill effect must be accepted as the same for the treatments to be compared. Such a state of balanced commitment to treatments is statistically unlikely to exist for any individual clinician (Freedman, 1987). It may be true that, based on existing scientific evidence, this state is a reasonable *consensus* position of knowledgeable researchers or clinicians (Passamani, 1991). But the individual doctor is more likely to incline one way or the other (Hellman and Hellman, 1991). Even if the clinician is unwilling to concede that one treatment is superior to the other at the beginning of the trial, this would be likely to change progressively as the trial results accrued, unless the two were, in fact, precisely equivalent in efficacy and risk of complication. However, the design of a trial is such that the clinician is denied access to these accruing results, and has therefore to abrogate responsibility for stopping the trial to a committee which has to rely on statistical data for the group rather than on the characteristics or wishes of the individual patient, or the preference of that patient's own doctor.

Even if the choice of treatment cannot be reasonably supported on scientific grounds, if it is based on an 'irrational' preference of the patient, or on a doctor's sincerely held view of the patient's best interests based on clinical experience, it must nonetheless be factored into the decision-making. For example, a woman may have strong feelings about radical mastectomy, a man about a colostomy. The options must therefore be clear to the patient and fully respected when obtaining informed consent.

Finally, even if the random allocation of treatment is accepted as ethical, its mode of administration may not be optimal for the individual patient. A randomised controlled trial requires that the treatments under test be administered according to a standardised regime. This may not be in the patient's best interests, since a therapeutic regime usually has to be individualised, often by a process of trial and error (Waldenstrom, 1983). It should be noted that the converse can also be argued—that the patient stands to benefit from participation in a trial since supervision and delivery of care are likely to be of higher than average quality (Stiller, 1992). Nevertheless, it is difficult to deny that the clinical contract is such that the doctor must, at all times and with no exceptions, exercise personal clinical judgment on behalf of the individual patient (Hellman and Hellman, 1991).

IS CONSENT TRULY 'INFORMED'?

The need for informed consent is universally conceded, although it has been suggested that the procedure of obtaining agreement should be made less stringent since the process can be seen as 'cruel' to patients in some instances (Tobias, 1993). Those who espouse the utilitarian viewpoint still have to contend with the difficulty of obtaining consent which can be said to be truly 'informed'. The legal model requires complete disclosure which, in research as in clinical practice, is scarcely feasible given that possibilities of adverse effect are essentially infinite. Where is the line to be drawn? In any case, to what extent can a patient ever be said to be 'fully informed' (Barber, 1981: 335; Baum, 1993). Patients cannot realistically have access to the full background of information available to the research team. Even if they did, how could they understand information in a controversial area at the boundaries of medical knowledge? How could they interpret its significance for themselves? Even if all these difficulties could be overcome, could we be confident that information could be conveyed 'objectively' by the research team?

The conduct of a randomised trial, including recruitment of the study population, tends to be seen as a technical matter to which the skills of epidemiology are relevant. The process of obtaining informed consent, however, involves other dimensions. Even the most independent of citizens may be seriously threatened by illness and disempowered by the clinical context. Hence they may be very vulnerable to suggestions, especially those made by their medical attendants (Jonas, 1981: 254). Even with good will and skilled presentation, there is much experience in psychology, clinical practice and elsewhere demonstrating that the way in which a person comprehends and responds to a question or proposition can be highly dependent on their own experience and the way in which statements and questions are framed (Cocking and Oakley, 1983: 294; Tversky and Kahneman, 1981). Hence the process of informed consent could be inadvertently distorted by the researcher. In addition, there can be personal and social determinants of a patient's decision which presentation of an informed consent form and a cursory explanation cannot probe. Hence ethical issues must be considered in their specific context (Hoffmaster, 1990: 250; Fox, 1990: 211), according to the personal circumstances and experience of each patient, and according to the nature and requirements of each trial. The best that can be hoped for is an honest, open, documented and witnessed dialogue between patient and researcher. There will always remain an element of discretion in what is discussed and how, and an element of trust in the patient's decision to participate. This places a heavy obligation on the researcher to ensure good communication and on the ethics committee to ensure that the issues are represented in a comprehensive and balanced manner.

THE CURRENT STAND-OFF

The need for randomised trials has been accepted without reservation by the British National Health Service (Anon., 1992). Their desirability appears to have been generally accepted by the medical profession; nor do individual doctors, in general, appear to have strong ethical objections to randomisation. They continue to allow their patients to participate in trials or encourage them to do so although there is evidence that clinicians themselves are not always willing to have their own treatment randomised (Shenkin, 1991: 234). On the other hand, there is evidence that doctors pick and choose whom they are willing to refer for inclusion in a trial. In a randomised trial of coronary graft surgery, patients with the most severe coronary artery disease were under-represented (Anon., 1984). The likely explanation is that clinicians were less willing to refer such patients for randomisation (Rahimtoola, 1985).

The community by and large appears to accept the value of clinical trials. There has even been a suggestion that there is discrimination involved in the lack of representation of women in trials (Mohiuddin and Hilleman, 1993). Reporting of trials in the media is generally favourable, in the spirit of the continuing march of medical science. Only a minority of patients refuse to participate in most published trials, suggesting that most accept randomisation on the recommendation of their own doctor. Occasionally the choice of treatment may happen to involve some aspect about which the patient does have strong feelings. In the case of cancer, the right of the individual to have treatment not tested by randomisation is a problem. In some such cases, only a small minority of patients may express willingness to participate in trials (Wittes and Friedman, 1988). Some people have a strong aversion to surgery, perhaps based on the death of a loved one during or after an operation.

What is surprising, given that the results of randomised trials are so often the subject of media reports and given the prolonged debate in the medical literature, is how little we know about the attitudes of members of the community and of clinicians to human experimentation, and especially to recruitment into randomised trials. Given the cautious attitudes of most research ethics committees, frankly unethical studies are likely to be rare. What is lacking at present, however, is insightful understanding of what is actually going on in the field, or any systematic attempt to garner such information. There is an urgent need for more empirical research involving clinical cases. To what extent are the recommendations of ethics committees actually implemented? Is informed consent tailored sensitively to the patient's understanding and circumstances? Do subjects actually understand the trial and their part in it, and to what extent? Is there any suggestion of bias in the research team's presentation? Is the language of the informed consent document comprehensible, and to whom? Are patients in any way discouraged from considering their own 'non-rational' values? Are they vulnerable to suggestion in particular settings? One factor leading to this dearth of empirical studies is the limited contact between the disciplines of moral philosophy on the one hand and of sociology and anthropology on the other (Hoffmaster, 1990: 250).

THE WAY AHEAD FOR ETHICAL TRIALS

Sir Francis Bacon long ago proposed that our research methods should evolve and improve (Bacon, 1954). The randomised trial, as the most rigorous method for studying treatment effectiveness, remains the intellectual and legal gold standard for drug evaluation. The problems of such trials, ethical and otherwise, should therefore provoke attempts at innovative study design. Attempts have been made to ease the difficulty of obtaining consent and to increase the response rate of potential trial recruits by pre-randomisation (Zelen, 1979). Treatment is first allocated at random without the patient's knowledge, then offered on the basis of this chance allocation. However, this does nothing to overcome the problem of informed consent, since this is denied to the patient on the basis of chance. Nor can account be taken of the possibility of personal and other non-technical influences which might operate if the patient had a choice. A method of allocation of treatment has been proposed which will allow randomisation but arrange for care by a clinician who has a preference for the allocated treatment after consultation with the patient (Korn and

Baumrind, 1991). This offers no panacea, however, since the study design is complicated and only a minority of studies would be suitable for technical reasons.

Given the problems and the expense of trials, hence the need for parsimony and economy, attempts are being made to maximise their clinical impact by careful documentation, by synthesis of their individual results using the technique of meta-analysis and by wide dissemination of the results through international networks. There has also been advocacy for a more rigorous use of non-randomised methods of assessment of therapeutic outcome which pose fewer ethical problems. Observational studies utilising an historical control group have been applied to drug evaluation (Horwitz et al, 1990), but this approach has not caught on. Cohort studies of patients selected for coronary graft surgery on clinical grounds, using a database to document outcome and related variables, have provided information which is clearly complementary to that obtained from randomised trials.

Although the randomised controlled trial is dominant in studies of therapeutic intervention—especially for drug evaluation, less often for surgical procedures—in the evaluation of diagnostic tests, non-experimental methods such as the impact of a test on diagnosis and management are needed to establish their clinical contribution (Guyatt et al, 1986). Here the question of informed consent for participation is not controversial, since management is observed but not altered.

Finally, it is worth noting that the technique of randomisation has also been used to test whether or not a particular drug is working in an individual patient or whether or not a symptom is a side effect of treatment. In difficult circumstances like these, the introduction and withdrawal of the drug on a random blinded basis, an N-of-1 study, can answer the question (Campbell, 1994). Despite its rigorous structure, such a trial is conducted in order to test treatment in the individual patient, although it is obviously possible to combine results to test a particular drug as a kind of case series reporting effects of an intervention. Not surprisingly, as Gordon Guyatt reports in this volume, research ethics committees have classified the N-of-1 study either as clinical research or as routine care in a somewhat idiosyncratic way. However, for other kinds of case reports concerning patient care, such as reporting the accuracy of a diagnostic test or clinical or laboratory findings in a particular disease, no such permission is deemed necessary.

INDIVIDUAL RIGHTS OR SOCIAL COMMITMENT?

When participating in a randomised trial, the clinician is on the horns of the dilemma, caught between the inalienable rights of the patient to individual care and a commitment to advance medical science. Generally the rights of the individual will prevail over those of the society except in extreme circumstances like war (Jonas, 1981: 237; Fox, 1990: 207–10). A solution with appeal is therefore to look to the patient's motivation to willingly contribute to the community rather than continuing our obsession with the rights of an individual living in an atomistic society.

Assuming that the ethical dilemma of the doctor's clinical role and the need for clinical trials cannot be entirely overcome by further developments in study design, it would seem reasonable to suggest that there could be a dialogue in the community analogous to that surrounding donation for organ transplantation (Adedeji, 1993). Specific groups in the community could be encouraged to support, even insist upon, inclusion of members in trials in the interests of ensuring that interventions of potential interest to them would be properly tested and that the results would be pertinent to the group. Given that societies and sports teams regularly ask for some sacrifice of personal autonomy in the group interest, is it so unreasonable that society should do the same in the case of medical research provided that the concession is truly voluntary and valued as a gift? If the community accepts in principle the importance of evaluation involving randomisation, patients who are already aware of the issues could then be approached by someone other than their doctor, discuss the specific issues with their own doctor, then decide whether or not they wish to volunteer as an act of generosity. Those who feel more strongly may wish to be identified in advance as willing to be approached in case of illness. In either case the gesture would be in the spirit of altruism, seen as a form of community service. Even here, however, the ethics of the manner of soliciting recruits have to be considered (Jonas, 1981: 248).

WIDENING THE DEBATE

The tenor of the discussion so far might have suggested that the only problems facing laboratory and health services research were those of ethics committee approval and informed consent, and related broader issues including the responsibilities of doctor to patient and of individual to society. There are a host of other issues which we can do no more than note. For example, a researcher can deliberately relax admission criteria in order to recruit patients in large enough numbers; analysis can be biased by choice of a test solely for the purpose of achieving statistical significance; and results can be released prematurely and inappropriately without peer review through media channels. There are other matters of potential concern to the community. In his seminal exposé, Henry Beecher (1966) pointed to the fact that individual medical scientists are not immune from vested interests which can cloud their ethical judgment. At the broader societal level, the activities of the pharmaceutical 'trial industry' raise politically and ethically contentious problems of potential conflict of interest (Kunin, 1978; Relman, 1984). Another major focus of ethical concern in the health field has become the question of equity in the allocation of scarce health care resources (Fox, 1990: 203–6).

Since the middle of the last century, there has been competition between clinical medicine and public health for political dominance in the health field. We no longer expect to hear debate as bitter as that in the nineteenth century surrounding Edwin Chadwick, champion of the need to improve the social environments of the poor and opponent of doctors who sought to dominate public health (Porter and Fee, 1992: 252). Nevertheless, medical research, defined for so long as biomedical research, has been seen by many as dominating the allocation of health research funds. An important plank in the position of those who have criticised medicine of recent years has been that the contribution of basic science related to curative care has been over-sold (McKeown, 1979), and that we should expect diminishing community health returns from medical treatment in the future (Fuchs, 1975). Pragmatic pressure for change has also come from governments supporting epidemiological research with a view to cost containment.

Many Western countries are in the process of reviewing allocation of funds for health research. In theory there must be some particular balance of allocation, some formula which will optimise societal benefit by best serving the collective best interests of its members without injustice to any. This will require those responsible for allocation to strike a balance between 'basic' and 'applied' research, researcher-driven and contracted research, research in public health, biomedical and clinical research, research in hospital and in primary care, directed at disease or public health problem, related to the health of men or of women, of community at large or of minority group.

Relevant to this debate is an old scientific chestnut closely entwined with the advocacy of biomedical laboratory research as opposed to clinical and public health research. The debate concerns the respective yields to the community of 'pure' research conducted without a specific pragmatic objective, and 'applied' research which is goal-directed. The former has, without rational justification, been more highly valued in the scientific community in the past (Medawar, 1984). In fact, there is still very little empirical evidence on which to base policy for allocation of resources (Smith, 1987). In this setting, it is possible to use professional power, exercised in committee or by lobby, to intentionally distort allocation so as to accommodate vested interests. A cynical attempt to block reasonable reform could be seen as unethical since the resulting distortion of research priorities would deny the community maximum benefit and deprive certain groups of their rights.

CONCLUSION

It was misadventure in biomedical experimentation which initially challenged the capacity of traditional medical ethics to cope with ethical problems. Of recent years, however, the problems of ethics in experimental health research have focused on the randomised controlled trial, the accepted gold standard for testing the efficacy of health interventions. Some claim that such trials are fundamentally unethical because patients can never be used as a means to an end, or because the requirements of trials are fundamentally at odds with the responsibilities of the doctor looking after the patient. In general, however, trials are accepted as permissible with informed consent. There are serious problems in defining such consent, and in obtaining it. There is a pressing need for data on attitudes of doctors and of members of the community, as well as for empirical studies of the social transaction of obtaining consent. These problems of recruitment for trials might best be addressed by eschewing the current obsession with individual rights as the sole guideline and encouraging instead a more social perspective. This could be done by educating the public to view volunteering for trials as a valued social commitment, a gift in the form of relinquishment of autonomy. This would largely obviate the need for intellectual gymnastics required to cope with issues such as 'equipoise' and the practical problems posed by the role of the doctor and process of obtaining consent. At a higher level, an important issue is the lack of a consensus view on how research funds should be allocated. Unethical behaviour in this setting would be a deliberate, self-interested attempt to subvert the allocation process.

REFERENCES

Adedeji, O.A., 1993, 'Raised public awareness' (letter to the editor), *British Medical Journal*, 307: 1495–6.

Anon., 1984, 'Coronary artery surgical study (CASS): A randomized trial of coronary artery bypass surgery. Comparison of entry characteristics and survival in randomized and nonrandomized patients meeting randomised criteria', *Journal of the American College of Cardiology*, 3: 114–28.

Bachelard, G., 1984, *The New Scientific Spirit*, Boston: Beacon

Bacon, F., 1954, *Novum Organum* (Book I). In S. Commins and R.N. Lipscott (eds.), *Man and the Universe: The Philosophers of Science*, New York: Pocket Books.

Barber, B., 1981, 'The ethics of experimentation with human subjects'. In T.A. Shannon, (ed.), *Bioethics: basic writings on the key ethical questions which surround the major, modern biological possibilities and problems*, Ramsey: Paulist Press.

Baum, M., 1983, 'New approach for recruitment into randomised controlled trials', *The Lancet*, 341: 812–13.

Beecher, H.E., 1966, 'Ethics and clinical research', *The New England Journal of Medicine*, 274: 1354–60.

Burkhardt, R. and Kienle, G., 1978, 'Controlled clinical trials and medical ethics', *Lancet* 2: 1356–9.

Campbell, M. J., 1994, 'Commentary: N of 1 trials may be useful for informed decision making', *British Medical Journal*, 309: 1045–6.

Cocking, D. and Oakley, J., 1994, 'Medical experimentation, informed consent and using people', *Bioethics*, 8: 293–311.

Cochrane, A. L., 1971, *Effectiveness and Efficiency: random reflections on health services*, London: The Nuffield Provincial Hospital's Trust.

Fox, R.C., 1990, 'The evolution of American bioethics: A sociological perspective'. In G. Weisz (ed.), *Social Science Perspectives on Medical Ethics*, Dordrecht: Kluwer.

Freedman, B., 1987, 'Equipoise and the ethics of clinical research', *The New England Journal of Medicine*, 317: 141–5.

Fuchs, V.R., 1975, *Who Shall Live ? Health, Economics, and Social Choice*, New York: Basic Books.

Guyatt, G.H., Tugwell, P.X., Feeny, D.H. *et al*, 1986, 'The role of before–after studies of therapeutic impact in the evaluation of diagnostic technologies', *Journal of Chronic Diseases*, 39: 295–304.

Hellman, S. and Hellman, D.S., 1991, 'Of mice but not men: Problems with the randomised clinical trial', *The New England Journal of Medicine*, 324: 1585–9.

Hoffmaster, B.,1990, 'Morality and the social sciences'. In G. Weisz (ed.), *Perspectives on Medical Ethics*, Dordrecht: Kluwer.

Horwitz, R.I., Viscoli, C.M., Clemens, J.D. *et al*, 1990, 'Developing improved observational methods for evaluating therapeutic effectiveness', *American Journal of Medicine*, 89: 630–8.

Jonas, H., 1981. 'Philosophical reflections on experimenting with human subjects'. In T.A. Shannon (ed.), *Bioethics: basic writings on the key ethical questions which surround the major, modern biological possibilities and problems*, Ramsey: Paulist Press.

Kuhn, T.S., 1970, *The Structure of Scientific Revolutions*, 2nd edition, Chicago: University of Chicago Press.

Korn, E.L. and Baumrind, S. 1991, 'Randomised clinical trials with clinician-preferred treatment', *The Lancet*, 337: 49–52.

Kunin, C.M., 1978, 'Clinical investigators in the pharmaceutical industry', *Annals of Internal Medicine*, 89 (number 5 Pt 2, Suppl.): 842–5.

Medawar, P., 1984, *Pluto's Republic*, Oxford: Oxford University Press.

McKeown, T., 1979, *The Role of Medicine: dream, mirage or nemesis ?*, Oxford: Basil Blackwell.

Mohiuddin, S.M. and Hilleman, D.E., 1993, 'Gender and racial bias in clinical pharmacology trials', *Annals of Pharmacological Therapeutics*, 27: 904–11.

Passamani, E., 1991, 'Clinical trials—are they ethical ?', *The New England Journal of Medicine*, 324: 1589–91.

Fee, E. and Porter, D., 1992, 'Public health, preventive medicine and professionalization: England and America in the nineteenth century'. In A. Wear (ed.), *Medicine in Society: historical essays*, Cambridge: Cambridge University Press.

Rahimtoola, S.H., 1985, 'Some unexpected lessons from large multicenter randomized controlled trials', *Circulation*, 72: 449–55.

Relman, A.S., 1984, 'Dealing with conflicts of interest', *The New England Journal of Medicine*, 310: 1182–3.

Shenkin, H.A., 1991, *Medical Ethics: evolution, rights and the physician*, Dordrecht: Kluwer.

Smith, R., 1987, 'The roots of innovation', *British Medical Journal*, 265: 1335–8.

Stiller, C., 1992, 'Survival of patients in clinical trials and at specialist centres'. In C.J. Williams (ed.), *Introducing New Treatments for Carcinoma: practical, ethical and legal problems*, Chichester: Wiley.

Tobias, J. S. and Souhami, J.L., 1993, 'Fully informed consent can be needlessly cruel', *British Medical Journal*, 307: 1199–201.

Tversky, A., Kahneman, D., 1981, 'The framing of decisions and the psychology of choice', *Science*, 211: 453–8.

Waldenstrom, J., 1983, 'The ethics of randomization'. In K. Berg and K.E. Tranoy (eds.), *Research Ethics*, New York: Liss.

Wittes, R. and Friedman, N. A., 1988, 'Accrual to clinical trials', *Journal of the National Cancer Institute*, 80: 884–5.

Zelen, M., 1979, 'A new design for randomised clinical trials', *The New England Journal of Medicine*, 300: 1242–5.

PART III

SOCIAL SCIENCE
DISCIPLINES

The health social sciences cover a broad range of disciplines whose purpose is to analyse the relationship between the health of individuals and social structure. Social science health researchers often enter into the lives of their study participants to a much greater extent than researchers using experimental designs. As a result, the ethical questions researchers face are more likely to involve the minimisation of this intrusion. In addition to contributing to social science, consideration is often given to the ways in which research results contribute to the health of the participants them-selves, directly or indirectly through policy change.

Jeanne Daly introduces some of the broad issues which social scientists take into account in planning health research, including considerations of the impact on society and community, of the choice of research method and of the way in which the research is conducted. She argues that social scientists are particularly well placed to address a broad range of health research problems in a methodologically flexible manner, but that their methods are not well understood and their critical conclusions may not always be welcome.

The next three contributions demonstrate the way in which social scientists design research which is responsive to research settings, especially when research explores issues which are difficult for participants to discuss. Allan Kellehear addresses an alternative to collecting data in survey or interview format by the use of unobtrusive methods. Such methods have the advantage of using existing data to reduce the intrusion of the re-searcher into the private lives of participants. Thus researchers should first consider whether analysis of existing data sources might not resolve the research question without the need for further data collection. When such data is not available, Pranee Liamputtong Rice argues that qualitative methods are particularly appropriate for addressing delicate research situations. Her essay describes a project in which she was able to be flexible in her approach and lend a helping hand to a distressed study participant.

Bill Noble addresses research into hearing impairment to show that methodological and ethical issues intersect. Hearing impairment is usually assessed using standardised measures of function. He argues that clients of hearing rehabilitation services experience difficulties which are closely related to the way in which they live with others. The ethical issue is that researchers have to set aside standardised methods of assessment, and the interventions suggested by these tests, in order to focus on interventions more directly related to the specific needs of individual clients.

Terri Jackson focuses on the broader issue of health policy. She argues that social scientists need to recognise the way in which their research is implemented in health policy. Health economists have found a central role in the generation of health policy but they have often not considered the ethical impact of their assumptions or their 'tools of trade'. She identifies five key issues which pose ethical problems for economist researchers, with allocation of resources on the basis of average marginal benefit being of particular concern. The essay also raises larger questions about the way in which limits for health spending are set and about the social responsibility of health economists for the way in which their research translates into public policy.

9

Social science
Health research

Jeanne Daly

In doing research, the social sciences proceed in a substantially different manner from the biomedical disciplines. Biomedical and clinical research traditionally use focused, reductionist and positivist research methods. As the previous section shows, the laboratory sciences, argued to be basic, proceed with relative confidence that their procedures are understood and valued. Not surprisingly, given the link to clinical practice, these disciplines exercise a fair degree of control over the research which is conducted not only in medical settings but also in the health field more generally. Thus we as social scientists often have to persuade the medical hierarchy of the value of our research as science. The danger is that a too-narrow focus on meeting medical standards of scientific design may obscure ethical considerations which emerge in the process of conducting health research—considerations which the social sciences are well placed to address.

THE HEALTH SOCIAL SCIENCES

The health social sciences cover a broad and sometimes confusing range of approaches. Different issues of research ethics need to be faced as we make our way through three different levels of health research: the broader, societal level, where health research is planned and implemented; the level of research method; and the level of research process.

THE SOCIETAL LEVEL

If we as social scientists working in the health field feel persecuted by a lack of recognition of our contribution to health research, it is also true that the social sciences, especially sociology, can be seen as invading too much of social life. A recent article in an Australian newspaper reflects such criticism:

> We are in the thrall of sociological research that is predicated on the assumption that virtually anything can be explained by the application of competent statistical analysis. *As a result, every aspect of life is some sociologist's research project.*
>
> The truth is that the truths generated by sociological research define our lives. And they change them. They remove mystery, doubt, guilt, and above all complexity. (Gawenda, 1994) [my emphasis]

This criticism of sociology is directed at research into the family where sociology and social psychology may be seen as dominating what counts as 'scientific truth'. Just as economists' predictions can shift the direction of the share market, sociologists can change the way people experience their daily lives, and this presents a considerable professional temptation. In the health area the dominant group defining 'scientific truth' is medical rather than sociological, but we still need to be wary of the potential of social science research to become evangelical, invading and colonising this area of social life. Honest, responsible research practice requires that we resist the temptation to exaggerate our contribution to any field and that we recognise the contribution made by other disciplines. The same would, of course, apply to practitioners of any other discipline working in the health field.

The problem is, however, more complex. The scope for social science research seems unlimited and so we should, in diffidence, set limits to the research which we, as social scientists, should be doing. Obviously, the proper topics for research are only those that present unresolved problems which it is important to see resolved. In going about our research task, we should take note of the potential of our disciplines for turning anything people do into data. Some people may not want their lives dissected and exposed to public view. Where we do tread our way into people's lives, we need to be sensitive to the demands and constraints under which they live.

Given the common task of social scientists and clinicians in interpreting the experience of illness, there is the need to tread a common path. The danger this presents for the social science researcher who wishes to respond to the sensitivities in the field is that we may be captured along the way. Agency capture refers to the process of giving up the concerns of our own discipline to represent the views of other groups in an uncritical manner, giving them legitimacy by our apparently objective research procedures. On one hand, we can be captured by patient or community concerns. Indeed, in the social sciences there is a strong tradition which requires us to represent the often silenced views of the 'underdog', and there is a clear need to represent community concerns disregarded by clinical researchers who focus only on disease in the body. On the other hand, we may also be captured by the medical profession, lending our research tools, shorn of their critical concerns, to bolster the medical research task while losing sight of our obligations to the wider community. Social scientists, especially those from a Marxian tradition, may also see the medical profession itself as being subjected to the dictates of the 'medical industrial complex'. In that sense, the medical profession itself is a (relative?) underdog. Perhaps the biggest temptation is to become a handmaiden of the health bureaucracy, using our research tools to reinforce specific policy initiatives in an unreflective manner. In the present economic climate, health economists may be at greatest risk of this research sin. Certainly their skills are valued highly by health departments intent on finding a legitimate reason for cutting health-care costs. The social sciences, especially those with a strong critical tradition, are perhaps unique in training their students to recognise the political purposes which their research can serve.

RESEARCH METHOD

As soon as we go to the practical level at which research is actually conducted, the social sciences seem to fractionate into groups addressing different issues from different theoretical perspectives using different methods. This is the source of considerable confusion to those trained in the natural or biomedical sciences.

At one extreme we have those social sciences which devise measures of social activity such as the individual experience of illness and medical interventions. The measures devised by social scientists are useful, especially when they have been validated in a series of studies. Essentially these social scientists use survey methods in a manner quite comparable with the use of epidemiological method. The basic assumption of the method is that the researcher knows what is going on in the field and can construct a set of questions which gather data only about factors seen as relevant to the research question. Since data gathering is limited to defined variables, samples may be large.

While these quantitative methods have undoubted value, the choice of research method is far from arbitrary (Daly *et al*, 1992). Given the wide variety of problems encountered in health care, we need to be able to choose from an equally wide range of research methods, selecting that method which provides the most rigorous approach to the problems which we have identified. When we know very little about an area, we need to proceed in a more unstructured manner. As researchers, we need to ensure that these various paths to research are respected and understood by those working in the field and by those making decisions about research funding.

Qualitative research methods are the most difficult to describe and are commonly misunderstood by both funding bodies and ethics committees. This misunderstanding relates both to the scientific credibility of the methods used and to issues of ethics raised by the way in which researchers invade people's social lives to collect data. Qualitative research can be seen as the collection of 'slices of life' which are then dissected and analysed using categories and themes which emerge from the data and from social science theory. Subsequent data collection methods may be altered on the basis of this analysis. Since the method of data collection (including considerations of sample size) and the analysis of the data evolve during the course of research, they cannot always be specified in detail in advance. Such methods are unfamiliar to biomedical scientists, who may fear that the research is unscientific, potentially misleading, and therefore unethical. The use of qualitative methods has been addressed in detail in comparison with other methods of research (Daly *et al*, 1992), and it is perhaps not the responsibility of the social scientist alone to ensure that these methods are properly understood. Nor is it necessarily our task to provide members of research ethics committees with a format for telling the difference between a scientifically sound social science research proposal and one which is badly constructed and unlikely to contribute to our knowledge of health. It is, however, our responsibility to be able to tell good research from bad when asked to make that judgment.

If qualitative methods create difficulties for those outside the social science disciplines, these pale by comparison with that research which is explicitly based on the application of social theory to the health area, including critical theory and postmodernist deconstruction. Often researchers using these approaches do not collect data from patients or doctors but draw on historical records. The difficulties arise when research from these perspectives cuts from under our feet the firm ground painfully built up through years of research. Let me give one example.

David Armstrong is a British sociologist whose work concentrates on a meticulous analysis of the historical social context of medical knowledge (Armstrong 1983; 1984). Like many other sociologists, he argues that disease is socially constructed. This does not mean that there is no biological source of disease but that the actual disease label is a reflection of the social processes surrounding the person or people who have the biological lesion. This means that disease labels are fluid, open to changing interpretations: disease can 'change shape' in front of our eyes. In modern society, for example, medical care has increasingly sought out disease in well people, not only in their bodies but in their social relations. Thus we encourage people to present for screening programs and advise them about risk factors which they should minimise by changing their behaviour and their social lives. On Armstrong's analysis this can be seen as an extension of medical surveillance into the everyday lives of well people. They will be under pressure to 'normalise' their lives by reducing the risk of disease. They may be required to give up smoking, drinking or having sex, to palpate their breasts and their scrotums for hidden signs of the disease just waiting to strike. Thus they become docile absorbers of health messages.

The process of surveillance exposes people to the risk of iatrogenesis (Illich, 1976). The search for disease and potential disease also contributes to rising health-care costs. These concerns can be put to use in two ways. In the first place social scientists can use this approach for a more critical analysis of the processes of diagnosis and treatment. Such an analysis can show the lack of benefit for patients, and even for doctors, in what may otherwise be taken for granted as being of obvious benefit. An example is our critical study of patient reassurance in the context of echocardiography (cardiac ultrasound) in which we showed that an uncomfortably large proportion of patients were left more worried about their hearts after a normal test result than they were before they were referred to the cardiologist (Daly and McDonald, 1993). Armstrong takes the argument further. In many medical texts there has been an emphasis on whole-person medicine and on the need to deal with the psychosocial context of patients. The work of Balint (1957) is widely used to argue for a more humanistic approach to medical practice. Armstrong does not see this movement as progressive or liberating. He points out that it brings larger and larger areas of patients' and well people's social lives under medical surveillance and that the benefits to patient or society are not clear. This casts a grey cloud not only over what doctors are doing but also over the activities of social scientists working in the health field. Those social scientists who are working with medical practitioners to study the social lives of their patients, whether by survey or qualitative study, may be strengthening a system of surveillance, making doctors into ever more intrusive health police. If Armstrong is correct, then the social sciences are being colonised and exploited to the detriment of patients. With disease disappearing and reappearing like the Cheshire Cat, and with the risk of harming people through our research, the ethical way out may be not to work in the health field at all! This would also save us from the tedious problem of having to label some social science research projects as good and some as bad.

RESEARCH PROCESS

If we persist in doing research in the health field, we will need guidance on the human qualities which we, as responsible researchers, need to guide us on our path. What reassurance can we give that those who participate in our research task will not be harmed by the processes we use in gathering and analysing data? There is no simple answer. All researchers, whatever their methods, might do worse than to cultivate human qualities like prudence, honesty, humility and caring and bring these to bear on their research task. Especially when using the less structured research procedures, the researcher can be seen as part of the research instrument, and we have to depend upon the capacity of the researcher for collecting data in an ethical and responsible manner. This is where we need to take account of what Paul Komesaroff calls the microethical context. Following Komesaroff's argument, we need to address some global ethical requirements, namely that we satisfy the conditions for free communication between individuals, that we recognise the different discourses which derive from the social and cultural groups to which people belong, and that we have the ability to respond in a flexible manner to 'the contingencies of individual interchanges'. These skills, and responsibilities, need to be the focus of our professional training as researchers.

With these considerations addressed, social scientists have some quite distinct advantages. This is where we can benefit from being able to gather data in a flexible manner across the whole spectrum of social experience. But how are we to know what is the *best* data to collect? How will an ethics committee know that we are collecting appropriate data and that we are not just grabbing, in a pragmatic and greedy manner, whatever comes our way?

The strength of qualitative method is that it allows us to categorise data of different kinds from different contexts into one coherent analytical framework. Since there are few constraints on the nature of the data we can collect, we can react to what we find in the field and change the focus of data collection during the course of the study. These changes in midstream are not done in an arbitrary manner; there has to be a good reason emerging from the process of data analysis, which means that there is a need for more extensive data collection. An example from my research into women's perceptions of menopause provides an example. Early interviews indicated that the experience of menopause might be different for women who have not had children. The question then was whether there was a difference between women who had simply not had children and women who had made an active commitment not to have children. The sample of women interviewed was therefore increased to include religious sisters and lesbians. Such changes can also be made to make our methods more responsive to the needs of particular groups of people interviewed, especially those who are most vulnerable. We can alter the way in which questions are asked and the way in which we respond to what our participants tell us.

The concerns of medical members of ethics committees that much of social science research appears subjective and arbitrary can be addressed further. Social science research methods depend upon an agreed set of principles and beliefs about the nature and conduct of research. In this they are identical with laboratory research. The difference is that social scientists, working in a varied and complex social context, need to address much broader issues and need a more varied and flexible set of theoretical criteria to provide the basis for sound research. This closely resembles what clinicians do when they apply biomedical knowledge in the complex interactive context of clinical practice. Allowances and judgments have to be made to reach the correct, best, most scientific decision. In the social sciences these decisions are based on quite explicit, well-described and historically validated theories about social behaviour. Indeed, many of us believe that social scientists and clinicians tread the same turf. As a social scientist my belief is that we have theoretical frameworks for analysis of the social context of clinical practice which clinicians could find very helpful. A word of warning to those clinicians who think it might be a good idea to colonise us and rob us of our methods—social science theory, including the work of Foucault, Habermas and the postmodern theorists, is not acquired in a pleasant weekend workshop!

RETURN TO THE SOCIETAL LEVEL

In the biomedical disciplines it is rare for a research project to spell out its policy implications, perhaps because these are taken to be self-evident. In the social sciences the research problems we address often arise from the everyday health problems of consumers and, traditionally, we take account of the historical background of these problems and their social context. It is therefore a relatively simple matter to relate our results to the lives of the people most concerned and to the policy level. In doing so, we make it more difficult for others to place their own interpretations on our research, perhaps in subtle ways distorting our conclusions. This problem may be particularly important in making evident the limitations of our research, for example, in making clear the extent to which our conclusions apply beyond the immediate context of the study to the general population or to other social groups. Sometimes, if some of the results of our studies are likely to result in harm to a group of people, especially if they are already disadvantaged, it may be preferable not to publish these findings.

Social scientists are perhaps peculiarly well suited to the task of critically evaluating existing programs or popular responses to health problems. We are likely, in the course of this work of critical analysis, to identify false assumptions and over-enthusiastic implementation of health interventions without regard to the long-term effects on community health. Such findings should be made available to anybody who might need to know the results—although, in truth, some people might prefer not to know that, for example, a brand new treatment for a debilitating disease is based on a set of dubious assumptions. Despite the lack of acclaim for social scientists in this role as 'spoilers', we cannot ignore a return of our analysis to the societal level.

CONCLUSION

Clearly, any research done in the health field should aim to make a substantive difference to the way in which we see health, disease and the treatment of disease. The problem is to find the best way of ensuring that the changes which result from our research benefit the community. Sometimes we need to remove doubt and uncertainty, but at other times, there is the need to emphasise caution and uncertainty. The skills we need for a research task will be defined by the particular health issue we are addressing. The social sciences offer a range of approaches and methods capable of addressing substantive health issues, but the methods of research are not straightforward in comparison with experimental methods.

Given this variety and complexity, it is not our responsibility, nor is it the purpose of the essays in this section, to provide guidelines for an ethics committee to judge what is ethical and what is unethical research. Rather, our aim is to give a glimpse of the kinds of considerations which social scientists bring to the task of setting up good, scientific, ethical research. These considerations will alter as the field of research and the relative vulnerability of the participants change. The task of evaluating such research requires detailed knowledge of social theory and research practice. While some basic indications of a general approach may be given, it is no substitute for peer assessment of proposals.

REFERENCES

Armstrong, D., 1983, *Political Anatomy of the Body: medical knowledge in Britain in the twentieth century*. Cambridge: Cambridge University Press.

——1984, 'The patient's view'. *Social Science and Medicine* 18, 9: 737–44.

Balint, M., 1957, *The Doctor, His Patient and the Illness*, London: Tavistock.

Daly, J., McDonald, I., and Willis, E., (eds.), 1992, *Researching Health Care: designs, dilemmas and disciplines*, London: Routledge.

Daly, J. and McDonald, I., 1993, *The Social Impact of Echocardiography*, Canberra: Australian Institute of Health and Welfare.

Gawenda, M., 1994, 'Sociologists have taken the truth captive, and us too', *The Age*, 24 February: 13.

Illich, I., 1976, *Medical Nemesis: the expropriation of health*, Middlesex: Penguin.

10

Unobtrusive Methods in Delicate Situations

Allan Kellehear

Doing some social science research into health care are we? (very good). Going before an institutional ethics committee? (of course you are). Got all the ethics figured out: Consent; Confidentiality; Privacy; Safety of subjects; Responsible publishing of results (CCPSR—difficult acronym, that one). And the method, the interview or survey I suppose (what else is there?). Then, of course, I take it that you're not researching people from non-English-speaking background? (you are!). Then, of course, you're bilingual (you're not!). Still, there are probably co-researchers who are? (only you conducting the research, eh . . .). Asking any potentially embarrassing questions, for example, about sex, death, mental illness, religion, politics, employment, personal habits, social attitudes or knowledge? (you are!) Well, you really are in a bit of a pickle. Still, I guess you won't be asking too many of those questions (138 questions!!). Well, then, I assume you at least won't have to ask too many people these questions (850, eh . . .). Good luck—to you and your respondents!!

INTRODUCTION

Like much behaviour in other quarters of society, many of our social science habits are based on traditions and conventions. And yet it is not our conventions in research which are, in themselves, unethical. Even the laziness which prevents us from thinking beyond them, although lamentable, is not strictly unethical. However, when social science research conventions move in to delicate situations uncritically, or with little circumspection, ethical questions then arise. And since a lot of health research asks a lot of questions about our bodies or mental health, a lot of that health research is socially delicate.

The term 'delicate' in the context of health research refers to a situation which maximises the conditions under which a person might give offence, embarrassment or shame to another. Usually this involves a stranger or relative stranger discussing, in a direct manner, potentially embarrassing or sensitive topics that they might not ordinarily share with strangers or 'outsiders'. Furthermore, the conditions which might foster trust in the relationship, such as an ongoing relationship, equality of interpersonal power, or control over the destiny and form of the information, are minimal. I have just described the most common experience of people undertaking interviews and surveys in health research and, in that context, the most common way in which health research may become unethical.

It is not that 'consent' or 'rapport' are not obtained (and these items should never be confused with understanding or trust). Rather, it is the imposition of the situation of stranger directness and demand, a situation so frequently a part of survey/interview work. The interview is the creation of an unnatural social situation, introduced by a researcher, for the purpose of polite interrogation. It is this situation, delicate by definition, which is ethically questionable.

This situation, embodied nicely in my early cameo and regularly ignored by ethics committees of every sort, might be avoided if more thought were devoted to unobtrusive ways of conducting research. If we are unable to avoid direct, obtrusive styles of research in health, then we should be responsible enough to invent ways to minimise its potential intrusiveness. It is not possible to cover every possible situation which might be partic-ularly delicate, but what follows are five questions we might ask ourselves before embarking on a project. These questions address the main issues of researcher intrusion by encouraging a rediscovery of what appears to be the lost art of unobtrusive research.

DO I NEED TO DO EMPIRICAL RESEARCH ON THIS TOPIC?

So often, when preparing a grant proposal or simply conducting the initial literature review for a certain research area, we will gain a broad familiarity with past research. That review of the literature will alert us to the research done in an area but not necessarily to the range of sources or resources available in that area. This distinction is important. Reviewing past social science effort in the health area encourages a certain mind-set: We think in terms of results and findings rather than the data sources.

For example, you, as researcher, might find one published study of adolescent attitudes toward premarital sex and another study on adolescent attitudes toward unsafe sex. The data sets for both studies may be deposited with a national data archive. Examination of the two data sets may reveal question categories that may answer your own interest in, say, adolescent attitudes to same sex relations. Reviewing the published studies does not necessarily mean reviewing the potential range of either available data or unpublished results in a particular area. To obtain that information you must check the original record; that single step might secure the information or insights that you require, obviating the need for your own direct, empirical investigation.

In connection with this check of existing sources, the main ones you might consult are: national census data, other government department data; business and company records; registries such as public or probate records; and state or national data archives. Data archives, for example, contain a wealth of information. The Australian one contains data sets from agencies such as Gallup and Saulwick Polls and the data sets from individual research projects on, for example, the social characteristics of non-drinkers or Tasmanian holiday makers (Maher and Burke, 1991, Social Science Data Archives, Catalogue SSDA, 1991).

Some of these archival sources also contain collections of published sources such as newspapers and photos. In this connection, state libraries sometimes offer a CD-ROM service which allows you to sit at a computer terminal and browse thousands of photographs by topic or subject. Of further interest is the possibility of using other published sources such as handbooks, textbooks, policy documents, fiction or even receipt books to obtain insights into professional or health-risk behaviours. There is a copious literature on content, thematic or semiotic approaches to analysing these data sources (Kellehear, 1993a; Webb *et al*, 1981). There is also a range of computer software such as ETHNOGRAPH or NUDIST which can assist with sorting the material for you.

Personal documents such as diaries, letters, published sources of oral history (there is an international journal for this now) and photos are also useful data for secondary analysis. *Some* studies employing this wealth of material will show up in your 'review of the literature', but the potential range and value of the untapped material will not. You will need to consult a directory of resources for some of this, or inquire at the library or appropriate government services. You may save yourself a lot of time, and your potential respondents a lot of bother, if you can obtain your information in these ways.

There has been a lot written on the pros and cons of secondary research, a lot of it hokum. Secondary research, it is said, can lead to inherited methodological errors (however, interviews and surveys can lead to 'inherited' and 'coal-face' methodological errors). Material may be out of date (however, respondent memory in interviews may be faulty *and* out of date). Material might have been collected for different purposes by different agencies (however, survey and interview material may vary according to who collects it, depending upon the age, sex, or motivation of the researcher as attributed by the respondents). Some argue that secondary analysis has limited generalisability (but so has interview and survey data). Others argue that existing sources may decontextualise meaning (I had always understood that to be a standing criticism of interview and survey data before also noticing it in the literature on secondary analysis).

However, unlike much interviewing work, existing data can often provide good sources of longitudinal data; can be obtained unobtrusively; can be rechecked by others easily; can often be very cheap; and can often be historically or methodologically unique.

IF I STILL NEED TO DO EMPIRICAL RESEARCH, DO I NEED TO EMPLOY DIRECT METHODS?

Even if you cannot answer your research questions by combing the existing sources of colleagues, businesses, universities or governments, surveys or interviews are not necessarily the best ways to conduct empirical investigation.

As many colleagues from media or cultural studies, anthropology or geography will tell you, there are a myriad other ways to find out about people's lives. In audiovisual analysis, for example, one might examine contemporary or historical film footage. This can involve the study of popular films, or a thematic examination of national 'documentaries'. Television shows, news hours or advertisements also tell us about producers and consumers, not simply of television, but also of ideas and products. Television news constructs crime and politics to taste along the same broad lines as soap powder and breath freshener ads. Photographs used in popular or professional tabloids, magazines or journals reveal knowledge, attitudes and practices just as surely as any survey, and probably with more reliability.

The study of noise content and concentration can tell us much about social architecture and planning as well as crowd reaction and individual use of spaces. Health and safety research in workplaces and homes commonly uses, as a stock category, aspects of material culture such as people's personal items, clothing and accessories, motor cars and housing. Recently someone has examined the impact of the 'Slip, Slop, Slap' anti-UV exposure campaign in Australia, not by asking but by observing people and their clothing and accessories on sunny summer days (Threlfall, 1992). Studying the contents of domestic garbage bins reveals dietary habits and attitudes that people take for granted, forget or prefer not to mention. This checking of behaviour against belief is a real strength of the observation method in general.

When most researchers think about observation they tend to associate it with the study of gross behaviour, such as the study of shopping behaviour; or child–parent interactions; or football crowd reactions. But much useful data can be obtained by examining physical objects, expressive movements of face or body posture, or language use.

Furthermore, all major methodological approaches are applicable in these kinds of studies: from simple tallying-type content analysis to the type of semiotic analysis that might impress even Foucault at a cafe near you.

If a few or any of these approaches do not replace your desire or need to interview or survey, consider the possibility of adding them to your research design. Observations of behaviour can underscore beliefs but they can also challenge them. By using unobtrusive methods in a complementary way in your research design, you can cross-validate the findings, giving them greater credibility, complexity or both.

DO I NEED TO DO AS MUCH INTERVIEWING OR SURVEYING AS I ORIGINALLY SUPPOSED?

Combining unobtrusive methods does more than cross-validate, as any use of multiple methods might. Combining these methods with direct methods has other advantages. In this section I will explain how. As I have mentioned, the most artificial and self-conscious—and hence intrusive—way to do research is to interrogate people. However, if interrogating people on a wide range of sensitive topics is unavoidable, perhaps you should work on reducing the number of questions involved. The only question you must never surrender in health research is: Do I need all those questions? We have already covered the main unobtrusive methods. If these are little or no use to you, this does not necessarily mean you are stuck with direct methods in all their undiminished glory. There are *less* obtrusive methods even if the unobtrusive ones are unsuitable. Two examples come to mind.

First, action research—*doing research with others*—is a fine way to reduce the number of questions. A long interview schedule is quickly trimmed and shaped when you are working *with* rather than *on* other people. By working with the people you are interested in, you convey an important degree of social understanding by being part of their everyday routines and conversations. Being part of a group's life places you on a quick learning curve by inducting you into experience. When you have experience, many questions, especially the questions of outsiders, soon disappear and the questions that remain may easily alter because either they become different questions in your own mind or because now you know how to be more sensitive, or culturally appropriate, and therefore less intrusive. In this way, what are seen as delicate situations for outsiders may not be such for insiders.

The *quid pro quo* of this research approach, of course, is that the researcher's aims become shared intellectual and political property of the group you have worked so hard to become a part of. This means that control over the research project becomes shared (or 'dispersed' or 'lost', depending on the language of your politics). Nevertheless, even this experience is part of the research project, that is to say, the learning experience. But many people can see the benefits of getting to know others better without relinquishing control over the project. They want to become less interrogative in their methodological style, ask fewer questions, and become better acquainted with the experience and values of those they are interested in.

Participant observation is broadly similar to action research, but unlike action research, does not entail research *with* others but rather *alongside* them. Here, it is understood that the researcher's aims are not necessarily the same as what the group would like to see come out of the project. Indeed, the group is not encouraged to think about that issue. Instead, the researcher becomes a kind of friendly academic type who naively, but with good intentions and enthusiasm, participates in the daily life and routines of the group.

Both action research and participant observation have the advantage that a relationship based on growing mutual trust and knowledge may develop over time. This means that the researcher must have time to engage in this sort of relationship. Remember that data is a commodity of considerable worth in the modern marketplace. Good data in research attracts money, prestige, and publications. However, researchers who want these delights on the cheap, as it were, by extracting data without much personal investment in the people providing it, raise several ethical questions about the researchers' right to exist, not to mention the dubious quality of the data so gained. Perhaps so much of health research is 'delicate' because so many researcher/respondent relationships are fleeting and of poor quality. Is it possible that doctors are not alone in their reluctance to spend time with their clients?

DO I NEED TO INTERVIEW/SURVEY IN THE CONVENTIONAL MANNER?

If you have reached this far in your thoughts but still need to interview the usual suspects, do you really need to adopt a totally inquisitional style? There are many ways to encourage people to talk and to address your interests without an endless cycle of question and answer.

In this context, the highly 'unstructured' interview or questionnaire is an instrument less likely to create trust and reciprocity and more likely to give a respondent a sense of violation afterwards. Respondents who are allowed to ramble on about the simplest question, fuelled by doses of empathy and eye contact, are later left wondering whether they disclosed too much or imposed too much on the researcher's time and patience.

There are at least two other ways to encourage discussion without the forced ways of formal interviewing.

The first way to introduce discussion in a more natural way is to present respondents with material objects or photographs. The objects or photos do not need to belong to the researcher. They may belong to the respondent. Medical equipment or photos of particular procedures can be shown to people for comment and discussion. Family albums, work photos or objects can stimulate people to talk together about a whole range of interests, concerns and fears. As a social research strategy alternative to formal interviewing, the exchanges between researcher and respondent become more informal, natural and familiar to the non-research world of the respondent.

The second way to discuss sensitive matters with people is to employ experiential work. Sometimes, asking people to express themselves in a medium other than speech can provide them with a broader social vocabulary. Children, people from non-English-speaking background, the voiceless or the speech impaired, may all find this methodology less tiresome.

In this context, people might be asked to make collages from images obtained from magazines; to draw or paint pictures; to select poems or music; or to take a series of photos, all of which may express their particular experience, values, feelings or attitude. Remember that as academics we belong to a minority class of word workers. Many other groups do not work or play by privileging written or spoken communication. The arrival of film and television has ensured a long and growing membership for this visually more responsive group.

For others, especially for those whose first language is not English, other forms of expression may be more freeing. In a folk-music coffee house in Charlottesville, Virginia, hangs a sign which reads: 'Talking about music is like dancing about architecture.' It's right. This should remind all researchers not only about the limitations of language but also about the limited way in which some people employ it to express themselves. Not allowing for this limitation can restrict the validity of interview work while maximising the chances that respondents will feel awkward, foolish or embarrassed, particularly in matters they find sensitive or complex.

DO I NEED TO AVOID INTERVIEWING/SURVEYS AT ALL COSTS?

This question should not, of course, be posed in these terms. It is never a question of which method to favour or disfavour but rather of which methods address the twin concerns of effective and sensitive probing. Too often researchers concern themselves with the 'effective' side of the equation because the 'sensitive' side is too inconvenient. Pressures to publish, get promoted, get the PhD, or simply get results fast, turn the concern from 'effectiveness' to 'efficiency' and the issue of sensitivity to respondents gets shunted even further from our concerns. Ethical discussions are one of the few ways to recover, indeed rediscover, those concerns. But I do not mean to suggest that interviews or surveys, as direct methods, are always intrusive, ethically questionable, methodologically dubious. Interviews or surveys can in fact be the opposite of these things for some groups of respondents.

I conducted fairly structured interviews with 100 terminally ill cancer sufferers (Kellehear, 1990). More than a few of these people experienced chronic pain, nausea or vomiting. Many others suffered from chronic tiredness and inability to concentrate (I discuss the ethics of this research in Kellehear, 1989). Physical energy and mental concentration ability were scarce resources for these people. Participant observation, long unstructured interviews—indeed, any requirement that invited them to be equal participants in the research exercise—were not welcome. What might be considered less intrusive for healthy people would be nothing short of a nightmare for these seriously ill people.

Structured interviews or questionnaires traditionally take up less of the respondents' time. This is a strength when the respondents are people with meagre physical reserves. Such research instruments aid both memory and concentration, where these qualities are compromised, by being focused and logical in structure. And this is relevant not only to cancer patients (I discuss this topic at greater length in Kellehear, 1993b). People who are very old, chronically or seriously ill, dying or mentally impaired, may cooperate, and gladly, if the research experience is direct, directed, and brief. The short interview or survey is seen by many people in these circumstances as a mercy. Direct methods can be less intrusive than others in such cases.

Furthermore, your use of an instrument which they see as being considerate of their time and resources is in itself some signal to them of your values of reciprocity, an important foundation for building respondent rapport and confidence in you as a researcher.

Interviews and surveys may also be seen as less intrusive research methods by very busy people—doctors, nurses, nursing mothers etc.—who might prefer to avoid the prolonged presence of a researcher that observational work may require. The whole point to any consideration of methods in delicate situations, however, is the importance of focusing on the needs of those you wish to research. Only when research is designed away from the social character of ordinary everyday people, people who do not see themselves as research participants, does the research process become reified and imposing, and the researchers a social menace. And, as with all social menaces, these are the least attractive people to let loose on sensitive topics and situations such as those one regularly encounters in health research.

CONCLUSION

When research in the area of health reaches for people's most personal thoughts, such research may have little or no legitimacy. As researchers we are often present only by the good grace and indulgence of those who endure our questions. And it *is* endurance for many of them, because health research often takes the form of a barrage of questions from people respondents hardly know. They may be consenting respondents but we should be responsible for the social occasion, which is, consent notwithstanding, an intrusion.

Those who make light of the issue of the ethical problem of intrusion, do not, I believe, understand the related problems of privacy and confidentiality. Are we these kinds of people? Do we need these kinds of people in health research today? Unobtrusive strategies are not about being clever with methods but, rather, about being imaginative in light of our responsibilities to research participants.

The five questions discussed in this paper cumulatively outline one of the few responsive ways of making health research ethically responsible and methodologically sound. This is because it returns the problem of researcher intrusion to its rightful place, at the top of our concerns, and reminds us that the research act itself is the key ethical problem in research, and the one from which all our other concerns flow.

REFERENCES

Kellehear, A., 1989, 'Ethics and social research'. In J. Perry (ed.), *Doing Fieldwork: eight personal accounts of social research*, Geelong: Deakin University Press.

Kellehear, A., 1990, *Dying of Cancer: the final year of life*, London: Harwood Academic Publishers.

——1993a, *The Unobtrusive Researcher: a guide to methods*, Sydney: Allen & Unwin.

——1993b, 'Rethinking the survey'. In D. Colquhoun and A. Kellehear (eds.), *Health Research in Practice: political, ethical and methodological issues*, London: Chapman and Hall.

Maher, C. and Burke, T., 1991, *Informed Decision Making*, Melbourne: Longman Cheshire.

Threlfall, T.J., 1992, 'Sunglasses and clothing—an unhealthy correlation', *Australian Journal of Public Health*, 16, 2: 192–96.

Social Science Data Archives., 1991, *SSDA Catalogue*, Canberra: Australian National University.

Webb, E., Campbell, D.T., Schwartz, R.D., Sechrest, L. and Grove, J.G., 1981, *Non-Reactive Measures in the Social Sciences*, Boston: Houghton and Mifflin.

11

My Soul Has Gone:
APPROPRIATE METHODS FOR
A DELICATE SITUATION

Pranee Liamputtong Rice

This essay is about the contribution that qualitative research methodology may make in responding appropriately to delicate situations which can arise in conducting research in the area of women's health. It is based on the case study of a Hmong woman which emerges from my ongoing research project on cultural beliefs and practices concerning child-bearing and child rearing and reproductive health in Southeast Asian women. I will begin with a description of the study, then present the case study, and follow this with a discussion of the research methodology. The final section will discuss the way health-care providers resolved the woman's problem.

BACKGROUND

This essay reports the results of an ongoing ethnographic study of reproductive health among Southeast Asian women living in Australia. The study included members of the Hmong, Lao, Vietnamese, Cambodian, and Thai communities.

I conducted ethnographic interviews covering a number of issues concerning reproductive health, including the beliefs and practices related to child-bearing and child rearing, with 23 Hmong women in Melbourne, Victoria. Most of the women had given birth while living in Laos or in a refugee camp in Thailand as well as in hospitals in Melbourne. The women were individually interviewed in their own homes. All interviews were conducted in the Hmong language with the assistance of a Hmong-born bicultural research assistant (BL) who has worked for and represented the Hmong community in Melbourne for more than ten years and is well known and accepted by most Hmong in that city.

Informed consent was obtained after the nature of the research and each woman's participation were clearly explained to her.

Each interview was tape-recorded. The length of the interviews varied depending on the women's responses. In general, each interview took between two and three hours. Most women were interviewed once. There were, however, a number of occasions when I needed to obtain more information. Those women were then visited for a second time.

In addition, a participant observation method was used to allow me to observe and record more fully the cultural beliefs and practices of the Hmong and their experiences in Australia. I attended a number of Hmong ceremonies and participated in Hmong activities. The interviews and participant observations were conducted between May 1993 and February 1994.

A content analysis approach was used to discern patterns in Hmong women's beliefs and practices. Put simply, recordings of interviews were transcribed for detailed analysis. The transcripts were examined for the women's explanations related to the concept concerned. From these, several themes were derived. For the purpose of this essay I examined the women's explanations of childbirth and their concepts of the soul.

THE HMONG

Many Hmong women in Australia are refugees. They have been accepted as immigrants in Australia since 1975. However, the majority of them are recently arrived. The Hmong in Australia come from Laos, where they lived in tribal groups in the mountainous areas. Embroiled in the fighting between the US armed forces and the Pathet Lao, the Laotian Communists, the Hmong were forced to move out of their homelands in the mountains and flee to Thailand. The majority were accepted for resettlement in the US. In Australia the Hmong are concentrated in New South Wales, though there are some in Tasmania and an increasing number in Queensland. In Victoria, the Hmong live in close-knit groups, mainly in Melbourne, in high-rise public housing in Fitzroy, an inner-city suburb, and Coolaroo, an outer northeastern suburb.

In general the Hmong are much poorer than other Southeast Asian refugees. The majority are unemployed. Most Hmong had no formal education in Laos because of the war and their geographical position. Because most Hmong are recent arrivals, they are still learning English.

The Hmong are animistic and observe ancestral worship. They believe in reincarnation. They are patrilineal and patrilocal. The family names follow the clan system. There are nine clans in Melbourne.

The usual Hmong family is large. Most Hmong women in this study have four to six children and are likely to bear more. Traditionally, the Hmong put a high value on having many children, particularly boys, since they could help in farming and continue traditional practices such as worshipping ancestral spirits and caring for their parents in old age. The Hmong maintain such customs (except for the farming) in Australia.

The demographic characteristics of Hmong women in this study are presented in Table 1.

THE CASE[1]

Mai is 34 years old. She is married and has six children. Four children were born in a refugee camp in Thailand and two in Australia. Five of her children were born normally. However, when Mai had her last child she was told she needed a caesarean operation because the foetus was in a transverse lie. She refused. However, when she was told that a vaginal birth would threaten the life of the baby, Mai agreed to the caesarean. The operation was done under general anaesthetic and Mai was alone in the operating theatre as her husband was not allowed to stay with her. Since this birth, Mai has been unwell. She has seen a number of medical specialists, but they have not been able to find anything wrong with her.

Mai believes that while she was unconscious in the operating theatre, one of her souls, which has as its duty the care of her well-being, left her body and was unable to re-enter it. She believes that because she was moved out of the operating theatre and regained consciousness in a recovery room, her soul was left behind in the operating theatre. She strongly believes that the loss of this soul is the main cause of her ill-health because over the past ten months, she has had bad dreams two to three times a week. After each dream, she feels very ill and has bad pain. Her dream is always that she is wandering to faraway and strange places. She does not know where she is going since she has never seen these places before. She feels as if she is compelled to keep walking endlessly. Mai believes these are signs that the soul which has left her body is wandering in another world.

The Hmong believe that each person has three souls (*plig*). One soul is to look after the body when a person is still living. When the person dies, this soul travels to the other world and awaits the opportunity for rebirth. A second soul stays to look after the grave of the person after his/her death and is not reincarnated. A third soul travels to live with the ancestors in the other world (Lee, 1981; Symonds, 1991).

If all souls are in residence in the body, a person is well and healthy. A soul may wander off occasionally, but usually it is able to return to its body. Ill-health occurs when a soul leaves the body because it is frightened away for various reasons and is unable to find its way home. The causes of soul loss are many, for example, injury and wounds, a great fall, a loud noise, being alone in darkness, being unconscious, and feeling sad and lonely (Chindasri, 1976; Thao, 1984; Symonds, 1991). Common symptoms

Table 1 Characteristics of Hmong women

Characteristics	Number	%
Age		
20–30	6	26.09
31–40	8	34.78
41–50	4	17.39
over 51	5	21.74
Marital status		
Married	8	78.26
De facto	1	4.35
Widowed	4	17.39
Number of children		
1–3	4	17.39
4–6	14	60.87
7–9	1	4.35
10 or more	4	17.39
Level of education		
None	17	73.91
Primary	6	26.09
Current activities		
Home duties	16	69.57
Learning English for migrants	7	30.43
No. of years in Australia		
1–3	6	26.09
4–6	13	56.52
7 or more	4	17.39
No. of family members living in the house		
1–3	2	8.70
4–6	8	34.78
7–9	9	39.13
10 or more	4	17.39
Length of stay in refugee camp in Thailand (years)		
1–3	4	17.39
4–6	2	8.70
7–9	5	21.74
10 or more	12	52.17

include tiredness and weakness, headache and fever, loss of appetite but increased thirst, insomnia, and frequent dreams of being in 'a strange place and with a stranger.

To restore a person to wellness, a soul-calling ceremony (*hu plig*) must be performed at the place where the soul left the body. This ceremony is usually performed by a shaman, but it can also be performed by an older person who has knowledge of the soul-calling ritual (Chindasri, 1976; Thao, 1984; Symonds, 1991). It involves the burning of incense, an egg, a bowl of raw rice, and a live chicken. Traditionally, the ceremony must be performed either early in the morning or late in the afternoon. However, no specific date is required. The ceremony may take from ten minutes to one hour or even longer, depending on how long the soul has been lost and how quickly it agrees to come home.

To regain her health, Mai would have to undergo a soul-calling ceremony at the theatre in which the caesarean was done and where the soul was still waiting to be called back. I asked her if she had ever considered doing this. Her quick response was that it would simply not be possible. She said the hospital staff would not understand her customs and would refuse the request, especially as the ceremony involves a live chicken and the burning of incense. Her husband said he had not been allowed to accompany his wife into the operating theatre; how, then, would they be permitted to perform a ceremony alien to Western health-care providers? Because so much time had passed since the loss of Mai's soul, the family believed that it had by now been transformed into another living thing. As a consequence, her health was deteriorating.

THE METHODOLOGY

There have been debates about what is the most appropriate methodology in doing health research (Baum, 1994). Daly and McDonald (1992), for example, argue that most health-care research to date has focused on experimental studies and on quantitative data analysis. Would this case have been found in a randomised trial or other quantitative method based on a structured set of questionnaires? My experience suggests that this is most unlikely.

In conducting research to understand people in their social and cultural contexts, it is essential to see the social and cultural world from the people's point of view rather than from that of the researcher. This is particularly so when 'the researcher knows very little about a particular area and where the social contexts of people's lives is of crucial significance' (McDonald and Daly, 1992). In such a case, qualitative methodology has much to offer.

Yoddumnern-Attig *et al.* (1993) argue that the strength of qualitative research lies in its ability to help discover and understand the context in which actions and events occur. Qualitative information offers in-depth descriptions and a rationale for explaining the underlying behaviour of people. Qualitative methodology is also flexible. Bryman (1984:78) writes: 'Qualitative research is deemed to be much more fluid and flexible than quantitative research in that it emphasises discovering novel or unanticipated findings and the possibility of altering research plans in response to such serendipitous occurrences.'

The flexibility of qualitative research methodology allows the researcher to investigate further and to respond to the situation in a meaningful way.

How did I find out about this case?

In the interview, when Mai told me she had had her last child by caesarean, I prompted her with a question about the effect of this on her subsequent health. Mai said she had been sick for some time. I asked about the symptoms she had had since the operation. Mai said:

> My sickness is not like if you say that I am very sick, no I am not. If you say I am well, no I am not well either. I can't say that I have no appetite but I can eat a little bit . . . to keep my body going . . . One day I must sleep at least two times for me to have strength to get about. If I don't sleep like that then my back and lower back is very sore like something is hitting it.

I asked: 'Do you have anything further to tell me?' She answered:

> Yes, when I go to sleep at night I can't sleep on the side. If I do then it feels like my chest is very tight and I can't breathe so I must get up and sit for a while. If I sleep on my back I feel that my lower back is not touching the mattress or the bed that I sleep on. It feels like my back is lifted all the time. So sleeping for me is very difficult.

At this point I was alerted to the likelihood that some crucial issues underlay her explanations, particularly since she mentioned the feeling that her back was not touching the bed. I asked her what she believed to be the cause of her ill-health. Mai only mentioned that it was because of the operation. Was it the operation solely? I asked myself. Being from Southeast Asia myself and coming from the medical anthropology field, I well know that we have a number of cultural beliefs and practices related to health and illness. I said to Mai:

> In Thailand, a lot of Thai people believe that each person has souls and if we are frightened one of the souls may leave the body and the person will become ill and may die if the soul does not come back forever. Do Hmong people have concern about this?

Because I showed Mai that I had some understanding and appreciation of cultural beliefs and practices similar to her own, she quickly responded that soul loss had in fact caused her ill-health. Thereafter the interview was focused on issues of soul loss in Hmong culture, what is involved in the soul-calling ceremony, and the possibility of bringing her soul back.

This account has served to illustrate the process of discovery and the flexibility inherent in the qualitative methodology which allowed me to discover, probe further and find some solutions. If I had used a quantitative method I would not have uncovered this case.

THE RESOLUTION[2]

WHAT DO YOU DO WHEN AN UNEXPECTED EVENT LIKE THIS OCCURS?

I promptly had a meeting with my superior, the director of the Centre for the Study of Mothers' and Children's Health, and discussed the possibility of arranging to bring Mai back to the hospital to perform a soul-calling ceremony. The director immediately contacted one of the hospital staff. Through this intermediary, the deputy chief executive officer of the hospital agreed to the request, saying: 'The hospital is more than happy to do anything for the woman if this can help her.' She left the name of a person whom we needed to contact to make the arrangements.

I contacted the operating theatre manager to arrange for the soul-calling ceremony. I learned that the theatre was quite busy during the week, so I suggested to Mai that it be done on a weekend. Since the date was not important, Mai agreed to have the ceremony performed on a Sunday morning. At eight o'clock on one Sunday morning Mai, her husband and a shaman met me and my bicultural research assistant at the ground floor of the hospital with the essential ingredients, including a live chicken in a cardboard box. When we reached the operating theatre, the charge nurses were expecting us. They were very helpful and supportive. They showed Mai where she was put to sleep and where she regained consciousness. They even showed her the path along which she was taken to the operating theatre because they wanted to ensure that the ceremony was performed appropriately. At 8.30 a.m. the shaman performed a soul-calling ritual in the operating theatre. It took him about twenty minutes to persuade Mai's soul to come home to her. To ensure that the soul would not be confused about which body it belonged in, the shaman also performed the same ritual at the spot where Mai regained consciousness in the recovery room. This time it took him only ten minutes. Then we all went back to Mai's house to perform another ceremony. This one was to welcome the soul back to its home.

On Monday I did not have an opportunity to inform the manager about the Sunday ceremony. On Tuesday while I was interviewing in the Hmong community, he rang me at work to find out if everything was all right and if Mai was better. One of my colleagues, who was informed about the matter, passed on the message as well as thanking him and the hospital staff for their kind cooperation. The manager replied that it was the duty of the hospital staff to provide good care to women and that we did not need to thank them.

THE SEQUEL

Morse (1992:xi) writes:

> . . . to be immersed in qualitative research inquiry is fun and exciting. Although the process may be filled with many traps that trip the unwary researcher, the rewards are immense. Researchers get to know the participants in their studies as real people, become part of their lives and often make lifelong friends in the process.

As Morse said, since these events I have had much contact with Mai and her family. I am no longer seen as a researcher who wants to find out about their lives, but rather as a friend and a family member. I have been invited to family functions. Mai has asked me for advice, including advice on health-related and family matters. She also gives me her advice on health issues. Recently I accidentally burned my daughter with hot coffee. I told Mai and talked with her about my concern about the burn. She suggested I bring my daughter to see the Hmong magic man, who has a reputation for healing burns with magic. She told me what to bring to honour the healer and how to go about asking for help in Hmong culture. I followed her advice.

CONCLUSION

Qualitative methodology may be helpful in delicate situations. An example is when a person believes they are ill because they have lost their soul. I describe the case of a Hmong woman named Mai who had a caesarean operation in a Victorian maternity hospital and attributed her subsequent ill-health to her soul having left her body during the operation.

This case was found only because I used qualitative methodology. Such methodology allows a process of discovery. It also has the flexibility for the researcher to investigate further. This enables the researcher to help solve problems for the respondent. The hospital allowed Mai to re-enter the operating theatre to have a soul-calling ceremony performed. Thanks to this essential ceremony, Mai is now gradually regaining her health.

Practically, this case could have been prevented if Mai's cultural beliefs and practices had been taken into account when she was admitted to hospital. There is no doubt that a caesarean operation was essential for the survival of the infant in this particular case. However, it could have been managed differently. For example, an epidural anaesthetic might have been used, and Mai's husband could have been allowed to stay with her in the operating theatre so he would be able to call her soul into the recovery room for her.

Nevertheless, the agreement of the hospital staff to allow Mai and her family to perform the soul-calling ceremony as well as their concern about her well-being are positive aspects. They illustrate that mainstream health services can provide culturally sensitive care to consumers from different cultural backgrounds if they are informed about these cultural beliefs and practices.

Morse (1992) says that 'researchers' lives are enriched as participants share their stories, their suffering, and their lives' when they adopt qualitative methodology. I found this to be particularly true in the case described here.

ACKNOWLEDGMENTS

I would like to thank the hospital and its staff for giving permission and arranging for Mai to have the soul-calling ritual. I also thank Blia Ly for assisting in the interviews, Dr Judith Lumley for taking immediate action to help solve Mai's problem, and to Lyn Watson and Anne Potter for assisting in the preparation of this essay.

NOTES

1 The case study presented here has been published in the *Medical Journal of Australia*. See Rice, P.L., Ly, B. and Lumley, J., 1993, 'Childbirth and soul loss: The case of a Hmong woman', *Medical Journal of Australia*, 160: 577–8.
2 Part of the resolution is in the paper mentioned above.

REFERENCES

Baum, F., 1993, 'Deconstructing the qualitative–quantitative divide in health research', *Annual Review of Health Social Sciences*, 3:6–18.

Bryman, A., 1984, 'The debate about quantitative and qualitative research: A question of method or epistemology?', *British Journal of Sociology*, 35, 1: 78–93.

Chindasri, N., 1976, *The Religion of the Hmong Njua*, Bangkok: The Siam Society.

Daly, J., and McDonald, I., 1992, 'Introduction: The problem as we saw it'. In Daly, J., McDonald, I., and Willis, E. (eds.), *Researching Health Care: designs, dilemmas, disciplines*, London: Routledge.

Lee, G.Y., 1981, *The effects of development measures on the socio-economy of the White Hmong*, PhD thesis, Department of Anthropology, University of Sydney.

McDonald, I. and Daly, J., 1992, 'Researching methods in health care—a summing up'. In Daly, J., McDonald, I., and Willis, E. (eds.), *Researching Health Care: designs, dilemmas, disciplines*, London: Routledge.

Morse, J.M., 1992, *Qualitative Health Research*, Newbury Park: Sage Publications.

Symonds, P.V., 1991, *Cosmology and the Cycle of Life: Hmong views of birth, death and gender in a mountain village in Northern Thailand*, PhD thesis, Department of Anthropology, Brown University, Providence, Rhode Island.

Thao, X., 1984, 'Southeast Asian refugees of Rhode Island: The Hmong perception of illness', *Rhode Island Medical Journal*, 67: 323–30.

Yoddumnern-Attig, B., Attig, G.A., Boonchalaksi, W., Richter, K. and Soonthorndhada, A., 1993, 'Qualitative research: A process of discovery'. In Yoddumnern-Attig, B., Attig, G.A., Boonchalaksi, W., *et al.* (eds), *Qualitative Methods for Population and Health Research*. Bangkok: Institute for Population and Social Research.

12

BEHAVIOURAL RESEARCH IN HEALTH: INDIVIDUAL SUBJECT VS PERSON IN CONTEXT

William Noble

The question of taking individuals as isolated subjects versus taking them as persons in contexts has obvious methodological implications in terms of what researchers, and ultimately practitioners, will attend to concerning their participants or clients. This has ethical importance inasmuch as anything taken to be beneficial to another human being under, say, the isolated-subject approach, may be seen as less than beneficial when considered from the person-in-context approach. Psychologists in the positivist tradition are very much oriented to assessing features of individuals as isolated possessors of attributes varying in value (personality traits, IQ); inadequate attention has been paid to the historical, sociopolitical and microsocial contexts within which individual functioning is intelligible, an argument that has taken various forms (Bevan and Kessel, 1994; Danziger, 1980; John, 1994).

This chapter uses the particular case of research directed to the delivery of aural rehabilitation services to illustrate the force of taking an individualist rather than a contextualist approach. Doubtless, some features of what is discussed will be peculiar to that arena; the general issues surely apply to other forms of research work associated with health and well-being.

SOME FINDINGS FROM BEHAVIOURAL RESEARCH ON HEARING HEALTH CARE

The purpose of undertaking health research is to try to improve procedures for alleviating impairments, or at least to make their effects less disabling. I mention this rather obvious point only to establish that research on adult-acquired hearing impairment is closely bound to the context of rehabilitation. Classical approaches to such research have been very much centred on procedures for diagnosis and appraisal. Only a small proportion of the very large and increasing number of people with impaired hearing (Davis, 1989) are able to be relieved by surgical or medical means. The commonest form of impairment, degeneration of or injury to the receptor cells of the inner ear, is usually irreversible. One major aim is to derive formulae to allow optimum and consistent fitting of personal hearing aids (Byrne and Dillon, 1986). This is a worthwhile aim, even though several problems, endemic to the nature of hearing loss and to constraints on signal amplification, continue to frustrate the achievement of fully satisfactory prosthesis design and fitting (Plomp, 1978; 1994).

Hearing *impairment* can be defined in the World Health Organisation's terms (1980) namely as a departure from normal expectation in terms of functional tests. Impairments give rise to *disabilities* (actual everyday inabilities to hear properly) and *handicaps* (everyday disadvantages which result from those disabilities). Disabilities and handicaps due to hearing impairment have been documented in several different forms (Hétu *et al*, 1987; Jones *et al*, 1987; Noble and Atherley, 1970), with the basic method relying on self-assessment. Early investigation using this procedure was justified partly by a need to grasp the perspective of the person whose hearing was impaired (Noble, 1978). One may see in this line of argument some emphasis on the 'person in context' rather than on the 'individual subject'.

The term 'individual subject' is used to highlight a paradoxical feature of that approach. Such 'subjects' are held to be autonomous units, and are the focus of research attention as being the individuals with the disorder of interest. Yet their unitary 'individuality' is regarded as interchangeable with that of other 'individual subjects', enabling them to be assigned to one or another 'effects' group, their data contributing to average outcomes which are compared across conditions. This is 'nomothetic' analysis (Stewart, 1988), in which generalities are sought using samples whose inter-individual variability is treated as error ('unexplained variance'). Individuals vary in response to the same dose of whatever is making them worse or whatever is being used to try to make them better. Even so, if people suffer injury or disease, on average, to the extent of X, from exposure to dose A, they will probably suffer at least more than X, on average, from exposure to 2 x A. Variability despite this general outcome is put down to measurement error, or to determinants such as differences in physiology.

Part of the 'individual subject' approach entails establishing reliable and objective procedures for assessment of effects. In the case of hearing impairment, this takes the form of tests using standardised sound sources. Assessment of hearing disability and handicap is less uniform, although there is continuing advocacy (Demorest and DeHaven, 1993; Schow and

Gatehouse, 1990) for the use of psychometrically robust, hence standardised, self-assessment devices.

The 'person in context' is not a different sort of person from the 'individual subject', but rather a different way of considering that individual. It is an idiographic form of analysis in which the object of attention is the individual's functioning in specific contexts or across different ones. What may be 'error' in the nomothetic approach is precisely the source of interest in the idiographic one. There is another dimension, borrowed from anthropology, which distinguishes the two approaches. The 'individual subject', witnessed through the objective procedures of the researcher, attracts '-etic' forms of description (Harris, 1968)—the person's functioning is given in terms intelligible to the researcher; for example, a degree of hearing loss in terms of decibels. In the 'person-in-context' view, description is '-emic': from the perspective, and in the terms, of the person in question.

Taking one or other approach has marked consequences for outcomes in the behavioural health research enterprise. A recent Australian research project (Dillon et al, 1991a; 1991b) illustrates my case. The project was aimed at assessing the effectiveness of rehabilitation (typically, hearing-aid fitting) by a national provider of this service. It included a modified form of a standardised hearing disability questionnaire (Ventry and Weinstein, 1982), as well as a standard hearing test. The questionnaire covered a range of contexts in which difficulties in hearing might occur. A subset of clients also self-rated their abilities and difficulties across a number of settings in which listening or communication can occur, and in which different personal or social reactions may arise from communication failure. Finally, those clients were asked to nominate the most notable circumstances, to a maximum of five, in which they experienced difficulty, and to what extent they would like the difficulty in those particular circumstances to be reduced. Most people identified two or three situations only.

At the end of the exercise, participating clients and clinicians were almost unanimous in their view that the forms of self-assessment comprising standard sets of items and settings were a waste of time, covering as they did great realms of contexts of highly variable relevance for any individual. The simple inquiry, oriented to the precise contexts identified by each client, proved much more valuable as a needs and outcomes indicator. Furthermore, though results on the standard forms correlated with each other, and with the standard hearing test, the extent of difficulty reported in specific contexts identified by clients did not correlate with any of those tests.

From a nomothetic research point of view, this outcome looks like a mess. The preferred approach to rehabilitation is based upon the provision of personal prostheses, fitted according to carefully determined prescription rules based on a hearing test. But individuals report experiencing difficulties in specific contexts (and a common one reported in this study was trying to listen to television), the extent of which seems unpredictable from the tests that guide the fitting rule. From an idiographic research point of view this outcome is a triumph. By getting *very* precise as to contexts, we have the chance of identifying very precise remedies. Some of these remedies may not involve the fitting of a personal hearing aid—a significant matter, as I will explain later. You might say, Surely the answer to difficulty in hearing the TV is to turn the volume up. I will come back to that; it is a good example of needing to take the precise context of the individual into account.

SOME THEORETICAL BACKGROUND

ECOLOGICAL PERCEPTUAL THEORY

There is a classical framework which opposes the 'person in context' approach and defends that of the 'individual subject'; there is a more recent framework that justifies the 'person in context' approach. The classical arguments imply that the perspective of the person is a poor basis on which to assess their real needs. Thus, one response to finding a lack of correlation between individually specific and standard measures of hearing difficulty, is that it reflects the idiosyncratic, even distorted impressions of individuals about what it is they perceive. This idea is nourished by an argument from Plato (Flew, 1971) and Descartes (1988 [1641]) that our knowledge of anything is at best partial, that we are prone to error concerning what we perceive, and that we ultimately make up plausible versions of reality aided by the creative powers of the imagination. Such notions appear in contemporary cognitive psychology (for example, Nisbett and Wilson, 1977) in arguments that we have only a tenuous grasp of the workings of our minds, hence that we make up stories about ourselves and call them 'what we think' or 'what we experience'.

These views get generalised to the point of saying that people may have no real grasp of even their own everyday circumstances. Bloch (1991) has argued that it is pointless to interrogate people living in traditional ways about aspects of their everyday practices. This, he says, is because critical features of those practices are embedded as pre- or non-linguistic concepts in people's cognitive systems. Cognitive systems are instantiated as neural networks in their brains, and are inaccessible to verbal analysis (How could ordinary folk begin to unravel the workings of such complicated mental machinery?). The solution to the problem seemingly lies in the use of participant observation to get to the heart of other people's reality. (It did not occur to Bloch that reports then made to fellow anthropologists would have to suffer in the same way as was presumed for any responses to interrogation—see Noble, 1992.)

A position that can help counter these arguments is that taken by James Gibson. His extensive work in perception (Macleod and Pick, 1974), culminated in a text (Gibson, 1979) which used the term 'ecological' explicitly as a descriptor of this approach. The ecological approach gives no attention to the workings of the imagination to explain how we make out what there is in the world around us. Far from the idea that we construct plausible versions in our minds of what might exist, Gibson insisted instead that we tune in, like self-adjusting radio receivers, to structures of energy which are already coherent, and which need no further fashioning in the workshops of the soul. Thus, what is perceived bears explicitly on what exists (Gibson, 1967).

In this we have a version of the contrast between 'individual subject' and 'person in context'. The classical understanding of perception has the individual subject as the sovereign arbiter of what is perceived. In Descartes's system (1988 [1637]), the individual mind is a dimensionless genius that hovers immaterially in proximity to our physical body, accomplishing the task of constructing an inner reality. In Gibson's approach, the person is seen in the context of their environment. Perceiving is taken to be the expression of evolutionary change. Any mutation that increases the sensory power of an individual, even if only slightly, is selected. Because such an individual is likely to have a survival advantage over otherwise similar members of the same species, the genetic fingerprint of that individual, and with it their improved perceptual capacity, is likelier to radiate among succeeding generations.

This line of theorising makes perception a public activity, not a private construction. If the issue is to explain what is there to be perceived, then the fact of something's visibility or audibility to one perceiver affords that same potential for other similarly endowed perceivers. What is available to be seen from where someone is standing now is available to be seen by anyone who takes up the same point of observation. Furthermore, perceiving is part of activity in general. We see to act and act to see (Powers, 1989). We can see how to accomplish something in the course of monitoring our actions, such as when we steer a car to avoid collision or in walking through a crowded room. And we enable ourselves to see what we want by acting in ways that permit us to get nearer that thing, or to keep it in view.

Whether this theoretical position guarantees that people whose hearing is starting to decline can accurately chart such change is, I think, moot. But it does offer an antidote to the view that people are hostage to their own fancies and imaginings in what they experience in everyday circumstances.

SOCIAL CONSTRUCTION OF MIND

The example from Bloch brings us to the matter of 'mind' as the product of social interaction, an approach opposed to the private mind Descartes describes. A key figure here is Jeff Coulter (1979; 1989), who relies on the 'ordinary language' tradition of Austin (1961), Ryle (1949) and Wittgenstein (1958). The Gibsonian approach deals with sensory apprehension of the world; the ordinary language/social construct argument considers cognition in broader terms—what is involved in saying of oneself or someone else that they have, for instance, thought of something, or come to a decision, or found something amusing, or recognised a state of affairs, or imagined it.

There are parallels between the issues Gibson raises and those raised by Coulter. A prominent one concerns the public nature of language. The argument is that what we call thinking, deciding and so on, are names for achievements. Such achievements are claimed by or on behalf of persons, and are ratified by relevant others. To claim to be thinking, it is not enough to mimic Rodin's famous figure, chin resting on fist; the pose alone will not pass, in anyone's eyes, for thinking. You may say of someone striking it that they *look* as if they are thinking. But a claim to actually be engaged in thinking is believable only when an utterance is made, or something is done, which satisfies others' criteria for such achievement; 'thinking' is normatively constrained.

The first point to take from this is that cognitive activity cannot be ultimately private. We may wrestle privately with problems, but only as preparation for public expression regarding them. And it is unavoidable that our private musings should be couched in a common language. The second point is that cognitive terms such as thinking and deciding, refer to forms of activity. As perceiving is an activity, so are these other ways of orienting to the world. The final point is that we are inevitably removed from the 'individual subject' and again confronting the 'person in context'. The cognitive activities in question are open to public confirmation, amendment or disavowal, for they are activities judged against publicly sustained criteria of what it means to say of someone that they have been thinking, or have made a decision.

Coulter (1973; 1979b) provides a good example of how this bears on behavioural research on health, from studies of psychiatric practices. Psychiatrists, he says, are engaged in acts of ratification, not discovery. Psychiatric practice is devoted to the confirmation (and disconfirmation) of claims made by or on behalf of others about conduct of a kind taken to contravene acceptable community standards. Psychiatric practice carries over into clinical settings the normative judgments made by members of the community at large about the aptness or otherwise of the behaviour of other community members. This is not all that the larger practice of psychiatry consists of. When it comes to seeking causes for behaviour judged as crazy, the apparatus of biochemistry and/or family relations analysis may come into play. The clinician partakes of some of that in going beyond the (dis)confirmatory phase. What puts the clinician there in the first place is the occurrence of behaviour in the everyday world judged in that setting to be objectionable. When asked for a clinical opinion, the practitioner does not depart from normative evaluation in order to come up with an account. A descriptor, such as 'schizophrenia', may be applied to conduct judged as bizarre. Its dictionary definition may not be immediately known to everyone concerned. At no stage does this defining term displace phrases such as 'inappropriate emotional reactions' or 'disordered thought patterns' used to describe what the person, judged in ordinary ways as mentally ill, is expressing. Diagnostic categories are shorthand descriptions of the publicly evaluated character of the dis-turbed/ing conduct.

From theory to research

The mental illness example can be extrapolated to all forms of 'illness'. Illness is a behavioural posture in which someone claims, or a claim is made on their behalf, that they are not functioning normally. In the psychopathological arena, as with many other aspects of dysfunction, a claim made on behalf of a suspect individual may not be assented to by that person; indeed, the attempt to ascribe incapacity may be strongly resisted. Hearing clinicians are in very much the same boat as psychiatrists. Their task is one of ratification, not discovery; they *are* involved with the latter when it comes to questions of ascribing a cause to a complaint. The usual precursor of presentation at the audiological clinic is a complaint by someone, usually another family member, that the person fails to respond—or to respond appropriately—in communicative exchanges, or needs to have the radio or television turned up too loud for others in the household. That will not be an issue if the person watches television alone, or it may not attract *strenuous* complaint if the other person in the household also has a hearing impairment. This is why the problem with 'trying to hear the television' may not neatly be predicted from the measured level of hearing loss. Other complaints are about missing warning sounds such as the doorbell or telephone, or about diminishment of a shared social life, including loss for the other person in the household of an autonomous social life—that person having to act as interpreter for and protector of the person with impaired hearing (Hétu et al, 1993; Hétu et al, 1987).

Thus the particular context of a person's life intersects in subtle ways with the brute fact of impaired hearing, augmenting or softening the disabling and handicapping consequences that may potentially flow from the impairment. This may explain the absence of correlation between standardised forms of assessment of hearing, and appraisals by the person in question of the specific situational difficulties they encounter. More than that, though, and this bears on ethical and methodological points, the subtle fabric of individuals' needs, as well as the needs of those they live or work with, can be more effectively addressed when the details of their circumstances are appreciated (Noble and Hétu, 1994).

Another issue relates to the point about its being moot whether the person with an impairment has a ready grasp of all its features (Brassard, 1991). This concerns reluctance on the part of the complained-about person to acknowledge a hearing loss. The typical response by *researchers* who have observed the phenomenon of reluctance has been to note it as a factor to be recorded and assessed (Demorest and Erdman, 1987; Goldstein and Stephens, 1981). Goldstein and Stephens refer to the issue using the term 'attitude' to rehabilitation involving use of a hearing aid. They describe: 1) positive attitude; 2) positive attitude but with complications; 3) negative attitude but potentially salvageable, and 4) implacably negative attitude. Demorest and Erdman use the term 'denial', and characterise it as an obstacle to rehabilitative assistance. In both cases the matter is seen by the researchers as a problem to be overcome.

A different perspective on reluctance is provided by a study undertaken among a group of workers whose hearing was injured by occupational noise (Hétu *et al*, 1990). Some of them were persuaded to publicly disclose the fact of their impaired hearing. The unexpected consequence was that they were subjected to insults and jokes from fellow workers. Upon reflection, the findings of this research are not entirely surprising. As Erving Goffman said (1963), a rational response to threatened spoiling of the identity by stigmatising signs is control of discrediting information. The same dynamic is in play with regard to many conditions affecting conduct, including forms of illness.

Control of potentially discrediting information about one's hearing status may include avoidance of use of a hearing aid. One survey (Franks and Beckmann, 1985) found that the fear of drawing attention to the disability was among the commonest reasons for rejecting such a device. Many people are unwilling to wear such a publicly perceivable emblem (Kendon, 1981) of their discreditable status. The evidence of discrediting moves by fellow workers shows they can hardly be faulted for that. The strategic point is that procedures which pinpoint specific problems—listening to television; answering the telephone—may be able to offer remedies that avoid the need for a personal hearing aid. Examples are modifying the television to allow separate, ear-level amplification for one listener while keeping the room level lower, or a telephone with volume control. By such expedients an unwanted prosthesis may be avoided.

Precisely *because* people are in contexts and cannot readily escape scrutiny of their conduct, that is, because they are not 'individual sovereign subjects', they are at risk of being 'outed' as a result of research inquiries that do not see these contexts fully or appropriately. Reluctance to acknowledge a problem makes sense if such acknowledgment is likely to make a person the butt of other people's negative attitudes to the problem. It may be that more effort should go into making the community a little safer for us all to be imperfect in. There may be too much research into all sorts of health-care issues and not enough into what that may lead to in the everyday lives of the researched upon.

Yet the particularities of the person's context still give reason for celebration of that factor. Through attention to the details of context, appropriate remedies may be better identified. Paradox: attention to a person's context tends to make that individual rather more sovereign. Take the case of the research mentioned at the start. The results of this project may be said to subordinate the interests of the service-providing system, and the interests of researchers in obtaining standardised responses and measures, and to valorise the interests of the individual client of the service—hardly a dismaying outcome.

REFERENCES

Austin, J.L., 1961, *Philosophical Papers* (edited by J.O. Urmson and G.J. Warnock), Oxford: Oxford University Press.

Bevan, W. and Kessel, F., 1994, 'Plain truths and home cooking: Thoughts on the making and remaking of psychology', *American Psychologist*, 49: 505–9.

Bloch, M., 1991, 'Language, anthropology and cognitive science', *Man*, 26: 183–98.

Brassard, C., 1991, *Analyse de la perception de la perte progressive de l'audition chez des travailleurs d'une même entreprise*, Université de Montréal.

Byrne, D. and Dillon, H., 1986, 'The National Acoustic Laboratories' new procedure for selecting the gain and frequency response of a hearing aid', *Ear and Hearing*, 7: 257–65.

Coulter, J., 1973, *Approaches to Insanity: a philosophical and sociological study*, London: Martin Robertson.

——1979, *The Social Construction of Mind*, London: Macmillan.

——1989, *Mind in Action*, Cambridge: Polity Press.

Danziger, K., 1980, 'Wundt and the two traditions in psychology'. In R.W. Rieber (ed.), *Wilhelm Wundt and the Making of a Scientific Psychology*, New York: Plenum.

Davis, A., 1989, 'The prevalence of hearing impairment and reported hearing disability among adults in Great Britain', *International Journal of Epidemiology*, 18: 911–17.

Demorest, M.E., and DeHaven, G.P., 1993, 'Psychometric adequacy of self-assessment scales', *Seminars in Hearing*, 14: 314–25.

Demorest, M.E., and Erdman, S.A., 1987, 'Development of the communication profile for the hearing impaired', *Journal of Speech and Hearing Disorders*, 52: 129–43.

Descartes, R., 1988[1637], 'Discourse on the method', In *Descartes: Selected Philosophical Writings*, Cambridge: Cambridge University Press, 20–56.

——1988[1641], 'Meditations on first philosophy'. In *Descartes: selected philosophical writings*, Cambridge: Cambridge University Press, 73–159.

Dillon, H., Koritschoner, E., Battaglia, J., *et al*, 1991a, 'Rehabilitation effectiveness I: Assessing the needs of clients entering a national hearing rehabilitation program', *Australian Journal of Audiology*, 13: 55–65.

——1991b, 'Rehabilitation effectiveness II: Assessing the outcomes for clients of a national hearing rehabilitation program', *Australian Journal of Audiology*, 13: 68–82.

Flew, A., 1971, *An Introduction to Western Philosophy*, London: Thames and Hudson.

Franks, J.R., and Beckmann, N.J., 1985, 'Rejection of hearing aids: Attitudes of a geriatric sample', *Ear and Hearing*, 6: 161–6.

Gibson, J.J., 1967, 'New reasons for realism', *Synthese*, 17: 173–201.

——1979, *The Ecological Approach to Visual Perception*, Boston: Houghton-Mifflin.

Goffman, E., 1963, *Stigma: notes on the management of spoiled identity*, Englewood Cliffs: Prentice-Hall.

Goldstein, D.P., and Stephens, S.D.G., 1981, 'Audiological rehabilitation: management model I', *Audiology*, 20: 432–52.

Harris, M., 1968, *The Rise of Anthropological Theory: a history of theories of culture*, New York: Crowell.

Hétu, R., Jones, L., and Getty, L., 1993, 'The impact of acquired hearing impairment on intimate relationships: Implications for rehabilitation', *Audiology*, 32: 363–81.

Hétu, R., Lalonde, M., and Getty, L., 1987, 'Psychosocial disadvantages associated with occupational hearing loss as experienced in the family', *Audiology*, 26: 141–52.

Hétu, R., Riverin, L., Getty, L., *et al*, 1990, 'The reluctance to acknowledge hearing problems among noise exposed workers', *British Journal of Audiology*, 24: 265–76.

John, I.D., 1994, 'Constructing knowledge of psychological knowledge: Towards an epistemology for psychological practice', *Australian Psychologist*, 29: 158–63.

Jones, L., Kyle, J., and Wood, P., 1987, *Words Apart: losing your hearing as an adult*, London: Tavistock.

Kendon, A., 1981, 'Introduction: Current issues in the study of "nonverbal communication"'. In A. Kendon (ed.), *Nonverbal Communication, Interaction, and Gesture*, The Hague: Mouton.

MacLeod, R.B., and Pick, H.L. (ed.), 1974, *Perception: essays in honor of James J. Gibson*, Ithaca: Cornell University Press.

Nisbett, R.E., and Wilson, T.D., 1977, 'Telling more than we can know: Verbal reports on mental processes', *Psychological Review*, 84: 231–59.

Noble, W., 1978, *Assessment of Impaired Hearing: a critique and a new method*, New York: Academic Press.

——1992, 'Language, thought and confusion', *Man*, 27: 637–42.

Noble, W., and Atherley, G., 1970, 'The hearing measurement scale: a questionnaire for the assessment of auditory disability', *Journal of Auditory Research*, 10: 229–50.

Noble, W., and Hétu, R., 1994, 'An ecological approach to disability and handicap in relation to impaired hearing', *Audiology*, 33: 117–26.

Plomp, R., 1978, 'Auditory handicap of hearing impairment and the limited benefit of hearing aids', *Journal of the Acoustical Society of America*, 63: 533–49.

——1994, 'Noise, amplification, and compression: Considerations of three main issues in hearing aid design', *Ear and Hearing*, 15: 2–12.

Powers, W.T., 1989, *Living Control Systems*, Gravel Switch: Control Systems Group Inc.

Ryle, G., 1949, *The Concept of Mind*, London: Hutchinson.

Schow, R.L., and Gatehouse, S., 1990, 'Fundamental issues in self-assessment of hearing', *Ear and Hearing*, 11: 6S–16S.

Stewart, T.R., 1988, 'Judgment analysis: procedures', In B. Brehmer and C.R.B. Joyce (eds), *Human Judgment: the SJT view*, Amsterdam: North-Holland.

Ventry, I.M., and Weinstein, B.E., 1982, 'The Hearing Handicap Inventory for the Elderly: A new tool', *Ear and Hearing*, 3: 128–34.

Wittgenstein, L., 1958, *Philosophical Investigations*, Oxford: Blackwell.

World Health Organisation, 1980, *International Classification of Impairments, Disabilities, and Handicaps*, Geneva: WHO.

13

HEALTH ECONOMICS AND POLICY: ETHICAL DILEMMAS IN THE SCIENCE OF SCARCITY

Terri Jackson

Economics is not idly called the dismal science. The fundamental human problem which economists seek to understand and control is scarcity. Health economics is perhaps even more dismal, dealing as it does with both scarcity *and* human suffering.

In this essay, I want to consider some key concepts in health economics, indeed, in the discipline of economics, and begin to identify how the application of economic research in the real-world context of health policy raises ethical questions not often considered by researchers. In using the term 'ethics' I am aware that it can be used very narrowly (as in bioethics), or more broadly to include questions of the social responsibility of scientists for the uses and applications of their work. It is this latter understanding of the ethical obligation of researchers to be concerned with the social and political impact of their research, particularly the fairness of the distribution of health-care resources arising from work by health economists, which informs my use of the term 'ethics'.

In defence of the discipline, I should first acknowledge that there is a broad consensus among health economists that in most instances Adam Smith's 'invisible hand of the market' works very badly to allocate resources for health care. I do not intend to review the standard textbook explanations of market failure here, but the discipline has not been naive, nor have health economists been blind adherents to market-based approaches. In the face of market failure, however, health economics is primarily engaged in devising policy tools which will achieve the optimum distribution of the scarce resource of health care. And it is in this enterprise, I believe, that health economists have particular obligations, first, to be aware of ethical implications which arise from some of the conceptual tools of economics, and second, to ensure that the issues are not misrepresented to, or misunderstood by, policy makers.

THE SOCIAL CONSTRUCTION OF SCARCITY

Fundamental to health economics is the notion of scarcity: there will never be enough resources to provide every health-related service to every person who could be deemed to need that service. We would all concede that having expensive machines like CT scanners installed in each neighbourhood might occasionally be handy, and at the extreme, life saving, but that no society could afford such a health system.

Moreover, most would agree that, at a certain point of investment in health care, other needs (education, public housing, welfare benefits) have an equal or greater priority—although we might differ on what that point might be. Thus, I reject the ethical abdication of those who argue that economics has no legitimate role in health care decision-making.

Issues of scarcity face health economists as three questions: How much in total should a country or state spend on health?; Is the ratio of benefits to costs for any particular health intervention large enough to justify its use?; To whom should benefits be distributed?

In terms of the absolute level of national health expenditures, recent research by the OECD (Schieber and Poullier, 1991) has demonstrated in Western developed economies an association between a country's health expenditures and its gross domestic product. This has led many health economists to conclude that knowing a country's GDP can tell you the right proportion of GDP that country should spend on health care.

McGuire and his colleagues (1993), however, have challenged this conclusion, arguing that the 'seemingly positive exercise of analysing empirically the relationship between national income and health care expenditures carries normative overtones, which may stray all too easily into a concern with how much health care can be "afforded" (p. 124). They warn that: 'Value judgments, essentially over the form of ideal society envisaged, are required at every stage in analysing [the size of the health care sector]' (p. 125). While scarcity is an inescapable fact of human life, the declaration of any given level of health expenditure as too much or too little is fundamentally a social and political determination.

Similarly, when weighing the costs and benefits of health interventions, the decision that a particular marginal benefit is 'not worth the cost' is a value judgment. This is a point I will return to in discussing the fairly crude tools which health economics currently has to determine the marginal benefits of different kinds of health interventions. By providing comparative information about the relative costs of achieving given health benefits (cost per life saved with immunisation versus bone-marrow transplantation, for example), health economics is able to inform and focus such discussions, but ultimately the decision that one intervention is valuable and another is not cannot be made solely on economic grounds.

Not surprisingly, democratic societies have difficulty making what have been termed 'tragic choices' (Calabresi and Bobbitt, 1978). Politicians and their advisers are eager for technocratic solutions, ones which seem to resolve the inherent ethical dilemmas of scarcity in health care on the basis of technical expertise. Given the dominance of economics as *the* policy science over the past several decades, health economists are under considerable pressure to devise technical tools which disguise political responsibility, and thus to carry the ethical responsibility for health care rationing.

Preoccupied with demonstrating their cleverness in inventing means by which rationing of health care can be accomplished, health economists have not devoted sufficient professional attention to the question of appropriate system capacity, nor fostered public debate about whether or at what level health-care resources should be rationed.

THE GREATEST GOOD FOR THE GREATEST NUMBER

Complicating health economists' moral responsibility for the application of health economics research to real policy problems is the ethical principle underlying health economics: utilitarianism. Implicit in the discipline is the utilitarian assumption that health-care systems exist to maximise total 'health' output, that is, to provide the greatest health for the greatest number of people.

Health economics has been preoccupied over the past decade with the measurement of utility in health care. By utility economists mean not only the measurement of improvements in people's quality of life brought about by health-care interventions (although this is an important prerequisite to measuring utility), but also a better understanding of what *value* people place on different health outcomes and on the different dimensions of health.

This approach is meant to replace cruder measures of the benefits of health care. In the past, most attention was given to life saving as a goal of the health system, with little attention paid to the quality-of-life improvements which are the goal of many health interventions. One of the tools developed to further such research is the Quality Adjusted Life Year, or QALY, which is designed to capture both quantity and quality gains in a single measure.

The problems with this approach when it intersects with the policy process are largely unexplored—particularly in setting priorities for health care. My colleagues Jeff Richardson and Erik Nord at the Centre for Health Program Evaluation in Melbourne have identified two problems in the application of current approaches to priority setting using cost–utility analysis.

The first is that most health economists have assumed that measures of what people value about health-care interventions on an individual level can be generalised to reflect social values and judgments. Using a person-tradeoff approach, Nord and Richardson compared survey respondents' answers to direct questions about social values (in a situation of scarce resources, how many people receiving a particular treatment would you judge to be equivalent to one person receiving another—perhaps life-saving—kind of treatment?). They compared the results of these direct questions with the values yielded in previous QALY research which had addressed the question only indirectly, and found large differences for three of the four commonly used QALY instruments (Nord, Richardson and Macarounas-Kirchmann, 1993).

The second question they explore is whether there is broad public support for health-care rationing based on 'the greatest good for the greatest number'. A recent research project with the Monash University Bioethics Centre entailed a survey of ordinary people on just this question. Confronted with choices between maximising total health and allowing equal access to care (chance of being treated), respondents were reluctant to support simple utilitarian policy approaches which traded benefits at a lower cost multiplied across many people for benefits at a higher cost to a smaller group of patients. In other words, when respondents were asked to allocate a fixed budget between groups of patients requiring high-cost and low-cost treatments, they did not choose allocations which simply maximised total health benefits (Nord, et al., 1994). The authors note:

> As a minimum, these conclusions suggest a general willingness to make quite significant sacrifices in terms of 'efficiency'—health maximisation—to achieve goals of social justice. This, in turn, suggests that algorithms for the maximisation of 'social utility' such as the QALY league table should be treated with considerable caution. (p. 230)

Critics may argue that the hypothetical position of respondents is not the same as the more limited choices open to policy makers—ordinary people may shrink from distasteful but necessary 'tough' decisions. If we stand back from the research context, however, I think this study has important lessons for elected officials (and, one would hope, for their public-service advisors): QALY-type measures which seek to simplify decision-making, or perhaps obscure it behind technical rationale, may not gain wide support for priorities based on simple utilitarian approaches to maximising health.

FROM CETERIS PARIBUS TO CUI BONO?

A third problem arising from the interface of health economics and health policy is the concept of *ceteris paribus* or 'other things being equal'. This refers to the useful research technique of reducing the complexity of economic systems in order to understand particular economic questions; holding some variables steady while studying others.

Thus, for example, to measure the marginal benefit of a new technology, health economics makes the assumption that existing expenditures on health care are allocated in the most economically rational way, and that the only economic decision is how the *next* dollar is to be spent: in buying more of the existing conventional treatments, or in expanding the system's capacity to undertake the new procedure.

The real world, of course, is more complex than theory would admit, and other things are not equal. In the context of static or shrinking health budgets, most policy outcomes of economic research will have the effect of *reallocating* dollars from one use to another. The health economist's recommendations to change any distribution of resources are made in a *political* environment, and a fundamental question in politics is *cui bono?*, that is, who benefits?

Existing allocations of resources reflect entrenched interests, political compromises and accommodations among powerful players resulting in particular distributions of benefits. It would be naive in the extreme to believe that the new political enthusiasm for economic evaluation of health care was not itself a manifestation of the political struggle between 'corporate rationalists' (those who advocate 'rational' decision-making in medicine) and 'professional monopolisers' (those concerned to maintain medical dominance over decision-making) first described by Alford (1975).

The regulatory mechanisms open to health economists are vulnerable to distortions and perverse incentives not anticipated, or held constant in the realm of *ceteris paribus*. Once policy tools are created, the economist cannot expect to remain the puppet master, holding some strings while pulling others. Of course, this problem is not unique to health economics. It is the classic 'nuclear scientist' dilemma: advances 'in the lab' may have troubling applications 'in the real world'.

I believe the ethical health economist should consider four questions when translating research into social policy: How do the simplifying assumptions made in reaching a particular policy recommendation impact on its possible applications, What are its likely distributional effects, What are the foreseeable responses of powerful players disadvantaged by policy recommendations, and lastly, Who are the policy's political sponsors, and what are their interests in the matter?

AVERAGING MARGINAL BENEFIT

I've previously mentioned the comparison of costs and benefits in economic analysis, I now turn to the way in which economics conceptualises questions of relative costs and benefits for different health interventions. In particular, it is the potential use of *average* marginal benefit in health policy which I think has ethical dimensions not often considered when policy prescriptions for 'outcome based funding' or 'managed care' are advanced.

In a previous paper, I used Bob Evans's (1984) account of the economic concept of diminishing marginal returns (or the marginal benefits curve), to illustrate problems in resource allocation in health (Jackson, 1992). Figure 3 is a representation of this curve, and is helpful, I think, in clarifying what different people may mean when they support more widespread economic evaluation of health care.

Figure 3 can be applied to a number of different levels of the health system, and indeed it is confusion about which level of decision-making is appropriate to the application of marginal benefit criteria which leads in turn to differences about the ethical implications of various proposals to 'ration' or 'manage' health care.

For every unit of expenditure on health, you can (theoretically, anyway) estimate the amount of health gain—for this exercise I will use the previously criticised QALY, but one might also think of health gains in terms of units of well-being, or degrees of movement of arthritic joints. To simplify, I will also assume that the benefits are self-evident, although we know that in the real world some health benefits are valued more by individuals, and that there are differences in valuation between individuals and between cultures.

This curve suggests that the first dollars spent on health care—if they are spent with some degree of wisdom—buy great improvements in patients' survival time and/or quality of life. The first $1000 buys two QALYs, the second $1000, an additional year, etc. But as the vertical lines get shorter, additional investments buy smaller and smaller increments of health gain. At the fourth and fifth steps, $1000 buys less than half a year of quality-adjusted life. As the curve begins to slope downward, it is possible to think of health expenditures (heroic interventions, for example) where, in spite of small gains in quantity of life, there may be larger quality-of-life losses for the additional expenditure.

When applied to a single individual's treatment, the marginal benefit curve would lead to relatively unproblematic decision-making. The first unit of expenditure might be an appendicectomy or good prenatal care, yielding big health gains for money spent. In the course of the individual's treatment, the application of more dollars buys relatively less benefit higher up the curve. Thus, dollars spent for the last day of hospital care, when the patient is really well enough to care for him/herself, or the ninth x-ray

Figure 3 Marginal social value of health care

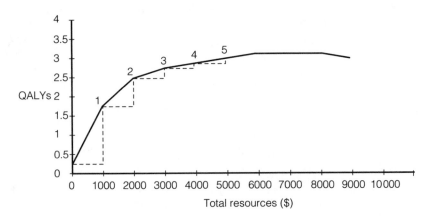

or blood test, would yield considerably less benefit per dollar invested. This has been termed 'flat of the curve' medicine in recognition of the fact that, at some point, additional inputs to the care of an individual will yield only the smallest sliver of additional health gain.

A second application of the marginal benefits curve is to the question of how much of any particular treatment should be provided—and thus, how many people will be treated. In some ways this is similar to the first sort of decision, but it takes account of the fact that not all patients are in a position to benefit equally from treatment. For Patient 1, spending $1000 gives good return, with nearly two extra QALYs as the result; for Patient 3, the treatment still costs $1000, but results in only an extra half QALY; for Patient 5, the treatment makes almost no difference in his/her quality or quantity of life.

It is important to note that predicting an individual's ability to benefit is not an exact science, and predictions based on characteristics shared with other patients raise many of the problems of average benefit described below. It is also important to realise that not all such decisions are life-and-death ones. For Patients 4 and 5, the small marginal benefit of the treatment may be either because they're too sick to benefit (the archetypal 'tragic choice'), or equally, because they're too well—as, for example, in unnecessary surgical procedures. When such marginal benefit analysis is used to prioritise access to health care, the ethical implications of these two situations are quite different.

A third use of the curve is in setting priorities among disease conditions or treatments. As a shorthand, we may term it the Oregon approach, after the US state which set out to use condition-specific prioritisation in allocating its Medicaid budget. It is important to note, however, that this policy approach to resource allocation is not limited to Oregon, but is also a part of New Zealand's recent health reforms, for example, in defining its package of 'core health services'.

When used in this way, different treatments—say prenatal care (1), hip replacement (3) and bone marrow transplantation (5) are placed on the curve based on the *average benefit* which patients derive from treatments. In both jurisdictions, access to therapies which are not judged to be cost-beneficial are still available to anyone who is in a position to pay for treatment, but not available to patients reliant on publicly funded programs.

The ethical problem with using the curve in this way is that no account is taken of the *individual* patient's potential to benefit: young leukaemia patients in their first remission (who have shown good survival rates) as well as older leukaemia patients in relapse (whose outcome is much poorer) (Handelsman, 1989) would both be excluded from publicly supported access to bone marrow transplantation.

In these systems, judgment of the ability of a patient to benefit is moved away from the level of the individual to groups of patients distinguished on clinical or demographic criteria. The calculation of both benefit and cost results in an *average* across the group, with an assumed normal curve describing the variation around the average. It is highly likely that for some groups of patients, say hip replacement and bone marrow transplantation patients, these distributions will overlap; individual bone marrow transplant patients will have a higher benefit-to-cost ratio than individual hip replacement candidates. Valtonen (1993) set out to test the homogeneity of total cost, and cost per QALY, for patients admitted to hospital in eleven commonly occurring ICD-9 (three-digit) diagnostic groups. He found considerable heterogeneity in terms of both costs and cost per QALY within the eleven diagnostic groups. In prostate cancer, for example, only 43 per cent of cases were correctly allocated to their predicted cost class, and only 38 per cent to their predicted cost:QALY class. Similarly poor predictive ability was found for slipped vertebral disc, cerebral thrombosis and cataract cases. In only two diagnostic groups were the costs accurately predicted for more than 60 per cent of patients, and in only three were predictions of cost:QALY accurate in more than 60 per cent of cases.

For the group of eleven diagnoses, costs were either over- or underestimated in 63 per cent of cases, and cost:QALY in 47 per cent. For patients with the lowest predicted cost:QALY (the best candidates for treatment), actual cost:QALY averaged twice the prediction. For the most costly groups in terms of cost:QALY (those most likely to be denied treatment), actual per-QALY costs were found to be 20 per cent less than predicted.

Because of the large errors in predicting cost:QALY, and the consequences of basing treatment decisions on these predictions, Valtonen concludes: 'it is not fair to treat an individual as a member of a group when this membership excludes him/her from treatment that he/she would receive on the basis of his/her individual cost-benefit indicator values if these were known correctly' (1993: 11).

Theoretically it may be possible to improve cost estimates, and to specify enough classes, or diagnosis/treatment pairs, to smooth out the discontinuities between classes: young leukaemia patients ranked before hip replacement patients with predicted poor outcomes. But short of individualised assessment (which such policies are designed to pre-empt), classes will always include outliers for whom the application of the average results in denial of treatment when patients in other classes, with less potential to benefit (and/or the means to buy out of the rationing system altogether), are provided treatment.

Public authorities, preoccupied with the increasing cost of health technologies, and dealing with the deliberate contraction of the public sector in developed countries during the 1980s, have embraced the notion of moving the locus of decision-making away from the individual and express considerable enthusiasm for decision-making on the basis of predicted 'health gain' for groups of patients. The challenge this poses for health economics is to ensure that policy makers understand the crudeness of the classes for which marginal benefit can currently be calculated, and the considerable ethical problems of prioritising access to care on the basis of *average* marginal benefit.

PROBLEM OF AGENCY

The final ethical challenge for health economics arises from the problem of 'agency' in health-care decision-making. This concept is commonly used to explain one aspect of market failure: that of imperfect information held by the consumer of health care. Because the technical complexity of most clinical decisions is so great, health economists have long realised that individual patients are not well placed to be the discerning, autonomous consumers of medical services which a market would require. It is acknowledged in health care that sellers of the service often make decisions on behalf of buyers, thus becoming their 'agents' in decision-making.

The agency relationship is used to justify licensing and regulatory mechanisms for groups of health-care providers as a way of limiting the potential for exploitation of patients. On the whole, health economists are very sceptical about the agency relationship, particularly when it is exercised by doctors. A large body of research demonstrates that, not surprisingly, doctors weigh their own as well as the patient's interests in coming to a treatment recommendation. In addition to possibly distorting patients' preferences, economists argue that decisions made are frequently unjustifiable in terms of the most rational use of scarce medical resources.

Bioethics has also worried about the agency relationship, particularly in circumstances in which patients are not competent to give consent for particular forms of care (shading from patients in coma to those whose ability to understand the choices available may be questioned). Compromises to individual autonomy, that is, where choices are made on behalf of the patient, are understood to be problematic in both ethics and health economics.

What has increasingly concerned me about the uses of economic evaluation in public policy is that health economists do not bring the same level of scepticism to their consideration of alternative agents. While they recognise that moving choices from patient to doctor is undesirable, the policy prescriptions they advocate (such as 'managed care') often would move such decisions even further away from the patient, up a line of bureaucratic decision-making.

The problem is that no policy maker sits in the *ceteris paribus* world of having no interests of their own, no utility of their own to maximise. This is not to argue that bureaucrats and politicians are intrinsically less ethical than doctors, only that they may not be more so. The ethical exercise of the power entrusted to public officials requires *disinterested* decision-making which balances on a case-by-case basis the social and individual costs of the range of clinical options available.

The most idealistic and ethical of health ministers (and all the public servants who carry out her policies) is not *disinterested*; she still has to take account of her own political interests, and those of her party, if she plans to continue to be the democratically elected ethical decision-maker. Managed care (in all its variants) moves the locus of decisions from 'scope of coverage' policy to individual assessment of entitlement, and the actual decisions from individual clinicians to state-employed care managers.

In the past our society has left doctors with full discretion to decide what kind of diagnosis and treatment a patient required. Increasingly, the more reflective members of the medical profession are joining a consensus that such latitude is no longer supportable, and that costs and ability to benefit must be considered in some way. But the critical question is: where else can decision-making be lodged so that agents' self-interest will not be played out, and/or where individual capacity to benefit can be considered in the treatment decision?

I think the answer lies in policy approaches which apply constraints to groups of doctors and groups of patients. In such a system, funding would be based on averaging in order to allow for individual clinical differences. Patient-by-patient clinical judgments (in place of *a priori* decision-rules) about an individual patient's ability to benefit from a course of treatment would be made in the context of an overall limit to expenditure for a group of patients under the care of a group of providers. This is not a well-developed proposal for a funding system which reconciles social cost and individual benefit, but the important point being made is that we should carefully consider the ethical implications of moving decision-making further from the doctor/patient dyad.

CONCLUSION

I argue that health economics has much to offer the policy process, the process by which democratic societies decide on priorities for public expenditure, and by which they create together the features of the society in which they choose to live. Five key features of policy-relevant research in health economics have been identified which raise problematic ethical questions.

The fundamental concept of scarcity is paradoxically real in the abstract, but artificial, or at least socially constructed, at any particular level of health expenditure. Health economists in general approach ethical issues on the basis of simple utilitarian principles of the greatest good for the greatest number, but these principles may not have wide support when applied in health care, and pose considerable technical problems of measurement and operationalisation. Theoretical propositions which are formulated and tested under the assumption of *ceteris paribus* may have unforeseen consequences when extended to the rough-and-tumble world of political decision-making. The tools to undertake resource allocation based on average marginal benefit are currently at a very crude level of development, and may have intrinsic limitations for use in the policy sphere. Finally, creating policy mechanisms to overcome problems in the agency relationship between patients and doctors may only exacerbate these problems by replacing one group of self-interested agents for another.

Each of these creates ethical dilemmas in extrapolating from research in health economics to policy development. Theoretically these problems can be addressed; in the perfect health economics, some would not arise. But in the imperfect world, economists must be careful to qualify their research findings, and be flattered but sceptical when results and techniques are enthusiastically taken up by policy-makers.

ACKNOWLEDGMENTS

I would like to acknowledge and thank Dr Erik Nord and Professor S.J. Duckett for very useful comments on this essay and an earlier paper from which this essay has been developed.

REFERENCES

Alford, R., 1975, *Health Care Politics*, Chicago: University of Chicago Press.

Calabresi, G. and Bobbitt, P., 1978, *Tragic Choices: the conflicts society confronts in the allocation of tragically scarce resources*, New York: Norton.

Evans, R., 1984, *Strained Mercy: the economics of Canadian health care*, Toronto: Butterworths.

Handelsman, H., 1989, 'Reassessment of autologous bone marrow transplantation', *Health Technology Assessment Reports (Number 3)*, Rockville: National Center for Health Services Research and Health Care Technology Assessment.

Jackson, T., 1992, 'Preserving what is right about the Australian health system', *Working Papers: Putting Health Back into Health Care*, Sydney: Public Health Association of Australia, 14–22.

McGuire, A., Parkin, D., Hugues, D. and Gerard, K., 1993, 'Econometric analyses of national health expenditures: Can positive economics help to answer normative questions?' *Health Economics*, 2: 13–126.

Nord, E., Richardson, J., and Macarounas-Kirchmann, K., 1993, 'Social evaluation of health care versus personal evaluation of health states', *International Journal of Technology Assessment in Health Care*, 9: 463–78.

Nord, E., Richardson, J., Street, A., Kuhse, H., and Singer, P., 1994, 'Do Australians want their health system to maximise health?', paper presented to the Conference of Australian Health Economists, 8 July 1994.

Schieber, G. and Poullier, J., 1991, 'International health spending: issues and trends', *Health Affairs*, 10, 1: 106–16.

Valtonen, H., 1993, 'Prediction of costs and benefits of hospital treatments', paper presented to the 14th Nordic Health Economists' Study Group Meeting, 19–20 August 1993.

PART IV

REPRESENTING COMMUNITY VIEWS

Previous sections have addressed the interests of community members who participate in research either indirectly (through benefits to science) or directly (by researchers being responsive to individuals' personal concerns). But the individuals who participate in our research are also members of communities and these communities are also affected, positively or negatively, by the research. Sometimes the community itself may be the focus of the research. This section addresses problems which arise when there is explicit recognition of the relevance of the research process to communities.

Hal Kendig's essay considers, from the viewpoint of an applied researcher, issues of social responsibility in the interplay between applied researchers, communities, and funding bodies. The apparently technical matter of selecting a research approach has implications which can work for or against a community's interests and communities have a major stake in how they are represented in research. However, they face substantial obstacles in participating in the setting of research agendas, and the institutional base of researchers and priorities of funding bodies can work against consideration of community priorities.

Ian Anderson focuses on the problems of conducting research in Australian Aboriginal communities. Despite the clear need for health care which will directly address the needs of these communities, the community-controlled Aboriginal health service suffers from a lack of funding to conduct its own research. This undermines the direct link between research and social change and frustrates the development of Aboriginal people's own academic research skills. Instead, the emphasis falls on making outside researchers responsive to their concerns. He calls for direct community research funding to ensure control over their own financial and intellectual resources.

The next contribution describes the dilemmas faced by three researchers who, as women, have an allegiance to the groups which are the focus of their research. Johanna Wyn, Judith Lumley and Jeanne Daly describe women's health research at various life stages as women undergo the transition to adulthood, to motherhood and to older age. They address the ethical issues of obtaining written consent from homeless young women, of working with community representative groups in the area of childbirth and of resolving the divergent needs of women and medical funding bodies in menopause research. Their aim is to keep the various experiences of the women themselves in the foreground of their research.

Rhonda Galbally focuses on problems of research funding in the area of health promotion from the perspective of consumers. She argues that the existing disease paradigm has to be changed if the interests of consumers are to be adequately represented. There has to be recognition of the interacting factors which contribute to ill-health, and strategies for health promotion should not focus on single risk factors but on the social settings in which consumers live. Her call is for better professional training, for an emphasis on compassion, empathy and respect for consumers in all health-care settings, and for funding decisions which reflect these values.

14

REPRESENTING THE COMMUNITY: ISSUES FROM APPLIED RESEARCH EXPERIENCES

Hal Kendig

There are few direct and easy connections between the classical treatises on research methodology and the practical demands and questions of applied research. I believe it is useful to speak from the viewpoint of a research practitioner. As with other areas of professional practice, we need to develop a culture (a shared set of understandings) which sets grounded prescripts to guide our everyday work (Imre, 1985). This demands attention to the *process* of doing research and how one can identify and address ethical issues and social responsibility in specific studies in particular contexts. While this essay presents examples from my own applied studies with older people, the focus is on generic issues which arise with research that relates to any constituency group.

Socially responsible research involves considerations which extend well beyond ethical procedures. Research ethics principally concern fair treatment of 'subjects', for example, the maxim that researchers above all do no harm. Social responsibility requires that researchers consider the broader consequences of their studies. Werner von Braun, the German then American rocket scientist, presumably was ethical in his physics experiments aiming for the moon; but one can question the social responsibility of the rockets falling short of his ideals and hitting London. Studies may have a 'disinterested' scientific purpose but their findings still are used or misused as ammunition by interest groups having quite different 'targets'.

'Pictures' of social reality painted by people of ideas have long had significant implications. History shows numerous exchanges, not always savoury, between intellectuals in courts and monasteries, and kings and other institutional elites. The former need money and other favours while the latter will pay for social legitimation of their power (Weber, 1947). During the rapid growth of government social research funding in the

United States in the 1960s, this tradition continued, with adverse effects on minority communities. For example, public money was poured into studying how the 'negro problem' arose from their cultural weaknesses and family breakdown; scant attention was devoted to the difficulties caused by economic and government structures (Piven and Cloward, 1971). Similarly, Estes (1979) has argued that researchers in the 'Ageing Enterprise' seek government funds which serve their own interests in ways that can work against the interests of older people.

Most social scientists, however, have echoed the enlightened belief that humanism and rationality will further good societies. Karl Mannheim (1936) believed that intellectuals had the 'objectivity' necessary to counter the horrors of extreme political ideologies in the early twentieth century. Some decades later Scott Greer (1969), an American sociologist, articulated a common view that social knowledge can empower disenfranchised social groups. A government elite at the time argued that the (Social) 'Scientific Estate' was a fundamental safeguard against totalitarian regimes (Price, 1965). Herbert Marcuse (1964) even went so far as to argue that academics, with their expert knowledge and 'disinterested' social positions, should virtually become the government and lead equitable societies!

Whatever one's ideological position on these matters—and irrespective of whether one works from a monastery or a university—it is virtually impossible to isolate the pursuit of knowledge from the world of social action and power. Social research data can become socially meaningful *information* useful in ideological and political struggles (Bulmer, 1982). Examining the social context of research assists in better appreciating the consequences for the people who are studied. The outcomes depend heavily on how academic researchers relate to government funders and community constituencies. Is it possible to conduct research which is true to the interests of all three parties?

RESEARCH AND COMMUNITIES

Complex issues arise when we interrelate communities, research, and values. While the term community often refers to spatial organisation, I will use it to refer more broadly to any social group which has some kind of 'shared fate' or common interest (Suttles, 1973). It is difficult to conceive of any single idea of 'the' community, given the varied interests of different groups, although the notion of 'the' public interest arguably is more defensible. Communities have a strong stake in any public representation of themselves and research has become a major avenue for acquiring and legitimating public knowledge. Researchers from different ideological camps agree that their findings can be significant in shaping social attitudes towards minority groups and in influencing government policies (Greer, 1969).

Research is a process of systematic thinking which builds knowledge (Kaplan, 1964). Investigations can test prior ideas, generate new ideas, and incorporate findings into established bodies of knowledge. The ongoing research process is a logical and technical skill which is not inherently political, ideological, or otherwise socially judgmental. But all research in practice has a social context. While all researchers must follow prescripts of good research conduct, social researchers must be aware that they are part of the phenomena which they study. Applied researchers have the added responsibility of deciding whether or not to challenge problematic definitions pre-set by government funders. They also need to anticipate how governments may wish to apply the findings.

Particularly with community-based research, major issues of values thus arise in setting up a study. In my estimation, it would take a serious misreading of Max Weber's (1949) classical writings to argue that research in the social sciences could be 'value-free'. That may be a politically convenient rationale for some sociologists, but values are central in deciding what is important to study and they lie at the heart of understanding why and how people do what they do. If researchers accept that their own values are inextricable from their research, there is an ethical obligation for researchers to make explicit their own values while at the same time limiting the intrusion of personal values into their interpretations of people being studied.

This essay is written from the viewpoint of researchers inside the academy looking to the outside in representing community views. The foundation for a successful relationship must be a common understanding and mutual agreement which respects the capacities and interests of all parties. Information generated by research is needed by researchers for publication, by governments for program development, and by community groups for lobbying governments and influencing public opinion. Difficulties are likely to arise when one or another party can impose its own views and interests. Problems commonly emerge when the parties think they have agreed but later find out that they have different understandings. The potential for difficulty is most serious when communities of interest have no organised group to represent them.

Academics in the health field need people *from whom* to collect information or *on whom* to perform clinical trials or program evaluations. Inherent in this language is the one-sided direction of benefits (academics need . . .) and the one-sided direction of power and authority (knowing academics 'act' on ignorant subjects). In our traditional research ethics, these one-sided relationships are ethical as long as subjects are informed and not hurt and the investigation pursues questions of academic worth (see basic methods texts such as Babbie, 1986). There is a rather diffuse assumption that good science will eventually benefit 'the community'. The public credence given to these ideas is shown by the rise of ethics reviews which support good ethical practice in universities (NHMRC, 1992).

In applied social science, I would argue that extensive interaction is highly desirable for both researchers and communities. Good science abstracts from the empirical world and research questions must have a firm grounding in experience (Kaplan, 1964). It is extraordinary to see methodology texts which imply that hypotheses somehow spring a priori out of thin air or, perhaps more bewildering, out of reviewing the literature on past studies. It would seem obvious that research benefits from practical input from people who are living the phenomena under study. Effective input starts before formulating research questions and continues through to conducting the fieldwork and interpreting and disseminating findings.

Research can also be important for social action by organised community groups. Activists may already know what the problems and solutions are, at least to their own satisfaction, but their knowledge cannot be accepted by wider circles unless it is confirmed by systematic investigation. Community groups seldom have the resources or technical skills needed to conduct significant studies by themselves. I can attest to several instances where a research project overwhelmed the advocacy responsibilities of a community group for years. I would suggest that independent research by community organisations is most appropriately limited to small-scale action research. This can document their views and experiences in relating to governments and other aspects of social life.

The usefulness of research findings to communities depends largely on who sets the questions. The power to initiate and/or direct an investigation, however, comes down largely to whoever puts up the cash, the time, or otherwise contributes to the enterprise. As will be discussed below, these relationships are largely defined by funding arrangements. In my experience, 'communities' seldom have much direct say before academic research plans are finalised in funding arrangements. Communities are involved mainly insofar as their group interests are invoked by others who set up research, or as individual participants after research questions have been set.

There are ways to institutionalise community involvement in research studies. Community input is occasionally sought in assessing proposals. Funders may require oversight by advisory or steering committees consisting of client groups, professionals, program managers, and other such interested parties. Representation by these interests is important in setting questions and again in commenting on the interpretation of findings. It is the researchers, however, who carry responsibility for selecting appropriate methods, designing instruments, conducting the analysis, and (in most cases) writing up the findings. It can be particularly difficult to explain to community groups why research generally takes more time and money than was expected, to yield findings which are perceived to be limited and highly qualified.

Community groups can benefit considerably from research when they proactively form partnerships with university researchers, lobby governments for funding, and apply the findings to policy. This is not easy but it is possible and it takes a willingness by advocates, practitioners, and researchers to accept the legitimacy of each other's values, objectives, language, and skills. Bodies such as the Australian Public Health Association provide a useful forum for working through common agendas and applying them to purposeful research. Key individuals from universities, government, and community groups can collaborate, in the ongoing development of their field, through research, practice, and policy which converges on the interests of constituency groups.

In summary, members of 'communities' must be far more than passive 'subjects' for university researchers. They are the legitimate 'owners' of their time and their insights and 'custodians' of their own interests in research on themselves. There is an important matter of civil rights in recognising that individuals' own understandings warrant a hearing in any enterprise aimed at understanding their actions. I would suggest that socially responsible research must involve representatives of organised constituencies.

CONDUCTING RESEARCH

Virtually every step in applied health research raises questions about how researchers relate to communities. Many of the central issues arise in setting the methodology, theoretically 'locating' the study, and interpreting and disseminating the findings. Too often research designs reflect the methodological experience of the researcher rather than the approach best suited to a study's purposes.

Only after study aims are carefully considered can methods be designed to fit the purposes and the resources. If there is little systematic knowledge available on the topic, one has to be wary of any design which imposes externally derived concepts that may have little applicability to the phenomena. When trying to understand human action, social responsibility would demand investigations grounded in the viewpoint of the individuals involved. Understanding the social consequences of health-care practice and service delivery similarly demands a focus on consumers rather than professionals, managers, and academics. Where the aim is to inform social interventions, it is particularly important to focus on what is potentially improvable and the barriers to better outcomes.

If one accepts these arguments, there is a strong case for qualitative methodologies which rely on key *informants* who structure the questions, concepts, and answers. There are a variety of options—including focus group interviews, in-depth interviews, and participant observation—all of which enable people to tell their own stories, from their own point of view, in the particular social context of their life (Minichiello *et al*, 1990). Explanations emerge from listening to what individuals say about their meanings, motives and actions and by searching for systematic sources of variation among them. The result can be good science as well as responsible, sensitive representation of a community.

Various quantitative methods such as surveys come into their own when one already knows a fair bit about a topic. A survey provides accurate estimates of 'how much' there is of something in the community and the results are useful in testing associations between variables (de Vaus, 1990). One of the limitations of surveys is that they can focus attention on individuals' characteristics, excluding consideration of the effects of prevailing social conditions or availability of services. Too often, funders and community representatives alike mistake the technical gloss of quantitative methods for sound science. For most complex social topics, a good understanding emerges only after taking into account information from both qualitative and quantitative investigations.

The theoretical stance of a study also has a major bearing on how accessible and relevant the findings may be for community interests. Good theory can provide an incisive ordering and explanation of phenomena under consideration (Kaplan, 1964). At its worst, ideological bias can masquerade as theory and arcane language can make a study incomprehensible to applied audiences. Explanation couched in abstract concepts needs to be 'unravelled' and applied for practical purposes. I would add that jargon can also render research inaccessible to critical review by academic colleagues!

Sampling limitations in health research have many adverse consequences for representing community interests. Just as much of psychology is based on testing undergraduates, so much of our understanding of health is based on captive, self-selected samples of patients and clients. In gerontology, there are appalling generalisations to all old people from studies based primarily on the 5 per cent or so who live in residential care (Kendig, 1988). This distortion is now being replicated through evaluations of community services which also focus on more-dependent people. As a result of sampling limitations, our knowledge base reinforces inaccurate social stereotypes of older people as dependent and negative attitudes towards ageing.

Even well-designed community surveys typically have only 60 to 80 per cent response rates. The 20 to 40 per cent who do not respond tend to be relatively more physically or socially vulnerable than those who do respond. A cross-sectional community care study obviously presents an overly optimistic view because it excludes those who were no longer able to stay in their homes. Given that virtually all studies have their limits, sound judgment is needed to draw conclusions which can be supported by the available research data.

Analysis of findings also has risks in regard to accurately representing communities. With qualitative studies, portraits of each individual can focus attention on idiosyncratic factors and divert attention away from powerful commonalities of experience. With quantitative studies, summary statistics mask the great diversity typically found within any population. As Pinker (1971) has observed, too many studies report descriptive findings and move on to moral exhortations, with little analysis of underlying causes of social problems. Too often analysis of data on vulnerable people pays little attention to the social and service context in which their vulnerabilities have emerged and are expressed in daily life.

At the writing-up stage, it is critical to think about responsibilities to communities. Preliminary findings can be greatly improved by providing written drafts for review by informants, respondents, and community advocates. With extended case write-ups from qualitative studies, we have benefited by asking informants to confirm that the draft represents the way they see themselves (Davison et al, 1993). With program evaluations and work with other organised entities, there are benefits from continual collaboration between researchers and the project staff (Kendig et al, 1992). It is important to have feedback from projects on the accuracy of interpretations, protection of confidentiality, and areas of potential misinterpretation and ambiguity in the report.

In my view one of the most important responsibilities in applied research is dissemination appropriate to multiple audiences. For program evaluations this typically involves a fulsome main report on methods and detailed findings, and a brief executive summary emphasising implications for services and policies. A burst of media presentations extends the public message. Publishing articles in professional and academic journals is a difficult test for applied research centres dependent on external funding for staff salaries. Another difficulty—for which I have no easy answer—is the tension between the short time frame required for government decision-making and the longer time frame necessary for academic quality. Quite often the most useful social and policy applications of research are made by researchers who continue in public debates for years after the research has been published.

INSTITUTIONAL CONTEXT

Universities, relative to other social institutions, offer a good institutional base for independent thought. Compared to the Australian/British traditions, universities in the United States have shown more pragmatic responsiveness—some would say political compliance—to various communities. Many state universities in the US were formed to support agricultural interests and now rely more heavily than ever on funds from industrial, charitable, and governmental interests. In the British tradition there appears to be little responsiveness to communities, while the American tradition is responsive mainly to those communities with a capacity to pay.

Academic careers are built primarily on scholarly achievements which do not relate very directly to representing community interests. Promotion requires scholarly rigour and originality as evidenced by refereed publications and peer review. Academic incentives are not necessarily at odds with community responsive research. Indeed, community involvement can heighten understanding and increase research funding. However, promotion criteria in universities pay little direct regard to community contributions and time is scarce for desirable but non-essential activities.

Australian universities are experiencing increasing direction from governments. While direct political interference is a worry, I believe there are benefits when universities have incentives to become more responsive to communities. As with any providers who rely on government subsidies, some counterweight is needed to the inbuilt pressures for the academy to allocate resources for inwardly focused purposes. In Australia, the jury is out on the extent to which basic research funding—most notably large grants from the Australian Research Council and the NHMRC—will be directed by national benefit as well as academic excellence. It is encouraging to see that applied research funds within government are setting incentives for building research partnerships with advocacy groups and community groups (Commonwealth Department of Community Services and Health, 1993). Important among these are the Health and Community Services Research and Development Grants (RADGAC); the NHMRC Public Health Research and Development Grants; and the Victorian Health Promotion Foundation. A particular issue in my field has been government consultancies. I believe that it is possible to align the purposes of universities (building knowledge) and governments (making and legitimating decisions) through studies which are socially responsible and responsive to communities. But these are not easy relationships. Although consultancies can focus on matters of social importance, they seldom involve the theoretical or methodological sophistication necessary to contribute much to academic careers. Some consultancy briefs cannot be accepted because they have predetermined answers, and time frames and budgets which do not allow for sound academic inquiry. Some contracts rule out independent publication. It is difficult to ensure that decisions about research agendas are made solely on academic grounds when your own salary or that of valued colleagues is at stake.

In Australia there has been relatively little research support from private foundations such as the British Nuffield Foundation or the major enterprises of the American Rockefeller, Ford, and Carnegie-Mellon foundations. Australia has remarkably little in the way of socially progressive philanthropy which funds applied research to further the interests of disadvantaged social groups.

I would suggest that postgraduate programs are especially important for universities in building research partnerships with communities. In the health field, most postgraduate students are experienced practitioners who have a keen appreciation of community needs. A postgraduate thesis, be it a minor thesis or a PhD degree, can be a very valuable way for practitioners to reflect on the experience and views of clients or consumers. A thesis requires the candidate's own time but is not heavily obligated to either a government program or an academic fraternity. Practitioners who become researchers are well placed to inform academics about the outside world, bringing the benefits of research out to communities.

REFERENCES

Babbie, E., 1986, *The Practice of Social Research*, fourth edition, Belmont California: Wadsworth.

Bulmer, M., 1982, *The Uses of Social Research: social investigation in public policy-making*, London: George Allen & Unwin.

Commonwealth Department of Community Services and Health, 1993, *Research Effort of the Department of Community Services and Health*, Canberra: Research Coordination and Support Grants Section, Department of Community Services and Health.

Davison, B., Kendig, H., Stephens, F. and Merrill, V., 1993, *'It's My Place': older people talk about their homes*, Canberra: Australian Government Publishing Service.

de Vaus, D., 1990, *Surveys in Social Research*, second edition, Sydney: Allen & Unwin.

Estes, C., 1979, *The Ageing Enterprise: a critical examination of social policies and services for the aged*, San Francisco: Jossey-Bass.

Greer, S., 1969, *The Logic of Social Inquiry*, Chicago: Aldine.

Imre, R., 1985, 'Tacit knowledge in social work research and practice', *Studies in Social Work*, 55, 2: 138–49.

Kendig, H., 1988, 'Research directions in social gerontology in Australia', *Issues in Gerontology: Proceedings of the 22nd Annual Conference of the Australian Association of Gerontology*, Sydney: Australian Association of Gerontology.

Kendig, H., Reynolds, A., McVicar, G., and O'Brien, A., 1992, *Evaluation of the Victorian Linkages Project*, Canberra: Commonwealth Department of Health, Housing, and Community Development.

Kaplan, A., 1964, *The Conduct of Inquiry: methodology for behavioural science*, Scranton: Chandler.

Mannheim, K., 1936, *Ideology and Utopia*, New York: Harcourt, Brace.

Marcuse, H., 1964, *One Dimensional Man*, Boston: Beacon Press.

Minichiello, M., Aroni, R., Timewell, E., Alexander, L., 1995, *In-Depth Interviewing: researching people*, second edition, Melbourne: Longman Cheshire.

National Health and Medical Research Council, 1992, *NHMRC Statement on Human Experimentation and Supplementary Notes*, Canberra: NHMRC.

Pinker, R., 1971, *Social Theory and Social Policy*, London: Heinemann.

Piven, F. and Cloward, R., 1971, *Regulating the Poor: the functions of public welfare*, New York: Vintage Books.

Price, D., 1965, *The Scientific Estate*, London: Oxford University Press.

Suttles, G., 1973, *The Social Construction of Communities*, Chicago: University of Chicago Press.

Weber, M., 1947, *The Theory of Social and Economic Organization*, tr. A. M. Henderson and T. Parsons, New York: Oxford University Press.

——1949, *The Methodology of the Social Sciences*, tr. E. Shils and H. Finch, New York: Free Press.

15

ETHICS AND HEALTH RESEARCH IN ABORIGINAL COMMUNITIES

Ian Anderson

Health research in Aboriginal communities is a relatively recent phenomenon. An interest in the ethical implications of such research is even more recent. Prior to the 1970s there were few published research reports on Aboriginal health, except for the occasional 'jab and run' serological surveys of remote communities. The changing nature of research on Aboriginal health has been situated within a broader shift in Australian colonial relations—over the past twenty years the relationship between Aboriginal people and the Australian nation has been transformed from a predominantly assimilationist form of colonialism into welfare colonialism. The key social processes which characterised this transition include the removal of constitutional barriers to Aboriginal citizenship following the 1967 referendum; the development of a national Aboriginal political movement focused on self-determination; and the development of a federal bureaucratic apparatus which administers Aboriginal programs and facilitates Aboriginal self-management. Assimilation colonialism, on the other hand, was characterised by the management of Aboriginal affairs by state governments, and by the exclusion of Aboriginal people from civic rights, except for those deemed 'almost whites'. This colonial system was associated with extensive systems of surveillance which closely monitored Aboriginal life practices.

The political circumstances created by this emergence of a new form of colonial relations enabled the development of an Aboriginal community infrastructure. Community controlled Aboriginal health services were created as Aboriginal communities successfully exploited new possibilities in collective life. Approximately 100 such services across Australia are among the most significant sites of primary health-care delivery to indigenous Australia. In parallel with the development of an Aboriginal primary

153

health-care system, academic institutions have demonstrated an increasing interest in defining Aboriginal health problems.

The growth of a significant body of Aboriginal health research has not been without historical antecedents. The principal, and virtually the only, academic discipline applied to Aboriginal people in the first half of the twentieth century was anthropology. Australian anthropology developed in alliance with the pre-1967-referendum systems of Aboriginal administration, but the political relationship between institutional knowledges such as anthropology, Aboriginal communities and systems of Aboriginal administration was complex and contested (Cowlishaw, 1990). This experience of the academy has had a powerful impact on the collective memory of Aboriginal communities. The health survey, the census taker, the keeper of public hospital morbidity records, all evoke memories of the anthropologist, the missionary and those police who were actively involved in the institutionalisation of Aboriginal children and the coercive regulation of reserve and mission life. In such a history the anthropologist of the 1930s blends easily with the health researcher of the 1990s, although the circumstances and intent may differ greatly.

Within the Aboriginal community there is a growing, though tentative, recognition that research can be a valuable tool if deployed appropriately. The significance of research was recognised in the National Aboriginal Health Strategy[1] (NAHS, 1989) with a chapter devoted to issues of research, including priority areas for research, and discussion in broad terms of ethical difficulties in Aboriginal health research. Many Aboriginal community agencies have signalled their desire for a more constructive relationship with the research establishment. This has driven, in part, a more proactive approach to defining an ethical framework for Aboriginal health research. The National Aboriginal and Islander Health Organisation (NAIHO)[2], in collaboration with the National Health and Medical Research Council (NHMRC), developed a set of ethical guidelines for research in indigenous Australian communities (NHMRC, 1991; Anon, 1993). Some states have developed their own research guidelines, and a number of Aboriginal and Torres Strait Islander controlled organisations have set up their own ethics committees (Maddocks, 1992). The NAIHO/NHMRC guidelines develop a broad framework for protecting Aboriginal people from exploitation by researchers. The guidelines include principles which govern:

1. The process of consultation and negotiation with Aboriginal communities, including appropriate steps and strategies in consultation to ensure that Aboriginal communities and their representative agencies have had the opportunity to make an informed assessment of the proposal.
2. Community involvement in research, in particular recommending that community members be offered the opportunity to assist in research,

that all community or individual resources be paid for, and that the community has an ongoing negotiating role as the project develops.

3. The ownership and publication of data. The guidelines are not rigidly prescriptive on these issues but recommend that negotiation over the conduct of research, the ownership of raw data and the rights of publication occur, and preferably be agreed upon, before the commencement of research. The guidelines do explicitly recommend that a community report be prepared and delivered on the completion of data collection and analysis—prior to publication of results. Further, the guidelines offer explicit comment on the use of data obtained from blood and tissue samples and the publication of results which identify individuals or communities. The emphasis is on the development of a transparent process of negotiation which leads to an agreed position for the particular study.

Following the publication of these guidelines it was suggested by some that they might stifle research initiatives (Maddocks, 1992). Anecdotally, this does not appear to be the case. In fact, the guidelines may actually be quite productive in terms of research effort. Most research projects are cooperative ventures which require the skills of local Aboriginal people and organisations in order to define points of access to particular study populations or suitable research strategies. Here local knowledge of community structures and processes is necessarily married with the researcher's skills in study design and implementation. There are of course projects in which the relationship between researcher and Aboriginal community is more abstract—such as those projects which mobilise data from statistical collections or which build theoretical models. However, even in the cases where relationships with Aboriginal people are more potential than actual, at some point the researcher will interact face to face with Aboriginal people and organisations.

If the research relationship is conducted within an agreed set of principles, then the risk of unproductive conflict is lessened. Used as tools of negotiation, ethical guidelines can assist in sustaining the development of a constructive relationship between the research establishment and Aboriginal communities and an explicit ethical framework may actually be quite liberating for all parties.

THE ETHICS OF BENEFIT

While the NAIHO/NHMRC guidelines have been productive policy developments, my concerns are with one aspect of the ethics of research partially dealt with in these guidelines: the ethics of utility, or benefit, to Aboriginal communities. Although the problem of the benefit of research to Aboriginal communities has been raised in discussions on research ethics, it has not been clearly defined how this may be assessed with respect to particular projects. This is a moral problem for two reasons. First, in the distribution of research resources questions about benefit cannot be resolved unless differences between alternative value systems are reconciled. Second, Aboriginal communities have such poor health status and poor access to health system resources that it is essential to maximise the potential of all resources. Here the ethical issues confronted by Aboriginal people are similar to those faced by others who engage with the research establishment from a position of marginalisation or disadvantage.

Protecting people from exploitation by research, ensuring that the research process is of maximal benefit to the Aboriginal community, and assessing the methodological rigour of research projects are, of course, interlocked issues and I am not dispensing with scientific rigour to focus on issues of benefit. A research study has little benefit to the community if it is not valid according to the criteria established by the research establishment. Such a project is a dubious basis for changing service delivery or for funding and policy arguments.[3] Nevertheless, at times the need for scientific rigour becomes a mantra for grant assessors—one which obscures the deep divisions within the establishment about what actually constitutes rigour. Rigour does not come in bottles as a defined entity with certain properties. If the scientists disagree about what constitutes a rigorous project, it certainly is not intuitively obvious to community groups who are the subjects of investigation.

The tension of reconciling the differences over what constitutes good science and what the community to be studied believes is acceptable is inherent in all research projects which deal with human populations. As Aboriginal people, our values, which have their own cultural and historical logic, shape the potential of all forms of inquiry. Once again, constructive relationships with Aboriginal communities may actually enhance the project's scientific value, as people in the community will be able to identify strategies to achieve the project objectives. An essential research skill in this arena is the ability of the researcher to work in a crosscultural context, balancing the demands of institution and community, defining commonalities and negotiating differences.

The ethics of exploitation are primarily concerned with the relations between the researcher and community. This relationship is inevitably characterised by differentials of power—with the researcher being in the position to scrutinise, observe and interrogate the researched, appropriating their experience to create symbolic capital. This is not a reflection on researchers' intent but rather a property of their social relationship with research subjects, and it remains regardless of whether the researcher works for an academic institution or is employed by an Aboriginal organisation— even though other social aspects of the relationship change according to the site of research. While the ethics of exploitation give the researched some protection, the problem of utility has broader structural implications.

Questions about the benefit of research processes involve issues of equity in distribution of research monies. Currently, resources are distributed primarily by apparatuses such as the NHMRC to universities, with Aboriginal communities remaining marginalised participants in the process. In 1991, for all current research projects in Aboriginal health, universities received 59 per cent of funding and Aboriginal health services 2 per cent (Henderson, 1994). These circumstances mean that research does not necessarily engage with the processes of community development, a necessary precondition if research processes are to enable improvement in both Aboriginal health status and services for Aboriginal needs.

WHO AND WHAT IS RESEARCHED?

The question of utility is, of course, highly contested. The subject which is of interest to researchers from their position within the academy is not necessarily of benefit to a service delivery agency within the Aboriginal community. The assessment of a project's benefit within non-Aboriginal institutions takes into account its contribution to a body of academic knowledge, its position in relation to institutional priorities, its contribution to institutional prestige and its ability to attract resources or be otherwise economically productive. In contrast, my position has always been that it is the researched, and not the researchers, who should be the primary beneficiaries. It is the researched whose privacy is invaded, who give their time and who allow themselves to be subjected to the critical gaze of the academy. If, in return, this process does not offer any potential for a better quality of life now or in the future, then research subjects are being unfairly exploited for the gain of the researcher. Of course, such issues are never so 'black and white', and benefit as assessed by the research establishment is not necessarily at odds with community needs. However, given the different social processes and priorities which govern the operation of community organisations, it is not surprising that they can also conflict. Here I want to clarify the important issues from the point of view of a community agency.

At both a NAIHO workshop in Alice Springs in 1986 (NHMRC, 1991) and in the NAHS working party report (1989), considerable effort was given to defining priority subject areas for research. Few would argue with either of these policy documents, which identified, for example, that research into cardiovascular disease, diabetes or alcohol and substance use was a priority in Aboriginal health. These are key areas of Aboriginal morbidity and mortality, so a project which enhances interventions in these areas is of potential benefit to Aboriginal communities. On the other hand, there have been few analyses of the actual distribution of research topics in Aboriginal health, but even a working knowledge of this body of literature would suggest that there is mismatch between study topics and health needs.

A content analysis of the *Aboriginal Health Information Bulletin*, a key publication in which research studies are reported, suggests major biases in the distribution of research effort (Lake, 1992), with a disproportionate regional distribution in the studies reported. Although 66 per cent of Aboriginal people live in urban and other urban populations,[4] only 14 per cent of studies have focused on these groups, while 24 per cent have focused exclusively on rural and remote communities. The most common study category was large population studies (14.5 per cent), followed by growth and nutrition studies (11.5 per cent). Circulatory system disease, the most important cause of excess mortality in Aboriginal communities, ranked 14th out of 19 subjects (1.5 per cent of the total)[5]. There have been no analyses of the distribution of methodologies employed. Although it remains to be demonstrated how generalised these observations are, Lake's analysis is suggestive of some major problems in the distribution of research effort.

However, these problems are not resolved by simply developing a priority list for Aboriginal health research. Given the high levels of morbidity and mortality in Aboriginal people, it would be difficult to find a research subject that could not be construed as a relative research priority. This may be less of an issue in assessing the relative value of two Aboriginal health projects. One could, for example, on the basis of the observations made above, make a case for ranking a project on cardiovascular disease above one on growth and nutrition. However, it would be difficult to assess the relative benefit of an Aboriginal research project compared with a non-Aboriginal project. What is the relative benefit of a project studying Aboriginal sexually transmitted diseases (STDs) relative to one studying cardiovascular disease in the non-Aboriginal community? One is a major cause of mortality for all Australians, but STDs are a significant cause of Aboriginal morbidity. Further, there is also the possibility that a proposed topic for study may be judged of low priority yet may be strongly advocated by an Aboriginal community agency because, at that moment, priorities within that particular community have heightened the likelihood of implementing a successful change in service delivery or other aspects of community life.

Further, this problem is not resolved only by assessing the relative value of research strategies. Attempts to define priority research areas have in the past identified quite particular problems within each category. However, many permutations are possible within each subject area. For example, the NAHS working party report (1989: 216) identifies one research priority as: 'investigation of the causes of gastroenteritis and the development of effective means of prevention and treatment'. Few would disagree with the overall thrust of this recommendation. However, two projects which fall within this broad thrust will not necessarily be of equal benefit to the Aboriginal community. Two equivalent proposals may differ in their impact on the researched community according to the social relationship of the researcher to the community. For example, there would be differences between a proposal developed by a metropolitan research unit and one developed by public health workers employed by the local community. The quality of the relationship between researcher and researched may affect the success with which the research strategy is implemented, and further shape the success with which project outcomes facilitate further action within that community. Differences in potential benefit are not only shaped by the methodology chosen for a priority research topic; the benefit is also related to the broader problem of the relationship between research processes and social change.

RESEARCH AND SOCIAL CHANGE

Recently, an assessor for a major funding body gave the advice that the body was interested in funding projects with demonstrable benefit for all Aboriginal Australians and not just those addressing 'parochial' community issues. This raises particular problems about how research beneficiaries are conceived. The local community is, of course, part of a larger entity, even though it may have a distinct health profile and access to resources. However, it is through local community relations that potential strategies may be developed to change the nature of the relationship between the research establishment and Aboriginal people. Here the key problem is to sustain productive research processes which enable the social change which Aboriginal communities believe necessary to enhance the quality of their lives.

The processes through which Aboriginal communities ask questions and seek answers are integral to how a particular community internally reorganises itself, its services, and its relations with non-Aboriginal Australia. It is not enough to understand the relationship between the diet of urban Kooris and heart disease. That knowledge must have meaning to the local community and form the basis of meaningful collective action. Individually and collectively, we need to choose how to make the minimum alteration possible in aspects of our social organisation, values or lifestyle for the maximum possible health effect. Constructive outcomes are possible if research problems are engaged within community processes. This does not mean that the same research questions must be asked in all sites. In one region people may take the insights developed in a study of the relationship between diet and heart disease, then develop the problem further. It is the process, not just the product, which is important.

As a result, assessing the potential benefit of research projects in terms of all-inclusive categories, such as 'all Aborigines', may actually exclude projects which are of considerable benefit to particular Aboriginal communities. Grant assessment procedures which match proposals to national priorities in Aboriginal health may overlook projects which are strategically important in terms of local community development. For this reason it is important that questions of benefit be first addressed to the defined community of study, and then placed in a more general context of Aboriginal health priorities.

In highlighting the importance of research utility within Aboriginal community development, I am not advocating only the so-called action-oriented research project. In a sense, all research projects are action-oriented. The problem here lies with the sort of action that is facilitated in the researched community. I take the position that different research methodologies promote different kinds of activities, and that improvement in Aboriginal health status will require a diverse range of activities. Theory development and model-building projects provide a basis for intervention-oriented studies. For example, models of illness causation facilitate those projects which examine strategies to prevent the occurrence of disease. Benefit, however, does not hinge only on project outcomes. The question of benefit is integral to the entire process, not just to the final results. Some projects may not offer an end product with a clear benefit, yet in the process of implementation, the skills of local workers may be developed or the community may begin to engage with a significant problem previously unrecognised.

It may be useful to think of the benefit of projects to Aboriginal communities in terms of the temporal phases of the research process, and divide them into immediate, directly consequent and delayed benefits.

IMMEDIATE BENEFITS

The immediate benefits of a research project may include enhanced skills of Aboriginal health workers; raised community awareness of particular health problems; or identification and treatment of individuals with disease. However, benefits of this kind do not lie dormant in the research strategy, waiting for action. Rather, potential benefits may be developed further within the research strategy design if such questions are seen to be essential to the overall integrity of the project. For example, rather than simply use Aboriginal health workers as research assistants or tools in the gathering of data, the research strategy would need to demonstrate how their skills would be developed throughout the project.

These benefits are best assessed in the context of the particular community. So, for example, it is not true that a project which employs a university-educated Aboriginal person is necessarily any more meaningful, or less tokenistic, than one which employs two non-university-educated research assistants. There are few Aboriginal people with formally recognised skills. Consequently, the opportunities for their participation in the research process are few. What is relevant here is not the qualification of the Aboriginal researchers but the extent to which the research project will develop the skills of Aboriginal co-workers.

DIRECTLY CONSEQUENT BENEFITS

Directly consequent benefits are the project outcomes. They include the data collected or the project results; the impact of published material; and new intervention strategies designed as a result of the research project.

There are a number of factors which affect the realisation of project benefits. In order to understand this, we need to conceptualise the link between the research outcomes and action. Research outcomes may promote action within a number of social realms, such as the bureaucracy or the Aboriginal community. There are, of course, numerous potential barriers to implementing research findings, such as limited resources or political processes opposing change. One key issue for the initiation of community action is the strategies used by the researcher for communicating results to the researched communities.

There are few reports of strategies to disseminate research findings (for example Hunter, 1993). It is important that research projects subject their dissemination strategies to public scrutiny. First, this would enable the development of the competencies necessary for this process. Second, it is important that there be a shift in attitude within research institutions where it would appear that the only outcome of career significance for the researcher is publication in a peer-reviewed journal. Creating *and sustaining* a meaningful dialogue between researcher and researched is integral to community development. This means that the interaction between researcher and community must be sustained beyond the time necessary for data collection and analysis.

The type of research methodology used shapes the way in which insights or critical leverage may be appropriately communicated to Aboriginal people. For example: a quantitative project may produce a set of data which can be easily communicated to the Aboriginal community as, say, a prevalence figure. The data may be subsequently used to initiate or shape action. The key information can be communicated while leaving validation mechanisms, such as a critique of the project's methodology, as a related but separate discussion. So we may be able to communicate that the prevalence of diabetes in a particular community is 10 per cent without necessarily engaging the Aboriginal community in a complex discussion on sampling frames. On the other hand, a qualitative project, using a method such as ethnography, may not necessarily produce an end product so easily summarised. The ethnographic text, with its many conceptual nuances, embodies particular theoretical strategies of representation. It is useful in building frameworks within which to better understand human action, but it is written for an academic audience. It is the ethnographic text which is assessed by the researcher's peers, and thus such research product may be of little value to a community audience who are mostly not university educated. Communicating the project outcomes to a community audience, requires the ethnographer to first imagine that the Aboriginal community is a necessary audience and then develop communication strategies accordingly.

I have considerably oversimplified the differences between quantitative and qualitative projects (they may, of course, be combined in one project). However, the point I wish to make is that strategies for the communication of results depend on the type of project being conducted. The benefits of a research project can be maximised if the process of dissemination of research findings is conceived to be integral to the entire process of research.

DELAYED BENEFITS

Finally, there are the delayed benefits—those which await further developments in intervention or which are a part of model building. These may be used in the training of future health workers or in stimulating further research questions. A theoretical model developed to explain the high prevalence of heart disease, for example, may not be of immediate value, but is important in the development of long-term thinking about the problem.

In the overall long-term development of Aboriginal health services, it is necessary to engage in a broad range of intellectual work, from abstract theory to the intervention-oriented study. The project which brings benefits earlier is likely to be favoured by the Aboriginal community. However, it is also possible that creative re-thinking of research strategies could bring long-term benefits even in apparently abstract research projects. Including these criteria of benefit in the assessment of the project's worth does not necessarily penalise any one methodological approach. Rather, it requires researchers to think creatively about how this problem can be addressed within their chosen method.

IDENTIFYING THE DANGERS

Another part of the process of identifying the potential benefit of a project is recognition of the dangers or potential damage of particular research strategies. Is the process going to accentuate internal community conflict? What is the effect of asking questions about women's parenting skills on their self-esteem as mothers? How will published reports be interpreted by the mainstream press, and is there a risk that they will be misrepresented to add currency to traditional colonial stereotypes? Such problems must be anticipated and responded to in strategy design and implementation. The NHMRC guidelines (1991: 8), for example, take a quite explicit position on the relationship with the media:

> Should the media solicit comments from researchers, once their work is in the public arena, researchers should first seek the consent of the community concerned. Comments to the media should be sensitive and professional and should focus on the research issues under consideration.

The potential hazards of a proposed research project may be avoided if researchers take time to consider the impact of their presence and their projects on Aboriginal experience.

MACRO-STRUCTURAL IMPLICATIONS

As I said at the outset, I believe questions of benefit are interlocked with determinations about the validity of the project methods, and mechanisms to protect the researched from exploitation. However, in the context of Aboriginal health, it is necessary to develop strategies to ensure that the impact of all research activity is maximised. While national priorities may, in broad terms, frame our assessment of a project's potential worth, it is also necessary to assess the benefit of a project in the context of local community needs. Here the key questions revolve not only around the project's methods, but also around the quality of the relationship between researcher and researched. These are, in effect, the key issues identified by Paul Komesaroff in this volume as belonging to the microethical level. However, as Komesaroff points out, we also need to address the relationship between microethical structures and the larger-scale structures of the society and culture in which they are embedded. This means that microethical issues cannot be resolved in isolation from broader shifts in the allocation of resources.

Here I want to return to an issue I highlighted earlier. What does it mean that the most significant sector involved in the delivery of primary health-care services (the community controlled Aboriginal health services) has virtually no funding to carry out its own research? It means that currently there is no necessary relationship between Aboriginal health research and the delivery of health services to Aboriginal people. More significantly, given that the Aboriginal health services are community controlled agencies, it means that the most appropriate organisational connection between research processes and community processes currently receives proportionally less funding for research than any other agency (except for the Aboriginal and Torres Strait Islander Commission and the

163

Australian Institute of Aboriginal and Torres Strait Islander Studies). With the current distribution of research funds, the link between research and social change is seriously undermined.

This also means that the processes through which Aboriginal values are inserted into the academy are undermined. If Aboriginal communities are unable to develop some control over academic processes such as research and education, the mobilisation of Aboriginal cultural experience within our higher education system will not occur. Aboriginal experience has a lot to contribute to intellectual activity—and has a useful role in providing critiques of theoretical frames, interpretative activity or study design. This also is a necessary step in producing research which is of greater utility to Aboriginal communities. Unless such research recognises the cultural context in which it is implemented or in which action occurs following its completion, it only partially engages with the problems it was designed to tackle. While Aboriginal people remain marginalised participants in this process we will remain dependent on the quality of researchers who seek us out, rather than being able to recruit researchers with the qualities to do the work we believe to be necessary in our communities.

The impact of Australian colonialism has been to stunt the development of the intellectual and symbolic capital of indigenous communities. It is now necessary to enhance the ability of Aboriginal people to determine the allocation of their own resources, including intellectual resources. This requires that barriers to direct funding of Aboriginal community agencies for research be identified, and that strategies for change be implemented.

NOTES

1 The National Aboriginal Health Strategy was developed following national consultations with Aboriginal communities, Aboriginal health services, state and territory agencies involved in the delivery of Aboriginal health services.

2 This was, at the time, the umbrella political advocacy forum for the nation's Aboriginal community controlled health services. It has since been superseded by the development of a new body, the National Aboriginal Community Controlled Health Organisation.

3 This position was actually adopted as a part of the Western Australian ethical guidelines on Aboriginal health research (Maddocks, 1992).

4 These populations are defined using Australian Bureau of Statistics criteria. 'Major urban' includes populations of over 100 000 and 'other urban' includes populations of between 1000 and 100 000.

5 Both these observed trends are supported by Henderson (1994) where he considers the distribution of NHMRC-funded research in 1991 (see NHMRC, 1991) as well as by Lake's analysis (1992).

REFERENCES

Anon, 1993, 'Brief communications: National Health and Medical Research Council guidelines on ethical matters in Aboriginal and Torres Strait Islander research', *Aboriginal Health Information Bulletin*, 18, 16–20.

Cowlishaw, G., 1990, 'Helping anthropologists: Cultural continuity in the constructions of Aboriginalists', *Canberra Anthropology*, 13: 1–28.

Donbavand, J., 1991, *Aboriginal Health Research, the classification of current research and research from the past decade that has been conducted into Aboriginal health,* Canberra: National Health and Medical Research Council & Commonwealth Department of Health Housing and Community Services.

Henderson, G., 1994, 'Priorities for research in social and environmental health: A discussion paper', Canberra: Australian Institute of Aboriginal and Torres Strait Islander Studies.

Hunter, E., 1992, 'Feedback: Towards the effective and responsible dissemination of Aboriginal health research findings', *Aboriginal Health Information Bulletin*, 17, 17–21.

Lake, P., 1992, 'A decade of Aboriginal health research', *Aboriginal Health Information Bulletin*, 17, 12–16.

Maddocks, I., 1992, 'Ethics in Aboriginal research', *Medical Journal of Australia*, 157: 553–5.

National Aboriginal Health Strategy Working Party, 1989, *A National Aboriginal Health Strategy*, Canberra: Aboriginal and Torres Strait Islander Commission.

National Health and Medical Research Council, 1991, *Guidelines on Ethical Matters in Aboriginal and Torres Strait Islander Health Research*, Canberra: National Health and Medical Research Council.

16

WOMEN'S HEALTH: METHODS AND ETHICS

Johanna Wyn, Judith Lumley, Jeanne Daly

Women researchers working in the area of women's health face a number of problems in representing the views of the women who participate in their research. At one level, the methodological and ethical issues involved in researching women are substantially the same as for any other group. The most fundamental concerns for the researcher are to protect the interests of the group being studied, to ensure that its members are not harmed and to ensure that the findings are valid. Broad methodological and ethical principles provide a useful guide to reaching these goals. However, general rules inevitably appear inadequate in the face of the specific circumstances of particular groups in particular research settings.

Women occupy both a central and a marginal place in our society. As the symbol of female (commercialised) beauty, young women have a central visual presence. Women are the focus of health promotion campaigns which subtly promote these commercialised norms of feminine beauty, thus giving rise to the problems described by Rhonda Galbally in this volume. At the same time, women are marginal in our society. In recent times, attention has been drawn to the systematic nature of the violation of women and girls, and their positioning as a powerless group in our society, by the increasing awareness of the rate of abuse of women (Hammer and Maynard, 1987; Angus and Wilkinson, 1993). In public health programs, this problem is substantially ignored in favour of screening programs, ranging from cervical cancer screening to mammography. Even with screening programs, there has been a lack of consideration of the way in which these are experienced by the women screened. Overall, there has been a lack of consideration of the social context in which diseases arise, for example, the *transmission* of sexually transmitted diseases in young women (Wyn, 1991). More recently, however, research funding priorities have focused our attention on the health of women during times of social transition: in particular the transitions to adulthood, to motherhood and to older age.

The problem we face as women's health researchers is to sustain a focus on the experience of the women themselves during these transitions. There is a substantial literature on transition to adulthood with its focus on youth and adolescence but, traditionally, young women have been rendered almost invisible in this research. Only recently has there been a more sustained focus on young women's specific experiences of the transition to adulthood (Griffin, 1985; Johnson, 1993; Wilson and Wyn, 1987), making their concerns and perspectives more visible. Childbirth has long been the focus of public health services and research but, in much traditional medical research, improving the survival rate of infants through techno-logical interventions during childbirth has taken precedence over concern for the experience of the woman giving birth. The rise of the consumer movement, starting in the 1970s, focused attention on the lack of response of childbirth services to women's needs (Oakley, 1993: Chapter 11), but we still lack information on what these needs are and how they vary in different groups of women. This remains true in those cases where women are particularly vulnerable because of problems such as post-natal depres-sion. Research into the transition to older age is dominated by a focus on the menopause. Coney (1991) argues that menopause offers rich profits for the pharmaceutical industry as the 'baby boomers' reach midlife. Again, the emphasis on medical treatment of this transition threatens to obscure analysis of the way in which women negotiate it.

It is in the conduct of research into the way in which women negotiate vulnerable periods in their lives that women's health researchers can make an important contribution, focusing on the implications of relations and discourses of power for women. By making the experience of women more central in our research, we can make a substantial contribution to inform-ing the community of women, to which we ourselves belong, of health policy. At the same time our research can contribute to the development of health policy and service delivery in the area of women's health.

As women and women's health researchers, we are well placed to address the experience of women at vulnerable stages in their lives. In some cases we ourselves have undergone or are undergoing the same transitions. This means that we are better able to gain access to research participants, who often feel more comfortable discussing intimate details of their lives with researchers who are likely to understand their problems. Our personal experience does give us an advantage in understanding of the subtleties of the experience, but this raises the issue that we may not be able to disentangle our own experience from that of the women who participate in our research—in positivist terms, these are issues of 'bias' and lack of 'objectivity' (Brown *et al*, 1994). Hal Kendig argues, ealier in this section, that we as researchers now accept that our own values are inextricable from our research but that we have an ethical responsibility to make our own values explicit in that research while limiting the intrusion of our personal values into our interpretations of the experience of others. These problems have been addressed in detail by feminist methodologists (for example, Roberts, 1981) and do not require further discussion here.

Even when women are vulnerable, they need not take a passive role in the research process. There are a number of ways in which a more active role can be promoted. In some projects a relatively unstructured research method can be used. After a clear statement of the research question, women can be asked to describe what they see as important, to the extent that they wish to contribute this information. This method of interviewing produces a wealth of data, which limits the number of participants in a study (the 'sample'). In other research projects, especially where it is necessary to obtain information on a small number of questions from a large group of women, a more structured approach is needed. In both cases researchers can involve community representatives in the design and conduct of the study and in both cases researchers should test the validity of the research conclusions with the participants.

The involvement of community representatives in women's health research is not an easy matter. Women at the same vulnerable stage of life do not necessarily constitute a 'community'. In the case of young women, they may identify with school communities or peer groups. On the other hand, the most vulnerable young women may be homeless, living socially isolated lives. During childbirth the health-care system may provide the opportunity for women to meet other women undergoing the same experience, and this area has seen the growth of self-help groups, but there is doubt as to the extent to which these organisations represent the views of women in general. In the case of women in midlife, there has been little formal community organisation and there is the additional problem that women may not wish to identify themselves as menopausal because of negative cultural attitudes to menopause.

If the women who participate in our research are experiencing extraordinary difficulties, they have an immediate and pressing need to be informed of the results of our research. For this reason we need to remain in contact with the 'communities' which participated in our research. However, this does not mean that they will necessarily welcome our conclusions. Where substantial disagreements occur, as a general rule, researchers should attempt to resolve disagreement or, failing that, acknowledge disagreements and attempt to provide an explanation for the various views and their implications for health policy.

With these as general guiding principles, we now turn to a more detailed description of the ways in which we addressed three very different sets of ethical issues in the course of conducting research with young women, with women during childbirth and with women in midlife.

YOUNG WOMEN AND ISSUES OF CONSENT

There are many health issues that are important to young women (such as diet, sexually transmitted diseases), but current funding priorities make it more likely that the researcher will come into contact with young women whose health is an issue because of their vulnerable and marginal status. Young women who are homeless, abused, AIDS sufferers or in poverty are among the most likely to be targeted, because they are seen to be the most 'at risk' of ill-health, and of transmitting infectious diseases to the wider population. For the researcher, this means that the diversity of young women's circumstances needs to be acknowledged, beyond the usual social divisions of ethnicity, social class and geographical location.

To put this another way, the concept of 'youth' covers enormous diversity. Differences in life circumstances, and in access to public resources and private support, are of fundamental importance to understanding the health outcomes and health needs of young women. Some young women negotiate the transition towards independent adulthood from a far more vulnerable position than others, lacking even the most basic support and advocacy of their parents or other adults who may act in their interests. Yet, because of their vulnerability, it is important that young women from these groups be featured in research on young women's health.

For the researcher there is a potential conflict between the duty to recognise young women's rights and interests and the benefits of drawing on their perspectives and experiences to inform health policy, service provision and education in the interests of serving the needs of all young women. The following discussion looks at two areas in which there are ethical dilemmas. It draws on a recent research project undertaken by the Youth Research Centre at The University of Melbourne, on young women (aged 16–18) and their knowledge and practices in relation to sexually transmitted diseases, and the implications of these for health-care delivery (Wyn, 1994; 1993; 1991). The two areas are identified with the aim of contributing to the ongoing debate about ethics issues involved in re-searching young women's health rather than of prescribing solutions.

YOUNG WOMEN'S RIGHTS AND INTERESTS: CONSENT AND ASSENT

At what age are young women 'adult' enough to make informed decisions about becoming the subjects of research? Does the provision of parental or other legal consent for minors mean that assent is not also required from the girl or young woman? Under what circumstances are parents or legal guardians unlikely to decide in the best interests of girls and young women? A systematic review of ethical issues involved in researching young people, based on experience in the US, found that 'no simple generalisations can be made across research settings, across the developmental span or across children' (Stanley and Sieber, 1992: 3). The authors concluded that re-searchers must use their own judgment in resolving such issues.

Young women are in the process of making the many transitions that will ultimately bring them to adult status. The transitions, although often equated with physical maturation, are complex and multifaceted. The complexity is illustrated by the differing legal and social definitions of 'youth' which apply for different purposes. Young people are not considered 'adult' by the Australian government until they are over 25, at which point they become eligible for adult rates of income support, although there are no legal requirements for parents to support their children's education beyond the age of eighteen (Hartley and Wolcott, 1994). However, legally they achieve majority at sixteen (age of consent), and eighteen (for voting purposes). These legal and bureaucratic 'markers' of status provide a guide based on professional assessment of the ages at which young people are able to make decisions for themselves, and they serve to protect young people from exploitation and risk. The extent of youth homelessness, however, has highlighted the reality that many Australian youth are living independently of adult protection. Economically, socially and culturally, they make their own decisions and fend for themselves, regardless of the legal situation.

Recognising the power relations which position young women as vulnerable and marginal does not imply that they are seen as 'victims', or in the category of 'at risk'. Taking a perspective on young women which places their rights as a central concern moves beyond the language of victimisation to acknowledging that they have economic, cultural, civil and social rights as identified by the UN Conventions of the Rights of the Child (Brownell, 1989). It is also increasingly recognised that young women have a life of their own, a right to be protected from intrusion, and also a right to voice their concerns (White, 1994).

The research reported here addressed the issue of young women and sexually transmitted diseases and involved interviewing young women who, by the age of sixteen, had been living independently of their families in transient accommodation for a number of years. Most of them had left school early, after a series of unsatisfactory school experiences. As a consequence most were not able readers, so their assent had to be obtained by reading the consent form to them. Although care was taken to ensure that all who agreed to participate understood the basis and purpose of the research, differences among the young women themselves meant that this process did not strictly follow a standard procedure each time. Where possible, parental consent was obtained to interviewing the young women about their knowledge, beliefs and practices in relation to sexually transmitted diseases. Inevitably, some of the young women were interviewed without parental consent.

POWER RELATIONS

One of the dilemmas in researching vulnerable people whose status in society is marginal is that the research may be conducted in a way which reproduces their marginality. This is one of the most fundamental concerns of feminist methodology, and, given the more powerful location of the researcher, is difficult to resolve. The face-to-face issue of appearing powerful in the interview process is frequently resolved by using peer interviewers. Beasley (1993) suggests working with young women to conduct their own research on issues relevant to them. The more difficult issue is that of having power over the interview material. This is especially complex in the case of researching young women from a range of circumstances and backgrounds, because they do not form a collective or community with which the researcher can engage and negotiate. The use of a 'steering group' or of 'critical friends' provides the researcher with alternative points of view for interpreting the data, but raises the question of whether one group of young women may 'speak for' another group.

To engage the interests and concerns of young women, their ambiguous status needs to be recognised, balancing their rights to voice opinions, to make decisions and to be heard against their right to privacy and to protection from risk or harm. For the young women themselves, the interview offered a rare opportunity to give their views, to have them heard and to reflect on the issue of young women's access to health services. The views they offered were systematic, thoughtful and widely relevant to health promotion strategies. One of the conclusions drawn by the project was that 'health services seldom challenged the taken-for-granted assumptions about gender which limit the active participation of young women in these strategies. In some cases, medical practitioners actively reinforced the marginality of young women' (Wyn, 1994: 37). The doctor–patient relationship and confidentiality were two of the most significant areas of concern to these young women, whose opinions and experiences provided a striking illustration of the consequences of power relations on young women's health.

The publication and dissemination of the research findings raises a further ethical issue. Because young women do not constitute a 'community', traditional forms of research reporting (such as academic journals) make it unlikely that they will have access to the findings. The researcher is faced with the difficult decision of how to make research findings of this nature accessible to those who made the research possible, and to those whose professional practice will be informed by the findings. In the case of this project, a strategy of reaching different audiences was followed. The research findings were published in an accessible form in the youth centre's series of research reports and working papers, which reach a wide range of young people, health workers and educators (Wyn and Stewart, 1991; Wyn, 1993). They were also published in more academic journals which inform health policy and debate about youth (Wyn, 1991; 1994). In addition, where young women were interviewed with the cooperation of schools, the schools were provided with a summary of the main findings (in a form which protected the anonymity of their students). This strategy ensured that the findings of the project were distributed widely to professionals who are in a position to place young women's concerns more centrally within health practice.

The points raised with respect to young women making the transition to adulthood also have some relevance to those groups of women who are vulnerable or marginal during later transitions. During the transition to motherhood, however, women are older, some are more articulate and the research and ethical issues change in response.

WOMEN AND CHILDBIRTH: WORKING WITH COMMUNITY REPRESENTATIVES

Women during childbirth may be seen as vulnerable in their exposure to a technologically controlled birthing process, but not generally to such an extent that they cannot consent to participate in, and indeed, make a considerable personal contribution to, research into the process of child-birth. While there is no identifiable 'community' of women in the case of childbirth, many—perhaps most—of the studies conducted in this area have found self-help support and advocacy groups already existing. Some are long established, national and well known (for example, the Nursing Mothers' Association). Some have a broad focus, such as improving services for children with disabilities or lobbying in relation to the welfare of children in hospital, but it is probably more common for a group to be organised around a single health problem which constitutes a particular source of vulnerability for women. Examples would be the Post and Ante-natal Depression Association (PaNDA), the Sudden Infant Death Research Foundation (SIDRF) and IVF Friends.

The immediate advantage of such groups is that they have an immediate interest in the results of research and can play a central role in dissemi-nating the findings to their members. They also have the potential to be more intimately involved in the design and conduct of a study. As the following research examples indicate, this is not always a simple process. Differences of interpretation, including differences about the appropriate time for making research findings public and even about the nature of an ill-health experience, are difficult to predict. While community participation may produce a beneficial effect, researchers can therefore not assume that this will always be the case.

In a recent study, the Melbourne Centre for Mothers' and Children's Health agreed to participate with 'A', a well-established support, advocacy and fund-raising group, in a case-control study of the disorder which is its primary interest. 'A' employed the research assistant who worked at its headquarters and worked with its counselling team on the approach to parents. Her work was designed and supervised from the Centre. Relationships between all the parties to this arrangement were excellent. When one year of a planned three-year study had been completed, the research assistant prepared a report for the board of 'A' including an analysis of the data collected so far. The next event, from the Centre's perspective, was a series of telephone calls from local and interstate newspapers following up a press release put out by 'A' based on the interim data.

As academic researchers, we had taken-for-granted assumptions about the conduct of a scientific study which were not part of the beliefs and practices of the community organisation, including issues about publication of preliminary results, authorship and responsibility. We had not drawn up a formal contract, nor discussed this issue with 'A', and had failed to communicate any of the very real concerns we had about the interpretation of the findings at this preliminary stage. This underlines the point made by Ian Anderson that there should be explicit discussion at the beginning of a project about publication and ownership of a study but that the issues which arise in each research project are likely to be different.

Postnatal and antenatal depression are a significant source of concern for women during childbirth. A research project was developed to follow up women whose scores on a self-report scale eight to nine months after giving birth suggested they had a high probability of being depressed, along with a group whose scores on the same instrument suggested that almost none of them were likely to be depressed. The intention was to interview the women twelve to eighteen months after the original contact in order to explore their experiences of being a mother, their physical health and emotional well-being, the social and instrumental support available to them, their own family history, work, leisure and 'time out'. The other aspect of the study was to ask women in both groups about their experiences of depression after giving birth, their views about contributing factors, and the help they had sought and received, and to assess their emotional well-being using the same scale as at eight to nine months.

The self-help and advocacy group 'B' accepted the invitation to join a reference group at the stage when we were designing the interview schedule. 'B' was very helpful over issues such as the training of the research team and the timing of the interview. The draft interview was piloted with members of 'B', all of whom had children around two years of age and all of whom had recovered from a depressive illness after birth. The final interview schedule was developed after comment from all reference group members, and the interviewer was given feedback about the nature and style of her approach.

'B' was dissatisfied with the final interview schedule, insisting on the inclusion of a large series of questions about women's experiences of premenstrual tension over their whole reproductive life. Despite detailed discussion about problems with the format and content of the questions and the difficulties of definition and more, the organisation withdrew from the study. The source of these difficulties was a substantial difference in interpretation. The self-help group was committed to a primarily biological view of depression and a particular biological view of 'postnatal depression'. The researchers were more interested in longer-term problems of the wider family and in the social context of women's emotional well-being. These differences of opinion had never been discussed explicitly within the reference group. Nor had we stated explicitly that the final responsibility for the project, and therefore the final decisions about how it would be carried out, lay with the research team.

The third, ongoing example of working with self-help, advocacy and support groups provides a contrast. The research project dealt with the long-term health effects on women of assisted conception, in particular the possibility that certain treatments might increase the risk of cancer. Its reference group had been established with more awareness of the need to have explicit agreements about roles and responsibilities from the beginning. The patient support group 'C' was a key part of the reference group and from the beginning one of its primary concerns has been the fear that public discussion of this question might harm the assisted reproduction programs.

More recently, as the reference group has continued to meet, the representative from 'C' has moved from a protective attitude towards the program towards a very firm stance about the responsibilities of program management to answer the queries or concerns which former patients of the program will have once the results of the study are published. In fact, providing a forum for all stakeholders to discuss the implications of the study, on a number of occasions, before there are any findings has done exactly what we had hoped a reference group might do: that is, contribute to a relationship between the participants which has enhanced understanding and promoted appropriate action.

These different experiences were difficult to predict. Having 'learned the hard way', we remain committed to the involvement of women themselves in the process of research, from the planning phase through to the final feedback of results. We now define the role of the reference group as follows:

> Each reference group acts in an advisory capacity to the research team, contributing ideas and advice at all stages of the research process, though responsibility for the conduct of the research, its analysis and publication rests with the researchers. Working with reference groups is an important way of receiving valuable input from a wide range of service providers, consumers and researchers and a way of facilitating discussion of our research aims and findings in practice settings.

However, it is clear from the experiences described above that each project will be embedded in different circumstances and processes in which the balancing of different and at times conflicting aims will be determined. The following discussion offers a view of the issues involved in this 'balancing act' in relation to health research on the experiences of women involved in the transition of menopause.

MENOPAUSE: WOMEN'S VIEWS VS MEDICAL NEEDS

While there is little in the way of community organisation around menopause, the health of women in midlife is of immediate concern for such women, especially those experiencing distressing health problems. Menopause is also of considerable interest to the medical profession, to which women commonly turn for help. Researchers can therefore be seen as having to address the needs of two 'communities': the 'community' of women undergoing a social and physical transition, some, but not all, of whom are vulnerable and marginal; and the medical profession, a highly organised and powerful community with clear parameters for judging which research has met its criteria of usefulness—these mostly involve publication in peer-reviewed, (preferably) medical, (preferably) international journals. Especially in the absence of community organisations, it would be all too easy to let the medical agenda predominate. This would substantially alter the research process and obscure one of the most important aspects of menopause research: the diversity of experience.

MENOPAUSE AND COMPLEXITY

Interviews conducted with 150 women showed that the experience of menopause is an extremely difficult one to represent in a way which does justice to the variety of the experience and the many contributing factors (Daly, 1994). Thus the first need is to do away with the stereotype of the 'menopausal woman' as necessarily vulnerable and marginal.

Some women in midlife glide their way through these years; most experience problems of one sort or another (the list is long) but manage to battle their way through; others again experience such difficulties that they feel unable to cope, even attempting suicide (Daly, forthcoming). In explaining these different experiences, we took account of the contribution to the women's experience of changes in their own physiology and in their family dynamics. At the same time, the options available to women are very dependent on their social and economic situations, and cultural attitudes to menopause vary enormously. While there is a web of these and other factors contributing to women's experiences of midlife, they are not able to be defined in any consistent manner. Thus, an extremely distressing experience may be attributed to one overwhelming problem or to the interplay among a number of things going wrong all at the same time. Women's distress may vary markedly over time or may be relatively unchanging for many years.

What emerges is a description of menopause which more closely resembles an impressionist painting than a scientific study. There are a number of sources of opposition to the representation of this complexity.

Researchers from the biomedical disciplines working in the area have viewed with scepticism the diversity of experience we found. They point to the fact that we used a volunteer sample likely to contain a preponderance of women with problems of various kinds. Moreover, the low-key, supportive manner in which the interviews were conducted would, they thought, *elicit* complaints. This problem could be avoided by a carefully constructed questionnaire which limited the range of responses to those seen as most relevant to the identification and treatment of the problems of menopause. Subtly, such arguments shift the research focus away from representing and understanding the rich complexity of women's experience towards a simplified *average* experience in which the good experience and the bad experience are conflated to produce a stereotypical 'menopausal woman' with 'symptoms' which cannot be explained except on the basis of biological change. 'Capturing' a random sample and extracting data about sensitive and controversial topics does, however, also raise issues of ethics discussed by a number of other authors in this volume.

An unstructured format and volunteer sample certainly placed limits on the study. We accepted that some women would not want to be interviewed and that there were issues some women would prefer not to discuss. Only about one-third of our participants took the initiative in discussing issues of sexuality or responded to the initiative of another woman in the group. We could, however, experiment with different ways of introducing the subject, an option not open to researchers using a standardised questionnaire. Instead of phrasing questions in the way commonly used in such questionnaires—'How often do you have penetrative sex?', for example—we could vary the questions to take account of who the women were. Thus, when we interviewed Catholic religious sisters, we were free to ask a more general question: 'What importance does sexuality have for you in your life?' This more flexible approach elicited valuable observations on the range of importance and meaning attached to the notion of sexuality, a result we had not anticipated.

Because we used an unstructured format, we do not know the extent to which our results are generalisable to midlife women as a whole. This meant that we had to set up close links with researchers conducting large surveys in the area so that the finely detailed knowledge we gained could be located within an overview of the experience of 'subgroups' of women defined by demographic and health variables.

MEETING MEDICAL NEEDS

In reporting a study of this kind, it is very difficult to meet the requirements of a medical journal. The methodological issues the study confronted are difficult and the results consist of analyses of sections of transcript which need to be quoted verbatim. Thus the word limit appropriate for studies based on standardised data is impossible to meet; nor could p-values be calculated to reassure the statistical reviewers to whom articles are commonly sent. The research method we saw as appropriate, and ethical, is so poorly understood in medical circles that reviewers used to assessing statistical niceties are almost certain to see the results as unscientific.

The main concern of the clinician is to enhance effective treatment. At present, in the view of the women we interviewed, medical treatment of the menopause is far from satisfactory. Thus women consult a range of practitioners, including natural therapists, and try a range of personal strategies for coping with midlife. These all have their successes and failures. Our conclusion, that these various attempts to 'help' midlife women should be coordinated, is not likely to meet with approval from medical practitioners focused on treatment of 'failing' endocrine glands. The study can therefore be faulted for failing to provide accessible insights into the treatment of the menopause for the medical profession.

MEETING WOMEN'S NEEDS

Many midlife women turn to medical journals for their information about menopause, but the wider needs of the 'community' are likely to be best served by less formal means of communicating results. During the course of the study, menopause was a topic of substantial media and popular interest. Informed of the study, the media provided a readily accessible way of communicating the results. The problems faced here, however, were similar to those raised by medical publication—the media wanted a succinct summary on 'treatment', and discussion of the complexities of the experience was not well received.

The lack of self-help groups in this area contributed to the difficulties of dissemination. On the other hand, public forums on menopause, in many cases run by women's health centres, are extremely well attended by midlife women and by sympathetic health professionals. These provided us with an opportunity to present our results and, at the same time, to seek comment on our findings. Women in isolated rural areas, where some of these forums have been held, are particularly appreciative of this form of dissemination and this offered the potential for changing community health practice in the area. Publication of the proceedings of these forums made our findings more widely available.

A DISSEMINATION STRATEGY

Providing feedback to groups of midlife women and their carers met with considerable success, but this process is very time consuming and will continue for many years after research funding has ceased. There is little allowance made for this as a professionally recognised form of dissemination, nor is it common for this longer-term strategy to be recognised in assessing the outcome of a research project.

The problem of satisfying the criteria for success in informing the medical profession remains unresolved. This will seriously jeopardise our future research funding.

CONCLUSION

In seeking to increase the visibility of women facing problems at various stages of life, the researcher confronts interwoven ethical and methodological issues. These issues cannot be resolved simply by the application of general rules; instead, they have to be resolved according to specific circumstances, depending on the judgment of the researcher. The researcher has to make informed decisions based on sound methodology, an assessment of the general principles of ethics, and the way in which these ethics play out in the context of the research being conducted. Central to our concerns as women has been our responsibility as researchers to the formal and informal communities of women who participate in our research and who are the primary consumers of our research findings. A key component in ensuring that our decisions are justifiable is public debate about both the research conducted and ethical problems associated with that research.

REFERENCES

Angus, G., and Wilkinson, K., 1993, *Child Abuse and Neglect, Australia, 1990–91,* Child Welfare Series no.2, Canberra: Australian Government Publishing Service.

Beasley, B, 1993, 'Young people researching their own cultures'. In R. White (ed.), *Youth Subcultures*, Tasmania: National Clearinghouse for Youth Studies.

Brown, S., Lumley, J., Small, R., Astbury, J., (eds), 1994, *Missing Voices: the experience of motherhood*, Melbourne: Oxford University Press.

Brownell, M., 1989, 'The impact of the new Convention of the Rights of the Child', *Youth Studies*, November: 48–53.

Coney, S., 1991, *The Menopause Industry: a guide to medicine's 'discovery' of the mid-life woman*, Auckland: Penguin.

Daly, J., 1994, 'Women's own voices: Pleasures and problems of menopause'. In R. Klein (ed.), *Menopause: the alternative way*, Geelong: Australian Women's Research Centre.

Daly, J., forthcoming, 'Caught in the web: The social construction of menopause as disease', *Journal of Reproductive and Infant Psychology*.

Griffin, C., 1985, *Typical Girls*, London: Routledge & Kegan Paul.

Hammer, J. and Maynard, M., 1987, *Women, Violence and Social Control*, London: Macmillan.

Hartley, R. and Wolcott, I., 1994, *The Position of Young People in Relation to the Family*, Tasmania: National Clearinghouse for Youth Studies.

Johnson, L., 1993, *The Modern Girl*, Sydney: Allen & Unwin.

Oakley, A., 1993, *Essays on Women, Medicine and Health*, Edinburgh: Edinburgh University Press.

Roberts, H. (ed.), 1981, *Doing Feminist Research*, London: Routledge.

Stanley, B. and Sieber, J., (eds), 1992, *Social Research on Children and Adolescents*, London: Sage.

White, R., 1994, 'Youth rights, social responsibility and the politics of denial', paper presented at Youth Affairs Conference, Brisbane, August.

Wilson, B. and Wyn, J., 1987, *Shaping Futures: youth action for livelihood*, Sydney: Allen & Unwin.

Wyn, J., 1991, 'Safe from attention: Young women, STDs and health policy', *Journal of Australian Studies*, 31, 94–107.

——1993, *Young Women's Health: the challenge of sexually transmitted diseases*, Research Report No 8, Youth Research Centre, University of Melbourne.

——1994, 'Young women and sexually transmitted diseases: The issues for public health', *Australian Journal of Public Health*, 18, 1: 32–39.

Wyn, J. and Stewart, F., 1991, *Young Women and Sexually Transmitted Diseases*, Working Paper no. 7, Youth Research Centre, The University of Melbourne.

17

Funding Health-Promoting Research: A Consumer Perspective

Rhonda Galbally

It is now generally recognised that the standard of health care is improved if consumers are allowed to have a say in decisions about their own health and treatment, and to have input into decisions about priorities and the allocation of resources. Some work has been done towards bringing consumers into the system, at both the individual and the community level. Australia's National Health Strategy (1993) recommends that areas and services should establish consumer advisory bodies to represent populations within the community, and that states and regions should resource self-help and community groups. Further, in response to this strategy, a national charter of health consumer rights has been established. The Australian National Consumer Affairs Advisory Council (1992) has argued strongly that the inclusion of consumer views be recognised by expert professionals and budget administrators. At the same time there is a growing emphasis on the need to ensure equity by the representation of disadvantaged groups on decision-making bodies, including ethics committees for health-care research.

These recommendations and consequent actions are certainly essential for the efficient provision of health care. However, if disadvantaged consumer groups gain representation on a range of bodies only to lobby for an increased share of available health resources, this is not enough. The benefits from a basic re-evaluation of the purpose of health care will fail to be realised. It is in this re-evaluation that key ethical issues emerge for health care and research.

RE-EVALUATING THE CURRENT PARADIGM

The first ethical issue to tackle is the way in which the dominant health paradigm reflects the cultural phenomena of valuing the 'body beautiful'. The creation of a body as close to 'perfect' as possible is a preoccupation pervading health care and setting much of the direction for health-care research. By contrast, health consumers, especially if disabled, chronically ill or ageing, live with the reality that their bodies are not perfect in a stereotypical sense and that no amount of medical intervention will make them so. These contrasting realities are reinforced by advertising, marketing and the media. There is a significant ethical concern implicit in decision-making which continues to fund research and health care that promotes this paradigm. Moreover, there is a certain futility in the enterprise of health-care research that fundamentally seeks to transform the bodies of individuals when, in the future, the number of people with disabilities and chronic conditions will significantly increase.

A similar contradiction exists within the culture of research and intervention for disease prevention. Attempts to transform behaviour, as though the behaviour of health consumers were abnormal or bad, deny the underlying causes of that behaviour as it relates to self-concept and self-esteem. For instance, the fact that one-third of young women are depressed bears a strong relationship to high-risk behaviours such as smoking, binge drinking, eating disorders, unsafe sex, and withdrawal from physical exercise (Vale, 1993). There are, then, ethical issues involved in funding research programs based on a single risk factor, often at the expense of research based on a more complex (but difficult to design) approach to the problem.

Attempts to 'normalise' bodies or behaviour also run a risk of creating other debilitating diseases. For example, obesity puts people at greater risk of such ailments as cardiovascular disease, diabetes and hypertension. However, health promotion programs focusing on obesity as a bad behaviour will fail and at the same time create a further risk. Such a focus reinforces low self-esteem which, in turn, can be seen as contributing significantly to conditions such as eating disorders and other mental illness (Galbally, 1993).

Thus the funding of programs focused on single issues such as obesity, without first funding research into the possible harm done by such campaigns, could be seen as unethical.

A second feature of the dominant health paradigm is the goal of postponement of death. This goal leads to a skewing of resources towards research on acute and expensive care, as well as on the prevention of diseases with high mortality in old age, which could be seen as unethical. Not only is this a waste of health-care resources but it has a pathological effect on society:

> People in the Western world have great difficulty in accepting the reality that we may get old, sick, disabled and die. We think of all those things as happening to someone else, and in all those denials we deplete ourselves of

Figure 4 Focus on obesity: a risk factor

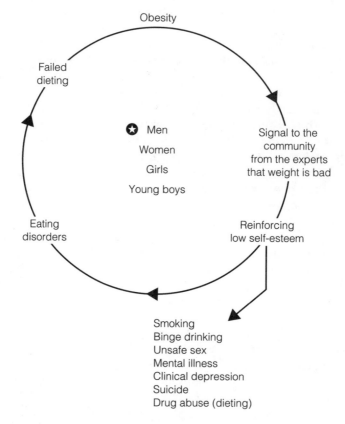

the very resources to deal with our own inevitable fallibility. And as long as we deny such vulnerability in ourselves, we will never be able to accept the disease and disability in others. (Zola, 1982: 12)

A NEW PARADIGM

An alternative health paradigm for a country with relatively high life expectancy is to accept the inevitability of age, declining function and ultimately death on a population-wide basis, and to use resources to ensure that people can live full, high-quality lives without having to endure endless, often unsuccessful attempts to 'cure' disease. This goal would require significant reallocation of funding.

However, within relatively affluent countries with high life expectancy, there are groups such as Aborigines who have a significantly lower than average life expectancy. The Australian Institute of Health and Welfare (1994: 28) states: 'The average life expectancy of a newborn Aboriginal boy is, depending on where he lives, up to 18.2 years shorter than [that of] his non-Aboriginal counterpart; the gap is up to 19.8 years for an Aboriginal girl.' From an ethical point of view this problem requires urgent attention and resources.

As a significant issue of ethics, in developing countries and Aboriginal communities alike, the emphasis of resource allocation must be on health promotion, prevention and primary health care. However, the state of all health, but especially Aboriginal health, must be analysed within the wider social, cultural and political context, as was recognised by the Royal Commission into Aboriginal Deaths in Custody (1991: 15):

> The contemporary situation of social disadvantage experienced by Australia's Aboriginal communities can only be understood in the light of their historical experience of dispossession, dislocation, disease, disemployment and the disabling consequences of these for community and family life.

It follows that risk behaviour cannot be understood in isolation from this wider context. Young people are said to take risks because they are young, or because their peers take risks, or because their parents provide bad role models. What remains unanswered is the fundamental question about risk-taking in relationship to young people's view of themselves, their future, their family, their self-esteem, that is, the deeper social, cultural and psychological context. A focus on mortality, morbidity and risk behaviour further excludes social factors such as educational status, employment status, income level, race, gender and age, as well as the significant impact of psychosocial factors on mental health, and the relationship of mental health status to total health status. The new paradigm, from a health-care consumer perspective, will therefore emphasise the 'whole' health status of specific population groups and see this as an ethical issue not only for health care but for health research funding.

Without this shift in emphasis to a concern for all the factors contributing to the health status of population groups, the interests of the health consumer will not be fulfilled. Health care itself will be inefficient and ineffective if the emphasis remains on risk factors, or parts of bodies, rather than on population groups. However, an emphasis on health promotion in itself requires a significant further paradigm shift. A characteristic of the health consumer movement is that, in general, it emphasises trying to ensure that the health-care system treats people with equity, dignity and appropriateness. What the health consumer movement has not tackled is the fundamental need to change the goal of the system itself. Changing the goal from one that promotes normal bodies and postpones death to one that promotes health also means disengaging people's need for the health-care system as such. In research this might mean that, for instance, measures of consumer attitudes such as patient satisfaction will need to be carefully designed so that they shift from being measures of dependency, a characteristic of the old paradigm, to being positive measures of independence from the health-care system. Research funding decisions can encourage this shift.

Analysis of the impact of the health-care system on the health of the consumer shows that many changes would be achieved if the fundamental assumptions of the dominant paradigm were different. When the aim of health care and the research behind it is no longer to 'normalise' bodies, we will cease isolating people from society for health care. For instance, institutionalisation or long-term hospitalisation for disabled or chronically ill people is premised on the desirability of using every medical means possible to promote normality and, with this emphasis, making the body much more significant than social, educational, or cultural issues as they affect the person. An emphasis on physical well-being requires the acknowledgment that health care and treatment are sometimes of less importance than psychological, educational or social factors (Galbally, 1992). Indeed, the chance of a good health outcome is increased by improvement in social and education status (Zola, 1983). Research which explores this shift in emphasis is urgently needed.

A CONSUMER HEALTH PARADIGM

Changing the paradigm for health care requires the transformation of health-professional research, education and training so that consumers are not used as objects. The current practice of displaying young children with medical conditions in front of students is shaming. It reduces a young child's capacity to differentiate between the invasion experienced within the health-care system and invasion as an aspect of abuse experienced in the community. The significantly higher rates of child abuse, including sexual abuse, experienced by children with disabilities and chronic illness in part relate to the destruction of natural modesty barriers by the health-care system in its focus on the child as an object for the purposes of health care and health-care research, as well as for the purpose of health-professional education (Temkin, 1994). The ethics implicit in such an approach must become of significant concern and should be reflected in funding decisions. Paradigmatic change for research and health care would also mean that people with disabilities or unhealthy behaviours were no longer labelled by their condition—'cerebral-palsied', 'obese', or 'a drinker'. Every time a label is applied, the humanity of the person is denied, self-esteem is assaulted, and inevitably the effectiveness of the health-care or disease prevention intervention will decline. Such an understanding should be reflected in funding decisions.

Both research and practice should recognise consumer involvement. There is no medical solution for many of the conditions with which people must live, but there are often a number of equally valuable treatment options from which consumers can select. It is therefore very important that the relationships between the researcher, provider and the consumer not only become more equal in power, but also reflect a mutuality of purpose—a joint attempt to open up the possibility of living life as fully and productively as possible. This means that the wisdom and instincts of consumers themselves and of their families must be given much more credence both in research and in health care. One way of effecting this change is to make medical records available to be annotated by the consumer.

At the same time, within the new paradigm, health care would take as a paramount goal the promotion of resilience (Rutter, 1987). It would be a significant indication of a paradigm shift if more research were focused on understanding how people survive with reasonable health under very adverse situations. We must learn more about the strengths, coping mechanisms, adaptation possibilities and resistance capacities of individuals, groups, families and communities. This provides an extensive research agenda.

A paradigmatic shift away from a focus on the individual and towards integrating the community will require research into organisational health so that every organisation in the health-care system becomes healthy in itself. This means that hospitals, medical and nursing schools, and primary care organisations such as community health centres, general practice and research institutions will become healthy organisations unashamedly promoting compassion, empathy and respect as primary values for the workforce, researchers and consumers. Programs devoted to these goals should be extended to all key settings in which consumers live, including the home, the family, workplaces, and schools. The impact of healthy or sick organisations on the health or sickness of individuals must become a key consideration in health care but also in professional training and research.

Health research and health care will require a new emphasis on the prevention of iatrogenesis. That disease can be created by contact with the health-care system is well known and identifiable via measures such as cross-infection and readmission rates (D'Arcy and Griffin, 1982). Examples of illness being created by health care include medical students and even medical practitioners interviewing patients in ways that increase anxiety or depression; the rapid turnover of psychiatric registrars so that psychiatric patients have no long-term contact with them, a practice known to have a negative impact on recovery rates; and adverse drug reactions, especially in the mental health area. In the interests of health consumers, iatrogenesis must become a top priority for research and prevention.

CONCLUSION

The new consumer health paradigm requires changes to the way in which health care is practised but also to the kind of research programs which are funded. The goal should be to ensure that the quality of life of all people, including those who are chronically ill and disabled, is as positive and productive as possible. Such issues of ethics should be made explicit in funding decisions, perhaps by subjecting all research proposals to an ethics impact analysis as follows:

AN ETHICS IMPACT ANALYSIS FOR RESEARCH AND HEALTH CARE

Do the research and health care harm people? Do they:

- contribute to isolation from society?
- treat people as objects, reinforcing shame, stigma and discrimination?
- increase exposure to invasion and abuse?
- reduce income-generating opportunities, education and training?

Do the research and health care strengthen people? Do they contribute to people:

- having higher self-esteem?
- becoming more resilient?
- trusting their own judgment and making informed choices (as opposed to giving informed consent)?
- living successfully in the community?

Do the research and health care open up systems of power? Do they:

- enhance the organisational health of health-care organisations and/or other settings in which consumers live, are educated and work?
- contribute to equity in access?
- contribute to a capacity for self-advocacy and advocacy by consumer, community and self-help groups?

REFERENCES

Australian Institute of Health and Welfare, 1994, *Australia's Health 1994*, Canberra: Australian Institute of Health and Welfare.

D'Arcy, P., and Griffin, J., 1982, *Iatrogenic Disease*, Oxford: Oxford University Press.

Dean, K., and Hancock, T., 1992 *Supportive Environments for Health*, Copenhagen: World Health Organisation.

Galbally, R., 1993, 'Prevention creating harm: How can we prevent a focus on obesity becoming a serious risk factor for other diseases', paper delivered at Australian Society for the Study of Obesity Conference, Melbourne.

Galbally, R., 1992, 'Does the health care system handicap young people with a disability?' Address to Australian Rotary Health Research Fund Conference, Canberra.

National Health Strategy, 1993, *Healthy Participation*, Canberra: National Health Strategy.

National Consumer Affairs Advisory Council, 1992, *How We Feel*, Canberra: Australian Government Publishing Service.

Oliver, M., 1984, 'The politics of disability', *Critical Social Policy*, 4, 2, 21–32.

Royal Commission into Aboriginal Deaths in Custody, 1991, *Report*, Canberra: Australian Government Publishing Service.

Rutter, M., 1987, 'Psychosocial resilience in protective mechanisms', *American Journal of Orthopsychiatry*, 57, 3, 316–31.

Temkin, J., 1994, 'Disability, child abuse, and criminal justice', *Modern Law Review*, 57, 3, 402–18

Vale, S., 1993, 'Teenage blues can often last for a lifetime', *Australian Doctor*, 30 April: 1.

Zola, I., 1982, *Ordinary Lives*, Cambridge: Applewood Books.

——1983, 'Towards independent living: Goals and dilemmas'. In I. Crewe and I. Zola, *Independent Living for Physically Disabled People*, San Francisco: Jossey Bass.

PART V

THE CLINICIANS' VIEW OF RESEARCH

While biomedical research solves some of the problems which arise in clinical practice, it falls to the practising clinician to put this research into practice in the clinic. Ian McDonald, in introducing this section, argues that clinical practice raises additional problems of research which are not addressed by the 'basic' sciences. Since clinicians are the best qualified to put into place those research projects which address the various problems arising in clinical practice, he sees it as their ethical duty to engage in 'research at the coal face'.

Alvan Feinstein believes passionately that clinicians should devise their own research procedures, not relying on methods and models devised by researchers in other fields. His view is that trust in mathematical models has impoverished research into clinical care with the result that it has now become of limited use in informing clinicians. While he is not prepared to see 'bad' research as involving issues of ethics, he believes that harm is being done to research, and to medical care, by a too-strong reliance on methods which purport to belong to the 'basic' sciences.

Howard Waitzkin addresses one of the most difficult problems encountered in clinical care and research into clinical care: that of helping patients to deal with problems which arise in their social contexts rather than in biological dysfunction. Clinicians often feel powerless to help patients confront these problems, which are seldom the focus of their research. Waitzkin describes the ethical and methodological considerations in conducting research into psychosocial issues in consultations with older people.

Peter Mudge focuses on the problems of conducting research in general practice. He argues that the clinical setting requires a flexible response to ethical problems encountered in 'clinical reality'. Similarly, in conducting research, a flexible approach is needed if we are to address traditional ethical issues like the doctor–patient relationship (including issues of patient autonomy vs physician responsibility), setting limits to life-sustaining treatment, and the allocation of health resources. These judgmental skills, appropriate to clinical care and to research, should be taught 'at the bedside' and in formal medical education. Mudge then addresses the problems encountered by a funding body dedicated to the promotion of general practice in Australia.

18

CLINICIANS STUDYING THEIR OWN PRACTICE: AN INTRODUCTION

Ian McDonald

Every clinical consultation touches on issues which could be of ethical concern. The same is true for clinical research. The need for moral probity in our dealings with patients in the setting of either treatment or research is obvious. Not so obvious is the collective moral obligation on clinicians to become critics and students of medical care. An important reason is that, under the current paradigm, 'clinical research' is tacitly defined as biomedical research undertaken in the clinical setting, and has not been taken to include the investigation of the processes and outcomes of clinical care itself. Implicit is the idea that clinical practice itself is not a subject suitable for academic study. This in itself tends to discourage clinicians from undertaking any form of critical academic appraisal of their day-to-day patient care activities. This is a remarkable example of ideological blinkering. The study of clinical practice is the very area of research in which the physician's insight and understanding are indispensable.

Only with the active participation of clinicians can the process of health-care reform systematically address those issues with respect to which modern medicine has been sharply criticised—reliance on technical decisions which lack scientific rigour, failure to communicate adequately with patients and inability to respond empathically to illness. With the best will in the world, the quality of patient care will not improve without research by doctors at the clinical coalface. Hence doctors owe it to their patients, and to the community in general, to participate in the empirical enquiry needed to improve the art and the science of clinical care. Moreover, in the modern state, medicine is no longer an island; it is linked more and more closely to the broader system of health-care delivery and to a web of political influences. Hence the clinician's responsibilities extend beyond the individual patient.

The medical profession is subjected to outside scrutiny and control as never before. In the interests of patients and in their own best interests, clinicians are now obliged to shoulder an unfamiliar responsibility. They must themselves cultivate a deep understanding of clinical care and its outcomes. Only then can they take part in the wider community debate over health and act as watchdogs to ensure that a bureaucratic agenda committed to cost constraint and regulation does not distort clinical objectives. This becomes more urgent as health funding is squeezed and the impact on quality of care becomes a political issue. Measures to improve the quality of clinical care in the long term will not be as readily achievable as those which simply 'reduce patient activity', or which cut corners and increase risk in a subtle way by piecemeal reduction of the quality of care and limitation of access to it. Clinical researchers today have an ethical responsibility to protect patients from potentially damaging cost constraints by studying and disclosing any adverse impact on patient care. Especially in the case of clinical medicine, with its focus on the individual, the clinician researcher may thereby be drawn into conflict with the public health profession or with government.

THE CLINICIAN AS STUDENT OF CLINICAL PRACTICE

It is up to some of the more academically oriented clinicians to take up the challenge of developing the methods, and of honing and applying the skills needed to subject clinical practice to scholarly intellectual inquiry. Research in clinical epidemiology provides data which contributes to the quality of technical aspects of clinical decision-making related to medical interventions. For example, the efficacy and risks of a new surgical technique, such as laparoscopic cholecystectomy (endoscopic removal of the gall bladder through a small incision) can be evaluated. Some clinicians already have the necessary epidemiological training to do research of this kind and to apply the results in their practices. Modern developments in information technology mean that this kind of information can now be made available to the clinician at the bedside via a computer terminal. Hence, for difficult decisions, the clinician has rapid access to relevant medical literature. This approach to clinical care, which emphasises efficient bedside retrieval of technical knowledge and its on-line application to clinical decisions, is known as evidence-based medicine (Anon., 1992).

Even those clinicians who clearly see the need for research and practice bolstered by clinical epidemiology, and perhaps by health economics and behavioural science, do not usually see the need to apply the knowledge and skills of sociology, of anthropology and of the humanities (for example, of ethics and epistemology) to similarly augment research into, and practice of, the art of medicine. What is required is that clinicians contribute their unique clinical perspective while taking advantage of concepts and skill derived from multidisciplinary cooperation involving all of these intellectual modalities. Many more doctors will then be able to cooperate in such activities as quality assurance or the evaluation of medical technology, or with an anthropological study of cultural factors influencing patient behaviour. Hopefully, all practitioners will be stimulated to reflect about what they do and remain open to suggestions for improvement. This new kind of clinical research is in its infancy. I will therefore briefly review its evolution so far, which has been in the form of rather fragmented responses. First we consider the historical evolution of the role of the specialist in internal medicine, the physician. This was the model, in turn, for the roles of the modern surgeon and general practitioner. This is necessary if we are to understand current attitudes, misunderstandings between disciplines and sometimes resistance to change.

THE EVOLUTION OF THE SPECIALIST PHYSICIAN

The pre-modern practitioner of physick was a university-educated 'Latined man', skilled in the supportive management of illness, cast in the mould of the Pythagorean gentleman (Jacob, 1987: 43–4), a tradition revived at the time of the Renaissance by Thomas Linacre, founder of the Royal College of Physicians of London (Jacob, 1987: 93). Such physicians subscribed to the ancient Hippocratic ethics of practice and adhered to the notion of fraternity which fostered apprenticeship medical education. Their training in the *litterae humaniores* was supposed to foster a humanistic outlook which included a sense of public responsibility (Jacob, 1987: 103). They were, of course, always a tiny minority among healers, their services unavailable to the bulk of the population—which might have been just as well in light of the blood-letting, puking and purging they purveyed!

The modern doctor has inherited problems and responsibilities which transcend those of the relatively impotent Hippocratic practitioner. The capacity of many modern therapies for iatrogenesis matches their potency for relief and cure. Illich (1976) highlighted the problem of iatrogenic harm from technical intervention, and broadened the definition to encompass what he called 'social' and 'cultural' iatrogenesis, metaphors respectively for the medicalisation of society (Zola, 1975) and for professional dominance (Freidson, 1970). What he did not emphasise was the serious mismatch between the modern doctor's training to treat disease and the problems presented, especially in ambulant care and the out-patient department, which form the bulk of medical practice. This is where most of the problems of unsatisfactory and costly medical care are to be found. This is where there is most need for clinical scholarship.

UNCERTAINTY AND INEFFICIENCY IN CLINICAL PRACTICE

Clinical medicine remains in large measure a craft skill. Certain knowledge, the *scientia* of the ancient world, is in short supply; uncertain knowledge, *opinio*, is the rule. Judgment and decision incorporate a substantial element of discretion. The decisions of the doctor, and those of the patient in seeking help, are subject to a wide variety of personal, social and cultural influences, motivations and interests. Action is rarely determined solely by a clear-cut appeal to cause and effect and recourse to technical intervention. First and foremost there is the need to distinguish between those people with organic diseases who can benefit from this powerful medicine and those whose primary problem is that they are anxious, depressed, sick at heart and socially disadvantaged, and those who are hypochondriacal or communicate their distress in the language of symptoms. What they do not need is an unnecessary electrocardiogram which yields a doubtful result or an inappropriate intervention such as coronary balloon angioplasty, which may do worse. Inconclusive or false-positive results can create doubt and anxiety as a threat to the quality of life, and unwarranted intervention can compound the problem. The nature and aetiology of illness are complex, and the doctor whose training has strongly emphasised biomedicine often has difficulty understanding the patient's perspective sufficiently to communicate the implications of illness or even to accept the need to do so (Toombs, 1992). Failure of the consultation as a social transaction is common and serious. It breeds patient dissatisfaction and courts lack of cooperation with treatment.

Arguably the commonest single medical negotiation of all, the attempt to reassure the worried patient with no demonstrable disease, often founders in the face of the patient's persistent doubts and misunderstandings, leaving a legacy of continuing medical consultations and repeated investigation (Daly and McDonald, 1993). A relentless search for non-existent organic disease is, of itself, fraught with an unavoidable statistical risk of diagnostic error, which can seriously compound the situation. All of this can add up to a substantial impairment of quality of life and to indirect costs which have never been factored into economic evaluations. And this risk is a cumulative one, since most people visit their doctor at least once each year and, on average, many times. The result of all this doubt and misjudgment is much harm, wasted effort and squandering of scarce resources. To add to these uncertainties facing doctors in clinical practice, a shifting culture has obliged them to adapt to a new emphasis on the autonomy and rights of the individual and on the ethical and legal issue of informed consent. Underneath runs a current of complaint about lack of humanism in medicine and about neglect of the psychosocial dimension of the clinical consultation, objection to what Katz (1984) refers to as 'the silent world of doctor and patient'. Not surprisingly then, there is pressure on the profession to recapture what are seen as the old skills of communication and empathy and to refine them in the light of the insights of the social sciences and humanities.

THE NEED FOR GRASS-ROOTS CLINICAL RESEARCH

Doctors could surely be persuaded that they have a responsibility as professionals to work to correct such problems. At the same time, however, we have to recognise its full extent. What is ultimately needed goes far beyond mere patch-up reforms. Major reform will require the emergence of a new paradigm, a new definition of health and perspective on health care, a fresh approach to clinical care, to medical education and to research. A quick look at the previous paradigm shift from the traditional to the modern scientific provides some insight into how difficult it is to implement major change in a community institution with ancient traditions. Until quite recently, the idea that the concepts and methods of epidemiology and of the social sciences should or could be applied to promote better understanding of what doctors and patients were doing, simply did not obtrude on medical consciousness.

At the end of the eighteenth-century Enlightenment, at the time of the French Revolution, science first impacted on clinical practice, mounting a radical challenge to the basic assumptions about the nature of disease upon which clinical techniques of diagnosis and treatment had rested for thousands of years (Foucault, 1973). The story of the subsequent rise of scientific medicine is generally well known. What is not generally appreciated is that the traditional Hippocratic clinical techniques of patient interview and physical examination, and subsequently even the deployment of modern investigations, have managed to elude the scrutiny of modern science. Yet even a cursory inspection of current textbooks of clinical examination reveals that diagnosis, as taught to medical students, remains in a nineteenth-century time warp. It is a curious mixture of sound empirical description, traditional belief and eponym garnished with a little biomedical understanding. It is almost entirely innocent of scientific scepticism, statistical rigour, psychological insight or understanding of the social context of illness.

THE SCIENTIFIC EVALUATION OF HEALTH CARE

In the late twentieth century, this lack of scholarly rigour with respect to clinical practice is surprising. In France, early in the nineteenth century, C.-P. A. Louis was already aware of the importance of documenting and counting empirical clinical observations (Faber, 1923: 39–43), and the basic concepts of inductive probability and statistics had also been applied to understanding the nature of illness and to the analysis of its clinical manifestations (Gutting, 1989: 122–4). But these ideas were virtually stillborn. In the early part of this century, management science evolved as the application of scientific principles to industrial organisation, but there has been no counterpart in medical practice. The medical fraternity had to wait until the 1960s for the rebirth of the idea that clinicians could make a scholarly study of what clinicians do, a radical thought attributable to Alvan Feinstein. He showed the relevance of the New Math and of the principles of probability to clinical diagnosis and choice of treatment (Feinstein, 1963; 1967), made a plea for the scientific definition of clinical concepts (Feinstein, 1987), and by showing how the quantitative methods of epidemiology could be applied to clinical decision-making, he became the founding figure of clinical epidemiology. Thus, it was a clinician who initiated a grass-roots critique of clinical care. Widespread recognition of its importance has come slowly, and, as Feinstein himself warns in this volume, the clinical epidemiology movement has been marred by excessive reverence for the certainty of mathematics, which has led to simple-minded attempts to directly apply the mathematical concepts of other disciplines, such as Bayesian probability, to the problems of clinical care.

While clinical doctors have, in the main, been twiddling their thumbs regarding the quality of medical care, governments and public health departments have moved to plug the gap by studying health from a political and bureaucratic perspective. In Britain, after the Second World War, Morris applied the concept of operations research and the methods of epidemiology to the study of health services (Morris, 1957), Hill introduced the randomised controlled trial as a method of drug evaluation (Hill, 1937), and Cochrane championed the widespread application of trials as an evaluative tool (Cochrane, 1971). In the United States, health services research appeared later, and in fragmented form. 'Health program evaluation' was a reflection of a more general concern that social institutions be more accountable, 'medical technology assessment' of apprehension about rising cost of intervention and, most recently, 'health outcomes research' was a response to a recognition of serious shortcomings of the way diagnostic and therapeutic interventions are deployed in clinical practice. The initial emphasis of such health-care evaluation on epidemiological methods has been challenged by economics and management science perspectives. This 'top-down' scrutiny has been driven by a political agenda which strongly emphasises cost constraint. Obviously sociology and anthropology should play major roles in the study of the interaction between doctor and patient and of the importance of social factors in illness. Yet the research interests of sociology took little or no account of medicine and health until after the Second World War (Gerhardt, 1987), and most research since then has been academic rather than grounded in the realities of clinical practice.

THE CLINICIAN AS ADVOCATE FOR COMMUNITY AND PATIENT

The clinician's ethical responsibility to practise efficiently in the modern era, to deploy technology skilfully and wisely, to communicate better with patients and to support them seems straightforward. Doctors also owe it to their patients to reflect on their actions with the objective of doing better. Here the physician can no longer rely solely on intuition, on practical experience and on traditional medical socialisation. The profession therefore has a duty to encourage clinicians to undertake formal study of their own practice, and to participate in research with the aim of improving it. The practising doctor may also be called upon to take on a role as advocate for the patient and profession during this era of reform. Governments, during a period of economic recession, have had to tread a narrow path between socialist ideals on the one hand and the forces of liberalism and economic rationalism on the other. Hence they have become highly sensitive to any escalation of either the cost of welfare or the cost of health care. Any political interest in patient welfare is related to the extent that quality of care surfaces as a political issue, as it has done with the introduction of cost containment measures which reduce length of stay in hospital. It is this preoccupation with cost which has brought the economist into the game to provide an apparently objective basis for the allocation of scarce resources.

Few would deny that health care has been profligate, and that there is a need for containment of costs. The incentives and objectives of public health departments, the health-care bureaucracy, management and administration must, at times, inevitably be in tension with those of clinicians and patients, who will promote the point of view of the individual. Indeed, doctors will have to stay constantly alert to the possibility of distorting influences on patient care. Financial exigencies can cause the objectives of bureaucrats and administrators to diverge from those of patients and of doctors, and the perspectives of epidemiologist and economist often fail to jibe with those of clinicians. The clear responsibility on doctors is therefore to defend the legitimate interests of the community and of their profession against such distortion. An important part of the clinician's moral obligation is to balance the bureaucratic 'top-down' perspective with grass-roots 'bottom-up' clinical input.

The assumption by doctors of a broader community responsibility implies more than cooperation with health services research. It also means initiating research, bringing to it the knowledge needed to frame the questions and interpret the clinical implications of results, and providing the experience to overcome practical constraints. The clinician-researcher has an obligation to ensure that what are legitimate priorities from the point of view of bureaucracy are not skewed by conclusions drawn from surveys or analysis of large databases remote from the intricacies of clinical practice, or from research inappropriate in method or design, or flawed in execution or interpretation. To study clinical care the researcher must accept that it is a matter of 'have problem find best method'—not 'have method will locate tractable problem' (McDonald and Daly, 1992). To employ inappropriate research methods is to run the risk of generating distorted and misleading conclusions as well as constituting an unconscionable drain on scarce research funds. Without adequate clinical input, what began as a justifiable and understandable attempt to reduce variations in the practice and cost of medical care—by implementation of a standard protocol, by administrative decision or by regulatory fiat—can increase the risk of harm to individual patients, even damage the fabric of clinical care. The economically driven decision to reduce staff numbers may subtly increase the risk of misdiagnosis or inadequate treatment. To close a hospital out-patient department will, for example, deprive medical students of the opportunity to learn how specialists go about making the crucial distinction between those symptoms which are and those which are not attributable to organic disease. Moreover, such measures cannot do more than marginally reduce the cost of care. Most of the excessive cost is related not so much to poor medical administration, or to such big-ticket items as magnetic resonance imaging or liver transplantation. Rather, it is the end result of the interaction between a myriad of suboptimal or inappropriate decisions in day-to-day clinical care.

The medical profession also has some responsibility to acknowledge the importance of social environment and of political decision-making to the health of the community and not be narrowly obsessed with disease in the individual. The observation that morbidity, disablement and premature death are closely related to social class and the distribution of wealth has been a constant prick to the conscience of the public health movement (Martin and McQueen, 1989). Clinicians have been notably silent on this issue in the past, but it has recently re-emerged in the form of editorials in the major clinical journals. Others go further. They allege that medicine has colluded with the state by defining the sick role in a manner which tends to support the status quo (Zola, 1972). These are difficult issues, apparently far removed from the mandate of individual practitioners. However, surely some moral responsibility rests on doctors to be aware of the general trends of thinking in these areas, and to ensure that the profession's voice is heard as an advocate of the public in matters relevant to health.

CONCLUSION

The modern doctor remains a pragmatist, committed to the treatment of the individual. The average clinician is not especially interested in the theoretical underpinning of medical care or in political machinations. The more thoughtful do exhibit curiosity about the way they practise, and occasionally pause in their daily routine to reflect on the validity and appropriateness of their customary methods. Few, however, ever cogitate on the intricacies of their own problem-solving activities, or attempt to apply the principles of statistical probability explicitly to diagnostic decisions, or the insights of psychology and sociology to the understanding of their patients' and their own judgments. The positive approach is to accept that there is a moral obligation on doctors to take up the challenge to improve clinical decision-making and communication in order to better satisfy their patients, protect them from iatrogenic harm and reduce costs in the process. Less worthy, but better than nothing, is the negative incentive—if we the clinicians don't do it, they will do it for us. 'They', of course, are the players in the bureaucratic critique of clinical care, driven by political considerations but with a legitimate stake in its efficient delivery. Unless balanced by sufficient clinical input, bureaucratic pressure for fiscal accountability is likely to be insensitive to clinical nuance and unsympathetic to clinical needs, overtly or subtly damaging to the interests of patients and to what is good in the profession. If the proper study of 'mankind' is 'man', then the proper study of the clinician is clinical practice. To study and improve clinical care is a moral obligation, an ethical issue.

REFERENCES

Anon., 1992, 'Evidence-based medicine: a new approach to teaching the practice of medicine', *Journal of the American Medical Association*, 268: 2420–5.

Cochrane, A.L., 1971, *Effectiveness and Efficiency: random reflections on health services*, London: The Nuffield Provincial Hospitals Trust.

Daly, J., McDonald, I.G., 1993, *The Social Impact of Echocardiography: opening Pandora's box*, Canberra: Australian Institute of Health and Welfare, Health Care Technology Series.

Faber, K., 1930, *Nosography: the evolution of clinical medicine in modern times*, New York: Hoeber.

Feinstein, A.R., 1963, 'Boolean algebra and clinical taxonomy: Analytical synthesis of the general spectrum of a human disease', *The New England Journal of Medicine*. 269, 929–38.

——1967, *Clinical Judgment*, Malabar: Krieger.

——1987, *Clinimetrics*, New Haven: Yale University Press.

Freidson, A.,1970, *Professional Dominance*, Chicago: Aldine.

Foucault, M., 1973, *The Birth of the Clinic: an archaeology of medical perception*, London: Tavistock.

Gerhardt, U., 1989, *Ideas about Illness: an intellectual and political history of medical sociology*, London: Macmillan.

Gutting, G., 1989, *Michel Foucault's Archaeology of Scientific Reason*. Cambridge: Cambridge University Press.

Hill, A.B., 1937, *Principles of Medical Statistics*, London: Lancet.

Illich, I., 1976, *Limits to Medicine. Medical Nemesis: the expropriation of health*, Harmondsworth: Penguin.

Jacob, J.M., 1987, *Doctors and Rules: a sociology of professional values*, London: Routledge

Katz, J., 1984, *The Silent World of Doctor and Patient*, New York: Free Press.

Morris, J.N., 1957, *Uses of Epidemiology*, Baltimore: Williams and Wilkins.

McDonald, I.G. and Daly, J.,1992, 'Research methods in health care: A summing up'. In J. Daly, I. McDonald and E. Willis (eds), *Researching Health Care: designs, dilemmas, disciplines*, London: Routledge.

Martin, C.J. and McQueen, D.V., 1989, 'Framework for a New Public Health'. In C.J. Martin and D.V. McQueen (eds), *Readings for a New Public Health*, Edinburgh: Edinburgh University Press.

Toombs, S.K., 1992, *The Meaning of Illness: a phenomenological account of the different perspectives of physician and patient*, Dordrecht: Kluwer.

Zola, I.K., 1972, 'Medicine as an institution of social control', *Sociological Review*, 20: 487–509.

19

MATHEMATICAL MODELS AND CLINICAL PRACTICE

Alvan R. Feinstein

Before turning to the subject of mathematical models, I should like to comment on a topic that often arises in discussions of ethics and research: Is bad research unethical?

ETHICAL AND SCIENTIFIC ISSUES

The immediate follow-up to that question, of course, is 'What is meant by "bad"?' Is it choosing the wrong topic? For example, I may think that mental illness warrants more research, but the investigator wants to study lupus erythematosus. Is it the type of inquiry? For example, is it bad to study explicatory mechanisms in molecular biology and good to study therapeutic interventions in patient care, or vice versa? Is it the type of intervention? Thus, is it better to do research in health promotion rather than disease prevention, and is the latter better than the more customary remedial forms of clinical therapy?

Is good or bad research determined by the choice of a research structure, such as a randomised trial rather than an observational study, or vice versa? Does the decision depend on the particular kind of observational structure, such as a cohort study, rather than a case-control study, rather than an 'ecologic' or 'secular' association study? What about the choice of basic data to be emphasised in the research? Is hard data, such as death and the results of laboratory tests, better than soft data, such as symptoms, functional capacity, emotional state, and satisfaction with life?

I would suggest that the answers to all of the foregoing questions are issues in science, in the architecture of research, or in scientific policy, not in ethics. I may disagree with the choices that you make or you may disagree with mine. You may think I am foolish or wrong-headed, and I may think you are deranged or demented, but we cannot call our quarrel an issue in ethics. If you do not do the kinds of research I would prefer, I can doubt the quality of your intellect, your social responsibility, or even your soul, but I cannot and should not assail your basic character, or call you immoral or unethical, because we disagree about a preferred scientific direction. Furthermore, regardless of which of those research topics or structure is chosen, the work can always be done well or badly. An ecological association study, although generally not an optimum scientific method, can sometimes yield a better and more convincing answer than an ineffectual or poorly designed randomised trial.

ATTRIBUTES OF 'BAD' RESEARCH

Turning from these policy issues, we can next consider some non-policy attributes that might make a piece of research 'bad'. The investigator might use an inappropriate model. This might mean, in the search for aetiological factors in non-organic disease, neglecting, in an Eastern culture, the possible loss of a soul in the operating room, while focusing, in Western culture, on interpersonal relationships.

The investigator might get unsatisfactory data, such as the information in oncological research that boasts of remissions and increased duration of survival, while reporting nothing about the concomitant misery, agony, or vegetating state of the patients receiving the allegedly miraculous chemotherapy.

A third problem is unwarranted conclusions. The investigator may have tortured the data until it confessed, or may have used a restricted set of information chosen because it was consistent with the desired conclusions. An example of this reasoning is the famous story of an investigator who observed that a person was drunk after having had a scotch and water, a gin and water, a vodka and water, and a brandy and water. As the common factor in all of those exposures, he decided, the water must have been the cause of the problem. Again, however, all of these defects I have just cited are not necessarily issues in ethics. They may be due to folly, wrong-headedness, or zealotry, but I would not necessarily want to call the investigators unethical.

The fourth problem, improper publicity, probably comes closer than any of the others to bordering or entering the domain of ethics. I shall confess my bias here as someone who grew up in the era when doctors kept their names out of the newspapers, and who still generally retains that belief. Nevertheless, when investigators today rely on getting fiscal support from political votes or from other sources which are affected by media publicity, and when the public routinely demands news of science and scientific research, many investigators have begun to release their results and contentions directly to the media, and many respected medical publications have also made special arrangement for these releases. Many physicians in the United States are quite unhappy that the prestigious *New England Journal of Medicine* sometimes seems to be a screening mechanism for news supplied via press releases to the *New York Times* and to the national television media. Their distress is heightened when allegations about a wonderful breakthrough or an accused killer agent appear in the media before clinicians have had a chance to see the original published paper about which they are being telephoned by patients. An even greater problem, however, is the false hopes raised by highly publicised breakthroughs that turn out to be wrong, and the false fears or hysteria produced by accusations that also turn out to be wrong, with subsequent effects analogous to someone shouting 'Fire' when a match is lit in a crowded theatre.

CLINICAL PROBLEMS IN MATHEMATICAL MODELS

Regardless of issues of ethics, however, separate problems can occur in clinical science when the research is done with conceptual 'paradigms' that are nevertheless unsatisfactory for medical realities. I shall comment on five sets of mathematical models that I believe, despite their popularity, have had some distinctive disadvantages in patient care.

RANDOMISED TRIALS

The first mathematical model is the randomised trial. Having once directed a biostatistical coordinating centre for cooperatively conducted randomised trials, I bow to no one in my admiration for their majestic accomplishments when they can be done and done well. They have made magnificent contributions to the science of clinical therapy; and they have allowed us today, for the first time in medical history, to provide documentary evidence that our pharmaceutical agents and a few other therapies are indeed efficacious. This evidence has been particularly valuable for pharmaceutical companies, public regulatory agencies, and perhaps governmental policy makers.

Unfortunately, however, the evidence usually pertains only to the average patient entered in the trial. The evidence has excellent internal validity for the therapeutic comparison conducted in the trial, but the external validity is not always satisfactory. In making decisions for individual patients, doctors usually want to know about specific clinical details for subgroups that are obscured in the aggregate average produced by the trial.

A separate problem of randomised double-blind trials has been their adverse intellectual side effects on clinical science. Because randomisation is expected to provide an equitable distribution of the heterogeneous clinical conditions in the baseline state of the patients, clinicians could escape the scientific challenges of creating a suitable taxonomy for classifying those clinical conditions. Because double-blind observation would allegedly prevent bias in the appraisal of outcome events, clinicians could also escape the scientific challenges of suitably identifying and classifying those events. We could use global rating scales to denote changes in conditions as good, fair or poor without having to identify what the changes were, or to establish criteria for their demarcation.

BAYES THEOREM

The second mathematical model is Bayes theorem, which has been offered and sometimes regarded as *the* basis for decisions in diagnostic reasoning. This model reminds me of another mathematical model I learned many years ago in physiology. The physiological model had a series of beautifully conceived, carefully planned, and splendidly executed equations that described the diffusion of fluids through the human body. The mathematical equations had just one minor flaw, however. They assumed that the human body was a spherical ball.

Different practising clinicians can cite various clinical and mathematical reasons for rejecting Bayes theorem and its mathematical cousin, diagnostic likelihood ratios. In my opinion, the fatal flaw is the assumption that certain mathematical indexes, called *sensitivity* and *specificity*, are constant for patients with a particular disease. Reality has shown that the assumption is wrong, and that these indexes are not constant. They vary for patients in different parts of the clinical spectrum of the disease. Since that clinical spectrum is not well classified, thanks in part to the intellectual escape permitted by randomised trials, the indexes of sensitivity, specificity, and likelihood ratios are generally imprecise, non-reproducible, and inaccurate. Bayes theorem and diagnostic likelihood ratios still survive because of the life support given by academic investigators. Among practising clinicians, however, this muddled model is becoming moribund. Clinicians still use probabilities in evaluating diagnostic tests, but the probabilities reflect results in specific clinical subgroups, not in a general statistical average.

DECISION ANALYSIS

The next mathematical model that has had its run of academic popularity is decision analysis. All practising clinicians, of course, analyse data and make decisions. The particular mathematical model called *decision analysis*, however, calls for a particular formal algorithmic strategy in which the quantitative probabilities attached to a particular possible event are multiplied by the quantitative utilities associated with that event. The mathematical product is a numerical probability–utility score that has no direct clinical or intuitive meaning; but the probability–utility product scores associated with diverse outcomes are then folded back or arranged in various other ways. The aggregate scores for each possible decision are then reviewed; and the best decision theoretically is the one that has the best aggregate score.

The decision-analysis model, after being originally developed in a school of business, was then imported and happily received in the intellectual environment of academic clinical medicine, although the model is alien to good clinical reasoning. All good clinicians think about a sequence of possible events, the pertinent probabilities of those events, and the associated utilities. But no good clinician multiplies probabilities by utilities to get an index that is folded back and used for an aggregate score. Although the model was developed in a business school, I have been unable to find any business that actually uses the model exactly as proposed. If time permitted, I could discuss a much simpler and more qualitative approach, based on avoiding chagrin (Feinstein, 1985), which I think is actually used by many businessmen and clinicians. The original decision analysis model, however, appears to have been effective mainly for getting grants and publishing papers. After about a decade of popularity, it seems to be going out of fashion. Perhaps the crowning blow occurred several years ago when the magnificence of decision analyses was doubted in an address given to the society that was founded to promulgate decision analysis (Detsky *et al*, 1987).

PSYCHOMETRIC STRATEGIES

I now turn to a fourth mathematical model: psychometric strategies. They have become particularly popular for constructing indexes for complex clinical phenomena such as functional capacity, health status, or quality of life. The psychometric approach is excellent for the psychosocial challenges at which it is aimed. In the psychosocial sciences, there are no alternative, objective sources of information, such as x-rays, biopsies, and laboratory tests; and the investigators usually do cross-sectional research that describes a single state in time, without engaging either in interventions to change those states, or in follow-up observations to observe the changes via cohort studies and randomised trials. Consequently, the psychosocial scientists have the difficult task of creating credible measurements that can seldom be validated by objective data, by subsequent events, or by concomitant judgmental observations. Without clinical clues or outcome correlations to show the importance of the individual components, and without the ability to determine accuracy, the psychosocial scientists concentrate on mathematical methods to establish 'validity', which has been defined for a bewildering array of diverse phenomena: construct validity, content validity, convergent validity, divergent validity, and many other forms of validity. A particularly important form of validity is devoted to the apparent homogeneity of the component items. The investigators would measure a 'construct'—such as happiness, racial prejudice, or intelligence—with a large number of items that could be regarded as all measuring the same thing if shown to be 'homogeneous' in a statistical index of correlation called Cronbach's alpha.

The approach, although apparently worthwhile in the psychosocial sciences, is not pertinent for clinical activities, where clinicians may deliberately combine non-homogeneous items to form composite variables such as the Apgar score and TNM staging systems, in which an array of items all measuring the same thing would be regarded as redundant and then trimmed to the most important components, rather than being statistically lauded (Wright and Feinstein, 1992). For clinical reasoning, importance would be determined from clinical correlations with concomitant and subsequent events, not merely from isolated statistical coefficients. Another major problem, originally noted by Nunally (1978)—a titan in psychometric activities—is that changes in state are difficult to discern from instruments containing a large array of single-state items. Nevertheless, changes in state are a prime focus of therapy and other clinical interventions.

Clinicians studying such clinical phenomena as relief of symptoms or improvement in functional capacity have invested enormous effort in constructing and applying psychometric indexes, only to find that the approach failed to provide adequate discernment of change. A particularly notorious failure of the psychometric approach occurred when it was applied in a futile effort to show that patients were more satisfied with care from family physicians than from specialists. Relying on a set of statistically validated but clinically irrelevant non-directive items, the instrument asked patients about their satisfaction with doctors in general, not with their own particular doctors (Feinstein, 1987b).

Perhaps the most glaring flaw in the psychometric approach has been its use to construct instruments for measuring quality of life. The instruments are almost all aimed at describing health status, but quality of life is not a health status. It is a patient's reaction to health status and to many other features of life, beyond health status alone; and it can be determined only by the patient, not by any statistical calculations or pronouncements of pundits (Gill and Feinstein, 1994).

The psychometric strategy may be splendid for the psychosocial goals at which it is aimed, but clinical goals require a separate, different clinimetric strategy.

ECONOMIC MODELS

I shall only briefly mention one other topic—medical economics—that is also regularly approached with unsatisfactory mathematical models. The term 'risk–benefit ratio' is constantly used as though it were really a ratio, despite the fact that the ratio is almost never actually calculated. The main problem that thwarts the calculations is that the risks can usually be quantified as costs, but benefits cannot be similarly quantified, and, in many instances, they are not even properly identified. How do we quantify the benefit of having pain relieved, or dying in a dignified, comfortable manner, or being able to walk normally again when prosthetic hip joints replace joints crippled by osteoarthritis, or becoming pregnant through in-vitro fertilisation, with a viable baby after years of unsuccessful efforts? In the absence of better clinimetric indexes and rating scales, these benefits are seldom articulated, and even when specified, they are not readily converted to monetary quantities for comparison with the economic costs of risks.

A second misleading or inappropriate economic tactic occurs during so-called cost–benefit or cost–effectiveness analyses, when the costs of a huge program of prophylactic interventions are expressed per patient rather than per program. For example, suppose we developed a program to prevent injuries in the home. In a community of 1 million families, the program of interventions might cost $300 per family, so that the total cost would be $300 million. A clinical trial might then be done showing that the community program prevents 20 major injuries a year, each of which would cost an average of $6000 in health care. The total cost of the extra health care would be $120 000. In a comparison of costs for *programs*, we would have spent $300 million to save $120 000.

The economic information is seldom presented in such a direct manner, however. Instead we might be told that the program is remarkably inexpensive because an expenditure of only $300 per family is obviously cheaper than a cost of $6000 per injury. There are many cogent non-fiscal reasons that are (and should be) involved in making decisions about the value of preventive programs. The decision-makers are not helped, however, when the fiscal data are presented in a misleading manner by referring to costs per person rather than costs per program.

I believe the main reason for all these problems is that modern medical schools, at least in English-speaking countries, have abandoned respect for the idea that clinical medicine contains intrinsic important challenges of its own, and that the challenges should be approached as basic problems in clinical science. Instead, medical students and many practising clinicians have been taught that clinical medicine is a secondary activity, deriving all of its ideas and procedures by applying the concepts and ideas of the so-called 'basic sciences'. For the explicatory decisions that deal with mechanisms of disease, the basic sciences are such fields as physiology, biochemistry and molecular biology. For the interventional decisions of patient care, the basic sciences are sometimes regarded as statistics, economics and sociology.

Clinicians are thus taught to be intellectual dunces who have no basic challenges of their own and whose main scientific role is to apply the ideas that emanate from the worthier and more profound 'basic sciences'. Since physiology, biochemistry, and molecular biology were historically derived from clinical medicine, many intellectual connections still remain; and the applications of these sciences can be meaningfully arranged. The other set of 'basic' fields—in statistics, economics, and sociology—were developed on their own, however, without any direct relationship to clinical challenges. Nevertheless, clinicians have been and are being taught to give unquestioning allegiance to these clinically distant methods, and to apply the ideas directly, without thinking about their subtle or egregious unsuitability for clinical challenges.

We might be able to offer some sort of mental rehabilitation for clinicians who suffer from this type of intellectual lobotomy. The best hope, however, is to produce a system of medical education and medical literature that will challenge clinicians to preserve and defend their own intellects, and to use those intellects for creating solutions to basic scientific challenges in their own domain. The basic challenges of patient-care interventions in clinical medicine cannot be solved by alien models, by the blandishments or 'guidelines' of academic nannies, or by the specious fashions of mathematical mandarins. Clinicians should make use of all the effective consultative help they can get, but should not abandon fundamental challenges that require direct clinical solutions from wise clinical intellects. The old maxim used to be, 'Physician, heal thyself.' The newer maxim we now need is, 'Physician, heal thy mind' (Feinstein, 1987a).

REFERENCES

Detsky, A.S., Redelmeier, D. and Abrams, H.B., 1987, 'What's wrong with decision analysis? Can the left brain influence the right?', *Journal of Chronic Diseases*, 40: 831–6.

Feinstein, A.R., 1985, 'The "chagrin" factor and qualitative decision analysis', *Archives of Internal Medicine*, 145: 1257–9.

——1987a, 'The intellectual crisis in clinical science: Medaled models and muddled mettle', *Perspectives in Biology and Medicine*, 30: 215–30.

——1987b, *Clinimetrics*, New Haven: Yale University Press.

Gill, T.M. and Feinstein, A.R., 1994, 'A critical appraisal of quality of quality-of-life measurements', *Journal of the American Medical Association*, 272: 619–26.

Nunnally, J.C., 1978, '*Psychometric Theory*, second edition, New York: McGraw-Hill.

Wright, J.G. and Feinstein, A.R., 1992, 'A comparative contrast of clinimetric and psychometric methods for constructing indexes and rating scales', *Journal of Clinical Epidemiology*, 45: 1201–18.

20

STUDYING NARRATIVES OF AGEING AND SOCIAL PROBLEMS IN MEDICAL ENCOUNTERS

Howard Waitzkin

As a sociologist, I have often criticised the medical profession for the power that it exerts. Yet as a practising physician, I find myself often feeling helpless to assist patients in solving the problems that bother them the most, and I know that many other colleagues in medicine feel that same way. These problems that we feel so powerless to solve, more often than not, are problems that have their roots in the social context of medicine, rather than in pathophysiological disturbances at the biological level. While we as doctors cannot always help patients with their physical problems, we run up against the feeling of powerlessness much more often as we confront their specifically social problems. In this essay, I would like to argue that, despite the difficulties in understanding (and researching) this problem, we cannot ethically ignore this paradox in patient–doctor encounters. I draw on research in which my co-workers and I are trying to clarify how patients and doctors process social problems as they talk.

When older people talk with doctors, their conversations often touch on social problems. Bereavement, financial insecurity, isolation, dependency, inadequate housing, lack of transportation, and similar issues cause difficulties for the elderly. In some cases, patients or doctors raise these issues directly. Alternatively, such problems may surface indirectly, in passing, or marginally, as doctors and patients focus on technical concerns.

Although physicians' responses to patients' psychosocial needs have generated criticism of the medical profession, little is known about how these troubles of communication emerge in the language of actual medical encounters. Research on patient–doctor encounters has seldom focused on the ways that contextual problems arise and get processed (Waitzkin, 1984; Kleinman, 1988; Mishler, 1984; Roter and Hall, 1989), and this gap in research appears also in the sparse literature on communication with older patients (Adelman, Greene and Charon, 1991; Greene et al, 1986; 1987; 1989; Haug and Ory, 1987; Rost and Roter, 1987; Rost et al, 1989). The study reported here asked how older patients and doctors deal with social problems in the discourse of routine medical encounters.

THEORETICAL APPROACH AND DEFINITIONS

Our research developed from a long-term, quantitative study of patient–doctor communication (Waitzkin, 1984; 1985; 1986). Although that project led to new information about communication in medical encounters, it also revealed difficulties on both conceptual and methodological levels. Conceptually, some of the most interesting and seemingly important features of recorded encounters involved concerns about contextual matters that appeared marginal or peripheral to the technical goals of clinical medicine. Such contextual concerns, which emerged in approximately two-thirds of the encounters that we studied, typically included comments about work, family, financial matters, or other issues outside the traditional categories that describe the content of medical visits (history taking, physical examination, discussion of diagnostic studies and treatment, patient education, and so forth). We initially had designated most of these concerns within a residual category of 'miscellaneous comments', a de-emphasis that later appeared to be an artefact of the method of categorisation that we had used.

We ourselves and other researchers on patient–doctor communication previously had emphasised the importance of psychosocial content of medical encounters and had argued that such content may hold crucial importance for patients even while physicians tend to overlook or de-emphasise it (Waitzkin, 1984). Yet we found that these psychosocial phenomena in medical encounters, which appeared marginal from the narrow perspective of medicine's technical goals, proved difficult to analyse or even to describe convincingly with the research techniques previously in use. In addition, distinguishing why contextual issues did appear in most encounters but did not arise in a minority of other encounters became another conceptual challenge.

In our initial attempt to study contextual concerns in medical encounters, we noted that this material usually touched on one or more themes. Contextual difficulties related to the process of ageing—such as social isolation, financial insecurity, and loss of community or material possessions—arose frequently in the encounters that we studied and proved especially striking. Problems related to gender roles at work and in the family often emerged as a contextual concern. For instance, women frequently referred to conflicting family and work responsibilities. Men often described economic hardship in supporting their families, as well as physical or emotional stress in meeting the requirements of their jobs. Patients also tended to mention contextual issues when they talked about smoking, alcohol, other substance use, and sexual behaviour. Our research group decided to look systematically at each of these contextual arenas. In this essay I discuss our approach and findings about contextual problems related to ageing.

Because we found that doctors rarely addressed contextual problems that their patients raised explicitly, we also faced ethical dilemmas as researchers. Specifically, we believed that it was inappropriate to intervene directly with physicians or doctors, since we aimed not to intrude into the patient–doctor relationships that we were studying. When we noted contextual problems that were not addressed, we could see no direct yet unobtrusive way to assist patients with these difficulties. For this reason, we decided to develop criteria that in the future could prove helpful to physicians and to patients in dealing with contextual difficulties as they arise. In the conclusion of this essay, I present some preliminary criteria that may help doctors and patients in responding to contextual problems in medical encounters.

In parallel to research on narratives outside the medical field, several investigators have applied conceptual and methodological perspectives of narrative analysis and sociolinguistics to the study of medical encounters. For instance, Mishler (1984) has identified the limitations of traditional quantitative methods and, based on an intensive analysis of transcribed tape-recordings gathered in our own prior research (Waitzkin, 1985), has identified two 'voices' in typical encounters. The 'voice of medicine', from this perspective, involves the technical details of disease and treatment, while the 'voice of the lifeworld' includes elements of the patient's everyday social relationships and activities that comprise the context of the medical encounter. Riessman (1990b) has extended Mishler's approach by calling attention to the 'strategic uses' of narrative for the presentation of self and illness during research interviews, and Viney and Bousfield (1991) have focused on psychosocial processes in a narrative analysis of transcribed interviews with persons affected by AIDS.

Other investigators have also applied narrative analysis to the study of women patients' experiences in medical encounters (Bell, 1988; Davis, 1988; Fisher, 1986; Fisher and Davis, 1993; Todd, 1989; Young, 1987). This latter research, while too extensive to review here in full, has revealed major problems in communication, especially within encounters that concern obstetrical or gynaecological issues. Such work also has revealed that patterns of language use related to gender tend to heighten power differences and contribute to conflict experienced by women in medical encounters.

Some researchers have examined narratives in medicine from interpretive perspectives that do not necessarily depend on the in-depth analysis of transcribed speech. In cultural anthropology, Kleinman (1988) has analysed the divergent belief systems that patients from different cultural back-grounds can convey in narratives of their physical symptoms and of how these symptoms are related to their social experiences; Kleinman represents patients' 'narratives of illness' through highly edited or summarised repre-sentations of talk, rather than through detailed transcriptions. In an interdisciplinary approach emphasising cognitive studies, Cicourel (1985) has described the 'prevailing knowledge' of technical medicine which tends to inhibit and to distort the meanings of patients' experiences during encounters with physicians. In the 'medical humanities', several investiga-tors have treated discourse in medical encounters as a form of story telling that resembles literature; they have used a literary approach to edited and summarised accounts of medical encounters (as opposed to the in-depth interpretation of transcribed speech) (Brody, 1987; 1992; Charon, 1989; Coles, 1989; Hunter, 1991).

In our own conceptual work, we have tried to build on prior work by adapting several theoretical strands from literary criticism, critical theory, and narrative analysis in the humanities and social sciences, to study the non-literary texts of medical encounters. While emphasising the sociocul-tural context of medical discourse, our theoretical analysis has taken a somewhat different approach from the related studies above, by emphasising elements of ideology, social control, underlying structure, and features of medical discourse that appear marginal on superficial reading. This approach focuses on story telling about contextual issues and on structural features of medical language that interrupt or marginalise the full expression of these issues, thus leaving them incompletely discussed or resolved (Waitzkin, 1989a; 1991a; Waitzkin and Britt, 1989). By developing a systematic methodological approach, we have learned that physicians do not simply tend to ignore contextual information about patients' lives, as previous research has revealed. Instead, we have moved beyond prior work to clarify a characteristic structure and sequencing by which contextual issues are handled in medical encounters. We have found that this con-ceptual approach is especially helpful to understand narratives of social problems in medical encounters with older people. A brief summary and definitions follow.

First, medical discourse occurs within a context that includes the cultural, economic, political, social, and psychological milieu of the medical encoun-ter. Our contextual focus, which links the analysis of narrative to the lived experiences of speakers outside the medical realm, derives from an emphasis in literary theory centred in the work of Bakhtin (1973; 1981; 1986) and more recent theorists influenced by him (Wertsch, 1991). In brief, this critical perspective emphasises the sociocultural embeddedness of written or oral discourse. For instance, Bakhtin (1986) identifies various 'speech genres', which are defined as typical forms of utterances that occur within specific sociocultural circumstances. Thus, in dialogue between professionals and lay people, a 'scientific' or 'technocratic' speech genre may clash with a genre of everyday speech. As Wertsch (1991) has pointed out in adapting Bakhtin's concepts to psychology, the use of discrepant speech genres can create a 'multivoicedness of meaning', which can be found not only in literature but also in the non-literary discourse observed in institutional settings such as education and medicine.

Ideology is a crucial sociocultural element that mediates the voices that arise within medical discourse. Although difficult to define simply, ideology comprises the ideas and doctrines that form the distinctive perspective of a social group. As Althusser (1971) has pointed out, ideology represents— on an imaginary level—individuals' relationship to the real conditions of their everyday lived experience. Subtle ideological features of medical discourse also illustrate what Lukács has termed 'reification'—the transformation of social relations into things or 'thing-like' beings that take on their own separate reality in people's consciousness. Through reification, according to Lukács, consciousness focuses on the concrete problems and objects of everyday life, while the 'totality' of social relations that lie behind these routine concerns escapes conscious attention (Lukács, 1971a; 1971b; Taussig, 1980). From this view, we have argued that ideology in medical encounters tends to remove from critical scrutiny those broader issues that are rooted in medicine's social context.

Ideological elements of medical encounters also contribute to social control, which refers to the mechanisms by which agencies of society achieve consent and adherence to norms of appropriate behaviour. Critics of the helping professions, such as Foucault (1975; 1977; 1978; 1985; 1986), have observed a gradual increase in social control through professional surveillance, in such areas as sexuality, criminality, and mental illness. Within modern medicine, social control occurs partly as a subtle feature of the discourse that patients and doctors exchange in their face-to-face encounters.

The discourse of medicine often contains an underlying structure—which we define as a consistent pattern of verbal elements that emerges in a similar way across medical encounters whose surface characteristics initially appear quite diverse. Predictably, such a structure seldom reaches the conscious awareness of patients and doctors as they interact (for a review of pertinent sources in structuralism—Jakobson, 1985; Lévi-Strauss, 1967; Saussure, 1986—see Waitzkin 1991b). Although prior critiques of medicine have noted difficulties in communication about contextual issues in medical encounters, we hoped to extend prior knowledge by looking for a consistent structure and sequencing of speech by which contextual issues are or are not addressed.

In this structure, elements of discourse that appear marginal based on superficial impression can become quite crucial, especially as these elements convey contextual concerns. Such elements typically appear in inconsistencies, breaks in logic, interruptions, silences, and absence of pertinent details. This post-structuralist view (Waitzkin, 1991b) is influenced by several key sources (Derrida, 1976; 1982; Jameson, 1981; 1991; Eagleton, 1978; 1993). While post-structuralist criticism has studied mainly the margins of philosophy and literature, a similar approach brings into focus what does and does not happen in the non-literary, spoken discourse of medicine. A post-structuralist perspective also emphasises ambiguity of meaning and encourages alternative readings of the same narrative material. This conceptual orientation allowing for ambiguity and alternative readings also influenced our methods of interpreting transcribed narratives.

METHODS

To study narrative material in medical encounters, we needed to ask: what is an appropriate method? During the late 1980s, when we initiated this phase of our work, we found no straightforward answer in prior research. From a critical appraisal of our own and others' studies of patient–doctor communication, we found major weaknesses in both quantitative and qualitative methods to address the concepts we hoped to investigate (Waitzkin, 1990). Recognising the historical tension in the social science literature between the traditional, so-called 'positivist' paradigm and the interpretive, 'naturalist' paradigm of research, we also realised the philosophies of science underlying these two models of inquiry are very different and often difficult to reconcile (Lincoln and Guba, 1985). In addition, emerging methodological discussion in narrative studies presented strong arguments that research on meaning and context in narrative materials requires in-depth analysis of transcribed speech and that traditional quantitative methods of categorisation and coding remain unable to accomplish key research goals in this arena (Mishler, 1986a; cf. Riessman, 1993).

Confronting these methodological difficulties, we have set forth several methodological criteria that, we believe, offer reasonable compromises in dealing with the weaknesses of earlier methods (Waitzkin, 1990). These criteria, presented in Table 2, guide the sampling of encounters, transcription of recordings, interpretation of transcripts, and presentation of transcripts and interpretations for publication. Our criteria in no way aim toward a goal of eliminating subjectivity in the research process; post-structuralist perspectives and recent advances in the philosophy of science have shown that such a goal remains elusive or impossible to obtain, even in quantitative studies (Lynch and Woolgar, 1990; Mishler, 1986a; 1991). On

Table 2 Criteria of an appropriate research method for the interpretation of narratives in medical encounters[a]

1. The discourse under study should be selected through a random sampling procedure to increase the degree to which it is 'representative' of discourse in similar settings and under similar conditions.

2. The sampled discourse should be recorded so that the primary recordings can be heard by other observers if interested.

3. Standardised rules of transcription should be applied to the recorded discourse in producing texts for subsequent analysis.

4. The reliability of transcription should be assessed by multiple observers.

5. Inductive procedures for interpreting the prepared texts should be decided in advance, should be assessed for validity in relation to theory, should address both the content and structure of texts, and should allow for alternative interpretations of similar textual material.

6. The reliability of applying these interpretive procedures should be ascertained by the participation of multiple observers.

7. If an interpretation is published, a summary of the transcript should precede its interpretation; within the interpretation, excerpts from the transcript should help substantiate the interpretive arguments; and the full transcript should be made available, for instance as an appendix, on microfilm, or on computer diskette, for the reader's review if he or she is interested.

8. If published, the texts and their interpretations should convey accurately the observed variability of content and structure across sampled texts.

[a] Further development of these criteria appears in Waitzkin (1990).

the other hand, we believe that these criteria offer a reasonable approach to important questions concerning method that should be answered in both quantitative and interpretive research (Lincoln and Guba, 1985).

In light of such concerns, we have implemented these methodological criteria in our recent research, based on a sample of audiotaped encounters involving patients and general internists. Our research group adhered to the cited criteria of an appropriate interpretive method in transcribing the tapes, carrying out interpretations, and presenting transcripts and interpretive conclusions for publication; further details concerning our methods appear in Waitzkin (1985; 1990) but are summarised here in Appendix 1; the standardised rules of transcription appear in Appendix 2.

A MEDICAL ENCOUNTER WITH AN OLDER PATIENT

The following encounter illustrates patterns observed in discourse involving older patients. An interpretive analysis of textual material requires space that inevitably restricts the number of encounters that can be presented, or even summarised, in an article of this scope. Because of space limitations, I have chosen here to apply the interpretive approach to a summary of, and excerpts from, an illustrative encounter. Although this encounter does not reflect the entire spectrum of encounters that we observed or that occur in clinical practice, it does show patterns that we have found to recur frequently. Age, of course, is not the only characteristic of patients or doctors that affects the processing of contextual material. In the conclusion of the article, we also allude to the impact of other characteristics, such as gender and social class.

This encounter, as well as others we have studied, inevitably raises the ethical question of how we as researchers might intervene to address the difficulties revealed in our work. That is, how might the structure and process of medical discourse be modified to improve on the conditions revealed here? While this question is not an easy one to answer, I discuss in the concluding section this study's implications for change.

LOSS OF HOME, COMMUNITY, AND AUTONOMY—AS REVEALED IN A MEDICAL ENCOUNTER

Summary: An elderly woman visits her doctor for follow-up of her heart disease. During the encounter she expresses concerns about decreased vision, her ability to continue driving, lack of stamina and strength, weight loss and diet, and financial problems. She discusses her recent move to a new home and her relationships with family and friends. Her physician assures her that her health is improving; he recommends that she continue her current medical regimen and that she see an eye doctor.

From the questionnaires that the patient and doctor completed after their interaction, some pertinent information is available: The patient is an 80-year-old white high school graduate. She is Protestant, Scottish-American, and widowed, with five living children whose ages range from 45 to 59; she describes her occupation as 'homemaker'. Her doctor is a 44-year-old white male, who is a general internist. The doctor has known the patient for about one year and believes that her primary diagnoses are atherosclerotic heart disease and prior congestive heart failure. The encounter takes place in a suburban private practice near Boston.

Although the patient values her independence, she also tries to maintain a social support network, which she describes without prompting in an incomplete narrative. Allusions to a support network usually arise within this medical encounter as marginal features, which the patient mentions in passing and which the doctor does not pursue in depth. Among her social contacts, R—, a friend, appears the most central. The patient tries to see R— regularly for lunch and other get-togethers. Socialising with R— brings her pleasure, advice, and support. For instance, when she describes her current nutritional status and medications, she says:

P: And I'm trying hard to eat a banana once in a while, trying to
    eat some tomatoes, and
D: uh

P: I ate a R— took me to lunch and I had an elegant lobster salad
     sandwich.   340

As a source of advice, R— has raised a question about vitamin A as a
factor in the patient's visual symptoms (lines 13–15). The patient also
mentions that R— has helped her to move and to buy clothing (lines 230,
298).

Family members figure less prominently as sources of support and also
create some rather burdensome obligations. Most of the family have moved
to other geographical areas. The patient keeps in touch by telephone and
mail, especially for birthdays, but she finds herself unable to do as much
as she might like, partly because of the number of people involved:

P: Well I should—now I've got birthday cards to buy. I've got seven
     or eight birthdays this week—month. Instead of that, I'm just
     gonna write 'em and wish them a happy birthday. Just a little note,
     my grandchildren.   100
D: Mm hmm.
P: But I'm not gonna bother. I just can't do it all, Dr.—
D: Well,
P: I called my daughters, her birthday was just, today's the third.
D: Yeah.   105
P: My daughter's birthday in Princeton was the uh first, and I called
     her up and talked with her. I don't know what time it'll cost me,
     but then, my telephone is my only indiscretion.

At no other time in the encounter does the patient refer to her own family,
nor does the doctor ask. The patient does her best to maintain contact,
even though she does not mention anything that she receives in the way
of day-to-day support.

Compounding these problems of social support and incipient isolation,
the patient recently has moved from a home that she occupied for 59 years.
The reasons for giving up her home remain unclear, but they seem to
involve a combination of financial factors and difficulties in maintaining
it. She first mentions the move quickly but then shifts to a visit with R—
and her shopping accomplishments:

P: And of course I'd been awful busy changing addresses, 'n-
D: Yeah.
P: And today, I've been to lunch with R—. And I've done all my
     week's shopping. And here I am.   80

During silent periods in the physical exam, the patient spontaneously
narrates more details about the loss of possessions and relationships with
previous neighbours, along with satisfaction about certain conveniences of
her new living situation. Further, as the patient speaks, the doctor asks
clarifying questions about the move and gives several of his usual pleasant

fillers. He cuts off this discussion by helping the patient from the examination table:

P: Yeah . . . .((moving around noises)) Well, I sold a lot of
   my stuff.   225
D: Yeah, how did the moving go, as long as (word)
* * *
P: And y'know take forty ni- fifty nine years accumulation. Boy, and
   I've got cartons in my closet it'll take me till doomsday to, ouch.   235
D: Gotcha.
P: But I've been kept out of mischief by doing it. But I've got a lot
   to do, I sold my rugs 'cause they wouldn't fit where I am. I just
   got a piece of plain cloth at home.   240
D: Mm hmm.
P: Sometimes I think I'm foolish at 81. I don't know how long I'll
   live. Isn't much point in putting money into stuff, and then, why
   not enjoy a little bit of life?
   [
D: Mm hmm, (words).   245
P: And I've got to have draperies made.
D: Now, then, you're (words).
P: But that'll come. I'm not worrying. I got an awfully cute place.
   It's very very comfortable. All electric kitchen. It's got a better
   bathroom than I ever had in my life.   250
D: Great . . . . . . Met any of your neighbours there yet?
P: Oh, I met two or three.
D: Mm hmm.
P: And my, some of my neighbours from Belmont here, there's Mrs.
   F— and her two sisters are up to see me, spent the afternoon with   255
   me day before yesterday. And all my neighbours um holler down
   the hall (words) . . . years ago. They're comin', so they say. So,
   I'm hopin' they will. I hated to move, cause I loved, um I liked
   my neighbours very much.
D: Now, we'll let you down. You watch your step.   260
P: You're not gonna let me, uh, unrobed, disrobed today.
D: Don't have to, I think.
P: Well!
D: Your heart sounds good.
P: It does?   265
D: Yep.

After the doctor mentions briefly that the patient's heart 'sounds good',
he and the patient go on to other topics. The doctor's cut-off and a return
to technical assessment of cardiac function have the effect of marginalising
a contextual problem that involves loss of home and community.

For the patient, the move holds several meanings. First, in the realm of
inanimate objects, her new living situation, an apartment (line 257 mentions a hallway), contains several physical features that she views as more

convenient, or at least 'cute'. On the other hand, she apparently has sold many of her possessions, which carry the memories of 59 years in the same house. Further, she feels the need to decorate her new home but doubts the wisdom of investing financial resources in such items as rugs and draperies at her advanced age.

Aside from physical objects, the patient confronts a loss of community. In response to the doctor's question about meeting new neighbours, the patient says that she has met 'two or three'. Yet she 'hated' to move, because of the affection that she held for her prior neighbours. Describing her attachment, she first mentions that she 'loved' them and then modulates her feelings by saying that she 'liked them very much'. Whatever the pain that this loss has created, the full impact remains unexplored, as the doctor cuts off the line of discussion by terminating the physical exam and returning to a technical comment about her heart.

Throughout these passages, the doctor supportively listens. He offers no specific suggestions to help the patient in these arenas, nor does he guide the dialogue toward deeper exploration of her feelings. Despite his supportive demeanour, the doctor here functions within the traditional constraints of the medical role. When tension mounts with the patient's mourning a much-loved community, the doctor returns to the realm of medical technique.

MOBILITY, AUTONOMY, AND VISUAL CAPACITY

From the start of the encounter, the patient complains about her vision and its impact on autonomous function in daily life. Although her cardiac symptoms have improved, she still feels 'rocky', by which she refers to her visual symptoms:

P:	But I:: feel kind of rocky.	10
D:	You are (word).	
P:	My eyes are bothering me. I can see perfectly, read signs, but R— [friend] said she wondered if I was eating right, and if I, a little vitamin A or something would, ah, when I go back, turn back from a bright lights, it looks dark to me, although I can see.	15

The patient attaches importance to eyesight as a critical aid for mobility and autonomy. At the age of 80, she still drives a car and wants to continue. She emphasises the link between vision and transportation immediately after the doctor refers her to an ophthalmologist:

P:	I drove my car yesterday, down Arlington Heights	
	[	
D:	Oh, dear. Eighty miles an hour again.	50
P:	No, I didn't. I went thirty.	
D:	Thirty.	

P: Yeah, down Mass Avenue.
D: Well, that's the first time in years you've ever slowed down to
    thirty.   55
    [
P: Nope
    Hm hmm.
    [
D: Yeah. Ha haa.

A negotiation that follows expresses several themes, which objectify and—
to use Lukács' term—reify the complex social conditions facing this older
person by converting them into a concrete professional decision about
physical capacity to use a car. First, the patient depends on her car for
many functional necessities and social contacts. She indicates these concerns later:

P: It's all right for me to drive a little bit if I feel like it?   365
D: I guess we're not gonna stop you.
P: Well, no, that isn't the question. It's whether you feel my—
                                      [
D: I, I think it's all right, yes.
P: Like going (words) shopping centre on Baker Street.   370
    * * *
P: (word) driving, I went to a funeral (words)   381
D: Yeah. Well, I don't if you use your judgment that way, sure.

The patient requests the doctor's approval for continuing to drive. His
response proves less than enthusiastic, as he uses the royal 'we' to note
that he will not invoke his legal responsibility, as a doctor and agent of
social control, to prohibit driving when physical incapacity predictably
might interfere with safety. As the patient begins to reply that the doctor's
stopping her 'isn't the question', she begins to clarify the question, but the
doctor interrupts (line 367). After the doctor gives tentative approval, the
patient alludes to the importance of using the car to go shopping and also
for social responsibilities like a recent funeral. Her car thus becomes her
means to buy the necessities required for independent living, as well as a
way to fulfil social obligations—among which the funerals of friends and
relatives figure prominently at her age.

The mobility that the patient's car provides then becomes part of a story
about functional capacity that the patient spontaneously narrates. As she
lives alone long after her husband has died and her children have departed,
autonomy in activities of daily living has become an increasing struggle.
For instance, she expresses pleasure in her ability to do housework, to cook,
and to feed herself:

P: Now I'll tell you what I did yesterday. Uhm, I did all my own   120

work, and I've been, been doing a fair amount of vegetable
cooking, getting better meals for myself.
D: Mm hmm.
P: I managed to get a whole tomato down this week.
D: There you are.   125
P: And a whole banana. Ha! Kidding. Well, . . ah, I took the car
out, then I came home, and I said, 'Well I've got (word)', so I
ironed.

Later she alludes to gratification in buying groceries on her own:

P: Still I'm getting better, I can, I can move around pretty well. I   215
went ramblin', picked a (word), oh I have two, three weeks ago,
all my groceries myself.

While the patient uses a humorous and ironic tone, she takes such
accomplishments seriously. The doctor punctuates the narrative with brief
conversational fillers ('Mm hmm', 'There you are', and so forth), which
convey tolerance and support for the patient's efforts to preserve autonomous function.

FINANCIAL INSECURITY

Worries about money come up at several points in the encounter. As
already noted, economic considerations are constraining her decisions
about decorating her new home. Further, desire to maintain mobility and
autonomy by driving a car also creates financial stress:

P: So, uh, I sha'n't do anything about buying something for myself
until I get my bills paid. So, and I suppose I was awfully foolish
to put my car on the road this year.   313

Driving thus increases financial pressures while helping her to maintain
autonomy.

The costs of medical care have also become a burden. Noting that her
insurance coverage remains incomplete, the patient describes a hospital
bill that has affected her ability to make needed purchases, for instance,
of clothes:

P: So I told R—, I said I'll go and get a dress at a time. I got a nice
bill from —Hospital yesterday. Two hundred and forty-one dollars.
((sniff))   300
* * *
D: How about Medicare?   305
P: I::'ve got, you see I didn't have Medicare D [sic], Doctor. A—
didn't think we needed it. And I was so, well, negligent I should
have had it. But I am registered for it the first of July.

Like many seniors, she regrets that she had underestimated the need for insurance.

Consistently the patient initiates consideration of financial problems. While the doctor seldom interrupts the contextual narrative, his style remains nondirective. The patient's financial difficulties thus remain unengaged and ultimately marginal elements of the discourse.

THE BODY'S DETERIORATION

The patient knows her age and its implications. She wonders about the wisdom of decorating her new home when the duration of her ability to enjoy it may be not very long (lines 242–244). Further, after mentioning her difficulty in keeping up with birthdays in her family, she assumes a pessimistic tone:

> P: I don't care, I never go to the movies, and I very seldom watch
>   movies on television even. So, . . . uh (word) oh, if I could only
>   (word) with my own self
>   [
> D: ((cough))
>   [
> P: and go like I used to. But what can you expect when I'm, when
>   I'm, when you're almost, when you're gonna, going toward 81?   115

A scenario of deterioration also appears in a discussion about weight loss and its impact on the patient's wardrobe:

> P: So I ironed. I had three dresses, which I'll never wear because
>   they're about that wide and I'm about that wide. If you want to
>   see something, come here, look at me.   130
> D: Uh huh.
> P: Look, look at that.
> D: Well, you've lost a little weight, huh?
> P: A little? I've lost about 20 pounds.

After the doctor questions her about her diet and performs a brief physical exam, the patient alludes to her continuing attempts to sew clothing for herself:

> P: Oh, the dress, good Lord, I've made my clothes for years. And I'm
>   heart broken because I had a couple of nice summer dresses that
>   I made myself, and, they're miles too big.   295

In short, the patient is experiencing distress about changes in her body and her image of it. As her body shrinks, she no longer is able to clothe it as she once could. The loss of such clothes that she has sewn for herself then blends with the effects of her other losses. The technical meaning of weight loss remains ambiguous, as the patient never questions the doctor explicitly about it, nor does he offer an explanation. For instance, a possible association between cancer and weight loss remains absent from the conversation. Further, while she has experienced a series of losses and verbalises a few depressed emotions, the patient does not mention the word 'depression'; likewise, the doctor neither asks about depression nor lists it as a possible diagnosis.

Throughout the encounter, death waits in the background. When the patient obliquely refers to the end of her life, the discourse does not encourage exploration of her feelings or plans about dying. In all this, an ideology of stoicism is maintained, as the patient stoically observes her own bodily deterioration (cf. Zola, 1991), and as the doctor listens supportively while she describes her attempts to transcend the sadnesses of physical ageing.

CONTEXT, IDEOLOGY, AND STRUCTURE

The socioemotional context of ageing predominates in this encounter. Typically, the patient initiates such topics; the doctor listens and enunciates brief verbal fillers that convey interest and support. Technical content gives way in most instances to extensive conversation about the experiences of ageing. Patient and doctor engage in warm and mutually respectful dialogue, as they both confront troubling issues that presumably remain beyond medicine's reach.

Several ideological assumptions become apparent. Coping with the vicissitudes of ageing remains a matter of individual responsibility. This ideological orientation emphasising individual responsibility is consistent with a dominant ideological pattern in US society (Sennett and Cobb, 1972). For the patient, preserving her functional capacity to carry out activities that are typical of women's social role—homemaking, shopping, cooking, feeding, sewing, and so forth—remains a high priority. In the face of physical deterioration and impending death, the dialogue objectifies and reifies the totality of the patient's contextual difficulties, even as it reinforces her stoical attempts to cope.

This encounter shows structural elements that appear beneath the surface details of patient–doctor communication, shown schematically in Figure 5. Contextual issues affecting the patient include social isolation; loss of home, possessions, family, and community; limited resources to preserve independent function; financial insecurity; and physical deterioration associated with the process of dying (A). Because of these contextual difficulties, the patient experiences loneliness, frustration, and anxiety, in addition to the physical troubles of heart disease, visual symptoms, and weight loss (B). In a visit with her doctor (C), she expresses concerns about contextual problems at great length. The doctor listens supportively, allowing the patient to describe her situation in detail and to emote about

Figure 5 Schematic, structural elements of a medical encounter involving loss of home, community and autonomy (encounter A)

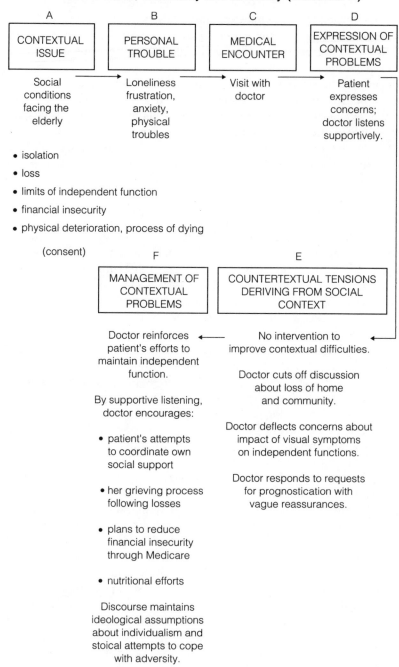

it (D). There is no intervention to improve any of the contextual difficulties that the patient presents. Nevertheless, tensions in the discourse arise that reflect medicine's presumed inability to affect the contextual issues that most trouble the patient. Facing these tensions, the doctor cuts off a discussion about loss of home and community and deflects concerns about the impact of visual symptoms on independent function by referring the patient to another specialist (E). To manage the patient's contextual problems, the doctor reinforces her efforts to maintain independent function, although a theme of social control arises about her uncertain ability to drive safely. Through supportive listening, he also encourages her efforts to coordinate a social support network, her grieving process following the loss of a home and community, her plan to reduce financial insecurity by registering for Medicare insurance coverage, and her nutritional efforts to resist physical deterioration. In these ways, the discourse maintains ideological assumptions that value individualism and stoical attempts to cope with adversity. Critical exploration of alternative arrangements to enhance her social support does not occur (F).

That such structural features should characterise an encounter like this one becomes rather disconcerting, since the communication otherwise seems so admirable. At an advanced age, the patient has retained a keen intellect and takes initiative to lead her life with independence and dignity. She shows no hesitation in voicing whatever questions and emotions seem pertinent. Likewise, the doctor manifests patience and compassion, as he encourages a wide-ranging discussion of socioemotional concerns that extend far beyond the technical details of the patient's physical disorders. Yet the discourse does nothing to improve the most troubling features of the patient's situation. To expect differently would require redefining much of what medicine aims to do.

CONCLUSION: AGEING AND THE DISCOURSE OF MEDICINE

Our study has moved in a somewhat different direction from prior research on patient–doctor communication in general and communication with older patients in particular. Conceptually, we have extended perspectives from narrative analysis in the humanities and social sciences to examine ideology, social control, underlying structure, and elements of medical discourse that appear marginal from the standpoint of medicine's technical goals. We have focused especially on problems of social context and the incomplete processing of these problems in medical encounters. Methodologically, after appraising the limitations of both quantitative and qualitative methods in studies of patient–doctor communication, we have applied a series of systematic criteria to guide our sampling techniques, transcription of recordings, and interpretation of transcripts.

Critical attention to contextual issues, despite their pertinence to the goals of overall patient care, remains marginal in such encounters. The technical world of medicine uses a speech genre, to cite Bakhtin's term, that does not lend itself well to a full exploration of contextual issues. In the encounters that we have studied, patients and doctors rarely discuss the social context in any detail, even when patients confront contextual issues that threaten their current and future well-being. Contextual issues related to bereavement, retirement, financial insecurity, social isolation, housing, transportation, and other life transitions affect patients to varying degrees. Although medical discourse encourages individual coping with these problems, it usually assumes that contextual constraints will persist in more or less unaltered form. When contextual issues do arise in medical encounters, the structure of discourse tends to cut off, to interrupt, and ultimately to marginalise their discussion, even though these issues create substantial day-to-day difficulties for older people.

Medical discourse also transmits subtle messages of ideology and social control. From the perspectives of Althusser's and Lukács' theories, this discourse fosters ideologies of stoicism and individualism in coping with contextual sources of adversity. A focus on reified, technical matters shifts attention from the totality of social relations that lie behind older people's difficulties. From the viewpoint of Foucault's work, professional surveillance of personal behaviour fosters social control, in such areas as the monitoring of potentially unsafe activities like driving and the modification of emotional responses to contextual conditions through psychotropic medication. That medical discourse conveys ideological assumptions and messages of social control, at least to some degree, remains dimly if at all perceived by older patients and physicians as they talk.

Patterns of medical discourse differ to some extent depending on the characteristics of patients and physicians (Davis, 1988; Fisher, 1986; Waitzkin, 1991a; Roter, Lipkin, and Korsgaard, 1991; Todd, 1989). From this perspective, we have found that social class, ethnicity, and race are associated with somewhat different speech patterns and contextual problems. For instance, less-educated, working-class patients take less initiative in questioning physicians about options and more often refer to financial limitations in dealing with contextual difficulties. Likewise, we have found certain associations with gender. Discourse with women patients tends to focus more on contextual problems of family life, while discourse with male patients touches to a greater extent on contextual difficulties related to work, especially when illness creates physical disability and a limited capacity to meet the physical demands of labor. Furthermore, in preliminary studies of differences between male and female physicians, we and others have found that female physicians tend to permit more extensive discussion of psychosocial problems, although interventions to change troubling contextual elements remain rare.

Issues related to ageing, of course, are not the only social problems that medical discourse mediates. From our studies of patient–doctor encounters, we have found that a broadly similar structure emerges as other social problems arise as well, especially those associated with gender roles and family life, stress and other illness-generating conditions of work, and social conditions that encourage self-destructive behaviours like smoking and substance use. In such instances, medical discourse tends to marginalise contextual problems for younger as well as older persons. At different stages of life, the contextual problems that appear in medical encounters vary somewhat. With younger men, for example, these problems often derive from challenging work demands, while for younger women, contextual issues involve not only work but also issues of gender roles and family life to a greater extent (Waitzkin, 1991a). On the other hand, we have found that problematic discourse about contextual issues becomes quite striking in encounters with older patients, whose biomedical and psychosocial difficulties tend to be closely intertwined.

To what extent should physicians intervene in the social context? As researchers, we recognised a certain ethical obligation to make suggestions for change. From this study, we believe that the processing of social problems in medical encounters with older patients warrants more critical attention. Elsewhere, suggestions for improving medical discourse by dealing with contextual difficulties have been spelled out (Waitzkin, 1989b; Mishler et al, 1989; West, 1984). Briefly, on the most limited level, we have argued that doctors should let patients tell their stories with far fewer interruptions, cut-offs, or returns to technical matters. Patients should have the chance to present their narratives in an open-ended way. When patients refer to personal troubles that derive from contextual issues, doctors should try not to marginalise these connections by reverting to a technical track.

Although such suggestions encourage more 'attentive patient care' (Mishler et al, 1989) and more acknowledgment of patients' contextual stories within medical encounters (Delbanco, 1992; Smith, 1991), some preliminary criteria also may prove helpful for physicians in deciding when and under what circumstances they could initiate, extend, or limit discussions about contextual matters (Table 3 presents a summary of these criteria). First, it is important to recognise that patients differ in their openness and desire for contextual discussion; physicians should take their cues here from the initiative of patients themselves in raising contextual concerns. For instance, in the above encounter, the patient introduces extensive contextual material, concerning loss of home and community, social isolation, transportation problems, financial insecurity, and nutri-

Table 3 Preliminary criteria to guide physicians in responding to contextual concerns in medical encounters

1. When patients initiate discussion of contextual issues, physicians should pursue this discussion rather than marginalising it and should offer contextual interventions.

2. When patients do not initiate discussion of contextual issues that clearly are present, physicians should inquire briefly if the patient wishes to discuss these issues and to take part in contextual interventions. Variability in patients' preferences, as well as patients' autonomy to refuse discussion and/or interventions, should be recognised.

3. In decisions about the time and costs devoted to contextual discussion, physicians and patients should consider evidence that contextual conditions affect treatment, prognosis, and functional capacity.

4. Practitioners should consider referral to social workers, psychologists, or psychiatrists, as opposed to dealing with contextual issues in the primary care setting.

5. Physicians should try to avoid the 'medicalisation' of social problems that require long-term reforms in social policy.

tional concerns. Rather than supportive listening alone, the physician here might respond more directly to these patient-initiated concerns, by mentioning interventions that could prove fairly easy to arrange: referral to seniors' organisations in the patient's new neighbourhood, home-care services including nursing and nutritional assistance, social work support to help with financial issues, information about transportation services, and efforts to coordinate care with the patient's family members and friends.

On the other hand, based on the lack of patient-initiated discussion of contextual concerns in other encounters, some patients might well prove resistant to such contextual interventions. Here, physicians could apply a second criterion that suggests several brief and non-intrusive questions inquiring whether the patient wishes to discuss specific contextual problems in more depth, and also whether the patient wants help in dealing with these problems. If the patient responds affirmatively, the physician then could ask if the patient wants to take part in contextual interventions such as home-care services, psychotherapy or other counselling, or increased social involvement through referral to seniors' or other organisations. Under these circumstances, physicians should remain sensitive to patients' differing desires and needs; some patients may prefer no discussion or contextual interventions.

In considering the time and costs devoted to contextual discussion and intervention, a third criterion suggests that doctors and patients consider effects of contextual conditions on treatment, prognosis, and functional capacity. Regarding the encounter described for instance, the geriatric literature provides extensive evidence that social isolation, lack of convenient transportation, financial insecurity, and inadequate nutritional support all worsen the functional capacity of older people (for example,

Reuben *et al*, 1992). When constraints or time and costs require prioritisation, existing evidence about the importance of specific contextual problems for health or physical functioning can help guide physicians and patients in targeting contextual issues for discussion and intervention.

As a fourth criterion, practitioners should consider referral to social workers, psychologists, or psychiatrists but should also evaluate whether specific patients would benefit more from dealing with contextual issues exclusively in the primary care setting. For some patients, experiences with mental health professionals prove unsatisfactory or financially prohibitive. If the patient agrees, for example, a doctor-initiated referral to a mental health professional might provide a way to address the socioemotional issues that could otherwise lead to prescriptions of a tranquilliser and antidepressant. On the other hand, mental health professionals' role in mediating socially caused distress has received criticism both outside and inside the psychiatric profession (Davis, 1986; 1988; Kupers, 1981; Laing and Esterson, 1964). Because many patients do not feel comfortable in seeking help from mental health professionals, primary care practitioners rather than psychiatrists will probably continue to see the majority of patients with emotional problems who present to physicians for care (Jencks, 1985; Kamerow, 1987; Wilkinson, 1986; Depression Guideline Panel, 1993). A broad mandate encouraging referrals to mental health professionals for people suffering from contextually based distress is not a solution. The education of primary care physicians, in both medical school and residency programs, should also devote much greater emphasis to contextual matters in medical encounters. The development of practitioners' skills in responding to contextual problems requires more attention to the nuances of referral procedures, as opposed to interventions that can be accomplished successfully within the primary care setting (Franco, 1993; Rush, 1993; Cohen-Cole *et al*, 1993).

As a fifth criterion, physicians should try to avoid the 'medicalisation' of social problems that require long-term reforms in social policy (Waitzkin, 1983). At the individual level, medicalisation can become a subtle process. For instance, there is a fine line between physicians' discussing contextual interventions and assuming professional control over broad arenas of patients' lives. Here it is important that physicians not imply that the solution of contextual difficulties ultimately becomes an individual's responsibility.

Clearly, it would be helpful if patients and doctors could turn to more readily available forms of assistance outside the medical arena to help in the solution of social problems, and current conditions do not evoke optimism about broader changes in medicine's social context. Such long-range changes will require time and financial resources, although not necessarily more than those now consumed in inefficient conversations that marginalise contextual issues. From our study, we are convinced that the contextual problems, especially those affecting older patients, warrant social policies to address unmet needs like those expressed in these encounters—needs for companionship, housing, transportation, nutritional services, financial aid, and support services focusing on life transitions like retirement and widowhood. Of course, these suggestions are not new. Yet it is evident that meaningful improvements in medical discourse between doctors and older patients will depend partly on such wider reforms.

There is some cross-national evidence, from observations in western Europe and Latin America, that greater availability of social support services facilitates a more explicit approach in medical discourse to contextual change for older patients. That is, in countries where services for older people are well organised and widely publicised, concrete opportunities for contextual intervention create more straightforward possibilities for dialogue (Waitzkin and Britt, 1989c). In the US, where contextual options are often limited, medical discourse confronts a narrower range of possibilities. Pending development of more responsive social policies, older patients and their doctors will continue to face the social context of ageing, through narratives that remain indirect, tense, or otherwise incomplete.

ACKNOWLEDGMENTS

This research was supported in part by grants from the National Center for Health Services Research (R01-HS02100), the National Institute on Aging (1-F32-AG 05438), the Division of Medicine of the US Public Health Service (PE–19154), the National Endowment for the Humanities (FA–22922), and the Academic Senate of the University of California, Irvine (Honorary Faculty Research Fellowship).

I am indebted to Stephany Borges, J. Hillis Miller, Mark Poster, Leslie Rabine, John Carlos Rowe, Jerome Tobis, and members of the Primary Care Research Seminar and Academic Geriatrics Resource Centre at the University of California, Irvine; and to Elaine Daunhauer, D.C. Peoples, and Georgia Taylor for technical help.

APPENDIX 1: METHODOLOGICAL DETAILS

In brief, a large (N=336) stratified random sample of patient–doctor encounters in internal medicine practices was selected. The study was approved by the institutional review committees at the University of California, Irvine, and at other institutions where data were gathered. Informed consent was obtained from patients and physicians who participated in the study. After encounters were recorded on audiotapes, questionnaires were administered to doctors and patients to obtain demographic, diagnostic, and attitudinal data, as well as information about the social context. The original recordings of medical discourse remain available in a database, to which other researchers can gain access. A smaller sample (N=50) was selected randomly from the larger sample of tapes for more intensive study.

For this phase of our research, the benefit of randomisation in constructing both the larger and smaller samples was to improve the representativeness of our narratives selected later for analysis; in addition, we hoped that random sampling would enhance our ability to arrive at interpretations that would be generalisable to encounters in similar settings and under similar conditions. On the other hand, we did not intend our use of randomised procedures for this phase of our work as part of an attempt to reach generalisable conclusions in the statistical sense. We also selected transcripts for publication in a non-random fashion by criteria that required the representation of variability in content and structure, as specified below.

After a training period, two transcriptionists used standard rules (reproduced in Appendix 2) to transcribe the full recorded discourse from all the tapes in the smaller sample. Although we decided operationally to use standard rules of transcription adapted from the work of other investigators, we also realised that transcription remains a problematic and never fully objective process that can proceed according to several different conceptual orientations (Mishler 1984, 1986a, 1991).

To assess the reliability of transcriptions according to the adopted convention, two research assistants separately read the transcripts as they listened to the original tapes of recorded interaction, before deciding on a final edited transcript to use for interpretation and later publication. Full transcripts of the encounters are available on request to University Microfilms International (300 North Zeeb Road, Ann Arbor, MI 48106; phone (800) 521 0600; research abstract number LD 10797).

For interpreting the transcripts, each research assistant scanned all the transcripts and noted those that dealt, in even minor ways, with the contextual issues under study; in addition to ageing, pertinent contextual issues included work; family life and gender roles; leisure, substance use, and other forms of pleasure seeking; and socioemotional problems. Within all transcripts, each research assistant flagged instances when either doctors or patients made statements that conveyed ideological content or expressed messages of social control, using the definitions given in the theoretical section above. The research assistants were to highlight nonverbal and quasi-verbal elements that might clarify a deeper structure lying beneath the surface elements of discourse. Interruptions, other cut-offs, de-emphases, shifts in tone of voice, silence, unresponsiveness to questions, and similar phenomena became special targets for this phase of the work. Here we were seeking the specific points in discourse when contextual issues might arise and how they might be either addressed directly or marginalised. By considering elements that were present, marginal, or absent, the research assistants were to prepare a preliminary structural outline or diagram that depicted how the medical discourse under study processed contextual issues.

After the two research assistants independently applied the above procedures to the transcripts, they and the senior members of the research group met together for several months to review the annotated transcripts and preliminary outlines or diagrams. We agreed to a surprising extent about the annotations that flagged instances of ideology and social control, as well as about which transcripts best illustrated the contextual issues of work, family life and gender roles, ageing, and so forth. On the other hand, we disagreed more about the underlying structures that we felt the transcripts revealed. In our meetings, we brainstormed about our disagreements and explicitly tried to avoid the discussion's being dominated by one person's views. We considered various quantitative ways to describe the degree to which we concurred or not (Viney and Bousfield, 1991); eventually, we decided that attaching a number would not convey either the strengths or the weaknesses in our group process of interpretation.

Throughout this process, we adopted a position influenced by a post-structuralism, that interpretation should accommodate ambiguity of meaning and should allow for alternative readings of the same textual material. Where members of the research group offered varying interpretations of a given transcript or passage, we noted these differences and included them in our working papers. This approach to ambiguity and alternative readings proves consistent with operational decisions about textual interpretations that other investigators in narrative analysis have reached independently (Bell, 1988; Riessman, 1990a; 1993). We also recognise the likelihood that other readers may produce distinct interpretations that we ourselves have not considered. To encourage further interpretive work, we have made the full transcripts accessible to researchers, as noted above.

After experimenting with many alternative formats, we took a mixed approach to presenting the transcripts and interpretations for publication. A summary of each transcript appears first. Within each interpretation, excerpts from the transcript help substantiate the interpretive arguments. Finally, full transcripts are available on request.

We dealt with variability of content and structure in the transcripts as follows. First, we grouped the 50 transcripts according to the predominant contextual arena, for instance the process of ageing, that the transcripts revealed. Within each contextual arena, we then selected two to four transcripts that illustrated a wide range of content and structure. Because of inherent space limitations in articles deriving from this phase of our work, we recognised that necessity of selecting a small number of transcripts for publication, based on substantive considerations rather than randomised selection. The substantive goal that determined this non-random selection was to present a wide range of content and structure, so that variability in the transcripts—including encounters that did not fully support our theoretical viewpoints—would be represented as accurately as possible. As noted above, although randomisation of the encounters sampled initially for in-depth study strengthened somewhat our ability to generalise about patient–doctor encounters, we recognised that this approach, coupled with the non-random selection of transcripts for publication, certainly would not permit statistical inferences from the traditional perspective of quantitative research.

From our sorting of transcripts, we also accumulated several in which we could not locate evidence of contextual concerns. Such encounters were 'negative cases', which did not yield any appreciable elements of content or structure that reflected the theoretical questions of interest. These 'non-problematic' encounters are considered at length in another publication (Waitzkin, 1991a).

APPENDIX 2: TRANSCRIPTION
CONVENTIONS (modified from Mishler 1984 and West, 1984)

1. Line Number 001 002 . . . 999
   Typescript lines are numbered sequentially from the first line.

2. Speaker D P
   D is doctor, P is patient. Speaker is noted at the first line of an utterance and at overlap points.

3. Turn/ Utterance Location
   Each new turn, that is, the beginnings of utterances by speakers in a sequence, generally starts at the beginning of a line in the transcript. Gaps and overlaps are indicated by appropriate markers.

4. Overlap [
   If a speaker begins to talk while the other is still talking, the point of beginning overlap is marked by a bracket [between the lines.

5. Silence . . . . (34)
   Silences within speaker utterances and between speakers are marked by a series of dots; each dot represents one second. Long pauses are denoted by number of seconds in parentheses. These silences are assigned to the previous speaker if they occur between speakers, that is, they are given the meaning of a post-utterance pause.

6. Unclarity (cold)/(. . .)
   Where a word(s) is heard but remains unclear, it is included in parentheses; if there are speaking sounds that are unintelligible, this is noted as dots within parentheses.

7. Speech features ?/.
   • Punctuation marks are used when intonation clearly marks the utterance as a question or as the end of a sentence.
   • If a word is stretched, this is marked by a colon, as in 'Wel:l'.
   • If a speaker breaks off in the middle of a word or phrase, this is marked by a hyphen -, as in 'haven't felt like-'.
   • ((softly)) ((change in tone of voice)). Double parentheses enclose descriptions, not transcribed utterances.
   • .hh, hh, eh-heh, .engh-henh. These are breathing and laughing indicators. A period followed by 'hh's' marks an inhalation. The 'hh's' alone stand for exhalation. The 'eh-heh' and '.engh- henh' are laughter syllables (inhaled when preceded by a period).
   • __ (Italics) or CAPS. Underline or capital letters are used if there is a marked increase in loudness and/or emphasis.

8. Names— (blanks)
   To protect confidentiality, blanks substitute for proper names.

9. Deletion in excerpt* * * (asterisks)
   Within excerpts from transcripts, three asterisks signify a passage from the original transcript that has been deleted from the excerpt.

REFERENCES

Adelman, R.D., M.G. Greene and R. Charon, 1991, 'Issues in physician–elderly patient interaction', *Ageing and Society*, 11: 127–48.

Althusser, L., 1971, 'Ideology and ideological state apparatuses', in *Lenin and Philosophy and Other Essays*. New York: Monthly Review Press.

Bakhtin, M.M. (Voloinov V.N.), 1973, *Marxism and the Philosophy of Language*, Cambridge: Harvard University Press.

——1981, *The Dialogic Imagination*, Austin: University of Texas Press.

——1986, *Speech Genres and Other Late Essays*, Austin: University of Texas Press.

Bell, S.E., 1988, 'Becoming a political woman: The reconstruction and interpretation of experience through stories'. In A.D. Todd and S. Fisher (eds), *Gender and Discourse: the power of talk*, Norwood: Ablex.

Brody, H., 1987, *Stories of Sickness*, New Haven: Yale University Press.

——1991, *The Healer's Power*, New Haven: Yale University Press.

Cappella, J.N., 1990, 'The method of proof by example in interaction analysis', *Communication Monographs*, 57: 236–42.

Cicourel, A., 1985, 'Text and discourse', *Annual Review of Anthropology*, 14: 159–85.

Charon, R., 1989, 'Doctor–patient/reader–writer: learning to find the text', *Soundings*, 2: 101–16.

Cohen-Cole, S.A., Boker, J., Bird, J., *et al*, 1993, 'Psychiatric education improves internists' knowledge: A three-year randomised, controlled evaluation', *Psychosomatic Medicine*, 55: 212–18.

Coles, R., 1989, *The Call of Stories*, Boston: Houghton, Mifflin.

Davis, K., 1986, 'The process of problem (re)formulation in psychotherapy', *Sociology of Health and Illness* 8:44–74.

——1988, *Power Under the Microscope: toward a grounded theory of gender relations in medical encounters*, Dortrecht: Foris.

Delbanco, T., 1992, 'Enriching the doctor–patient relationship by inviting the patient's perspective', *Annals of Internal Medicine*, 116: 414–18.

Depression Guideline Panel, 1993, *Depression in Primary Care*, Rockville: Agency for Health Care Policy and Research (AHCPR Publication No. 93–0550).

Derrida, J., 1976, *Of Grammatology*, Baltimore: Johns Hopkins University Press.

——1982, 'Tympan', in *Margins of Philosophy*, Chicago: University of Chicago Press.

Dreher, B.B., 1987, *Communication Skills for Working with Elders*, New York: Springer.

Eagleton, T., 1978, *Criticism and Ideology*, London: Verso.

——1993, *The Crisis of Contemporary Culture*, New York: Oxford University Press.

Fisher, S., 1986, *In the Patient's Best Interest: women and the politics of medical decisions*. New Brunswick: Rutgers University Press.

Fisher, S. and Davis, K., 1993, *Negotiating at the Margins: the gendered discourse of power and resistance*, New Brunswick: Rutgers University Press.

Foucault, M., 1975, *The Birth of the Clinic*, New York: Vintage.

——1977, *Discipline and Punish*, New York: Pantheon.

——1978, 1985, 1987, *The History of Sexuality*, vol. 1–3, New York: Pantheon.

Franco, K.S., 1993, 'Consultation-liaison elective for primary care residents', *General Hospital Psychiatry*, 15: 71–6.

Garfinkel, H., 1967, *Studies in Ethnomethodology*, Englewood Cliffs: Prentice-Hall.

Gee, J.P., 1991, 'A linguistic approach to narrative', *Journal of Narrative and Life History*, 1: 15–39.

Giddens, A., 1986, 'Action, subjectivity, and the constitution of meaning', *Social Research*, 53: 529–45.

Greene, M.G., Adelman, R., Charon, R. and Hoffman, S., 1986, 'Ageism in the medical encounter: An exploratory study of the doctor–patient relationship', *Language and Communication*, 6: 113–24.

Greene, M.G., Hoffman, S., Charon, R. and Adelman, R., 1987, 'Psychosocial concerns in the medical encounter: A comparison of the interactions of doctors with their old and young patients', *Gerontologist*, 27: 164–8.

Greene, M.G., Adelman, R.D., Charon, R. and Friedmann, E., 1989, 'Concordance between physicians and their older and younger patients in the primary care medical encounter', *Gerontologist*, 29: 808–13.

Haug, M.R., 1979, 'Doctor patient relationships and the older patient', *Journal of Gerontology*, 34: 852–60.

Haug, M.R. and Ory, M.G., 1987, 'Issues in elderly patient–provider interactions', *Research on Aging*, 9: 3–44.

Jakobson, R., 1985, *Verbal Art, Verbal Sign, Verbal Time*, Minneapolis: University of Minnesota Press.

Jameson, F., 1981. *The Political Unconscious: narrative as a socially symbolic act*, Ithaca: Cornell University Press.

——1991, *Postmodernism, or the Cultural Logic of Late Capitalism*, Durham: Duke University Press.

Jencks, S.F., 1985, 'Recognition of mental distress and diagnosis of mental disorder in primary care', *Journal of the American Medical Association*, 253: 1903–07.

Kamerow, D.B., 1987, 'Is screening for mental health problems worthwhile in family practice?', *Journal of Family Practice*, 25: 181–87.

Kleinman, A., 1988, *The Illness Narratives*, New York: Basic Books.

Kupers, T.A., 1981, *Public Therapy*, New York: Free Press.

Labov, W. and Fanshel, D., 1977, *Therapeutic Discourse: psychotherapy as conversation*, New York: Academic Press.

Laing, R.D. and Esterson, A., *Sanity, Madness and the Family*. Baltimore: Penguin.

Lévi-Strauss, C., 1967, *Structural Anthropology*, Garden City: Anchor.

Lincoln, Y.S., and Guba. E.G., 1985, *Naturalistic Inquiry*, Beverly Hills: Sage.

Lukács, G., 1971a, *History and Class Consciousness*, Cambridge: MIT Press.

——1971b, *The Theory of the Novel*, Cambridge: MIT Press.

Lynch, M. and Woolgar, S., 1990, *Representation in Scientific Practice*, Cambridge: MIT Press.

Marshall, V.W., 1981, 'Physician characteristics and relationships with older patients'. In M.R. Haug (ed.), *Elderly Patients and Their Doctors*, New York: Springer.

Mishler, E.G., 1984, *The Discourse of Medicine: dialectics of medical interviews*, Norwood: Ablex.

——1986a, *Research Interviewing: context and narrative*, Cambridge: Harvard University Press.

——1986b, 'The analysis of interview-narratives', in *Narrative Psychology: the storied nature of human conduct*, New York: Praeger, 233–55.

——1991, 'Representing discourse: The rhetoric of transcription', *Journal of Narrative and Life History*, 1: 255–80.

Mishler, E.G., Clark, J.A., Ingelfinger, J. and Simon, M.P., 1989, 'The language of attentive patient care: A comparison of two medical interviews', *Journal of General Internal Medicine*, 4: 25–35.

Mitchell, W.J.T. (ed.), 1981, *On Narrative*, Chicago: University of Chicago Press.

Mitchell, W.J.T., 1990, 'Representation'. In F. Lentricchia and T. McLaughlin (eds), *Critical Terms for Literary Study*, Chicago: University of Chicago Press.

Polkinghorne, D., 1988, *Narrative Knowing and the Human Sciences*, Albany: State University of New York Press.

Reuben, D.B., Rubenstein, L.V., Hirsch, S.H. and Hays, R.D., 1992, 'Value of functional status as a predictor of mortality: Results of a prospective study', *American Journal of Medicine*, 93: 63–9.

Riessman, C.K., 1990a, *Divorce Talk: women and men make sense of personal relationships*, New Brunswick: Rutgers University Press.

——1990b, 'Strategic uses of narrative in the presentation of self and illness', *Social Science and Medicine*, 30: 1195–2000.

——1993, *Narrative Analysis*, Newbury Park: Sage.

Rosenwald, G. and Ochberg, R.L. (eds), 1992. *Storied Lives: the cultural politics of self-understanding*, New Haven: Yale University Press.

Rost, K. and Roter, D., 1987, 'Predictors of recall of medication regimens and recommendations for lifestyle change in elderly patients', *Gerontologist*, 27: 510–15.

Rost, K., Carter, W. and Inui, T., 1989, 'Introduction of information during the initial medical visit: consequences for patient follow-through with physician recommendations for medication', *Social Science and Medicine*, 28: 315–21.

Roter, D.L., and Hall, J.A., 1989, 'Studies of doctor–patient interaction', *Annual Review of Public Health*, 10: 163–80.

Roter, D.L., Lipkin, M.Jr. and Korsgaard, A., 1991, 'Sex differences in patients' and physicians' communication during primary care medical visits', *Medical Care*, 29: 1083–93.

Rush, A.J., 1993, 'Clinical practice guidelines: Good news, bad news, or no news?', *Archives of General Psychiatry*, 50: 483–90.

Saussure, F. de, 1986 (1915), *Course in General Linguistics*, La Salle: Open Court.

Schutz, A. and Luckmann, T., 1989, *The Structures of the Life-world*, Evanston: Northwestern University Press.

Sennett, R. and Cobb, J., 1972, *The Hidden Injuries of Class*, New York: Vintage.

Smith, R.C. and Hoppe, R.B., 1991, 'The patient's story: Integrating the patient- and physician-centred approaches to interviewing', *Annals of Internal Medicine*, 115: 470–77.

Strauss, A. and Corbin, J., 1990, *Basics of Qualitative Research: grounded theory procedures and techniques*, Newbury Park: Sage.

Taussig, M.T., 1980, 'Reification and the consciousness of the patient', *Social Science and Medicine*, 14B: 3–13.

Todd, A.D., 1989, *Intimate Adversaries: cultural conflict between doctors and women patients*, Philadelphia: University of Pennsylvania Press.

Treichler, P.A., Frankel, R.M., Kramarae, C., Zoppi, K. and Beckman, H.B., 1984,

'Problems and problems: Power relationships in a medical encounter'. In C. Kramarae, M. Schultz, and W.M. O'Barr (eds), *Language and Power*, Beverly Hills: Sage.

Viney, L.L., and Bousfield, L., 1991, 'Narrative analysis: a method of psychosocial research for AIDS-affected people', *Social Science and Medicine*, 32: 757–65.

Waitzkin, H., 1983, *The Second Sickness: contradictions of capitalist health care*, New York: Free Press.

——1984, 'Doctor–patient communication: Clinical implications of social scientific research', *Journal of the American Medical Association*, 252: 2441–6.

——1985, 'Information giving in medical care', *Journal of Health and Social Behaviour*, 26: 81–101.

——1986, 'Research on doctor–patient communication: Implications for practice', *Internist*, 27(7): 7–10.

——1989a, 'A critical theory of medical discourse: Ideology, social control, and the processing of social context in medical encounters', *Journal of Health and Social Behaviour*, 30: 220–39.

——1989b, 'Changing the structure of medical discourse: Implications of cross-national comparisons', *Journal of Health and Social Behaviour*, 30: 436–49.

——1990, 'On studying the discourse of medical encounters: A critique of quantitative and qualitative methods and a proposal for reasonable compromise', *Medical Care*, 28: 473–88.

——1991a, *The Politics of Medical Encounters: how patients and doctors deal with social problems*, New Haven: Yale University Press.

——1991b, 'Text, social context, and the structure of medical discourse', *Current Research on Occupations and Professions*, 6: 79–108.

——1993, 'Processing narratives of self-destructive behaviour in routine medical encounters: health promotion, disease prevention, and the discourse of health care', *Social Science and Medicine*, 36: 1121–36.

Waitzkin, H. and Britt, T., 1989, 'A critical theory of medical discourse: how patients and health professionals deal with social problems', *International Journal of Health Services*, 19: 577–97.

Wertsch, J.V., 1991, *Voices of the Mind: a sociocultural approach to mediated action*, Cambridge: Harvard University Press.

West, C., 1984, *Routine Complications: troubles with talk between doctors and patients*, Bloomington: Indiana University Press.

Wilkinson, G., 1986, *Overview of Mental Health Practices in Primary Care Settings, with Recommendations for Further Research*, Washington: U.S. Government Printing Office (DHHS Pub. No. (ADM) 86–1467).

Young, K.G., 1987, *Taleworlds and Storyrealms: the phenomenology of narrative*, Dordrecht: Nijhoff.

Zola, I.K., 1991, 'Bringing our bodies and ourselves back in: Reflections on a past, present, and future "medical sociology"', *Journal of Health and Social Behaviour*, 32: 1–16.

21

PRIMARY CARE: ISSUES FOR GENERAL PRACTICE RESEARCH

Peter Mudge

In a discussion about ethical issues in general practice research, it is difficult to define a boundary between the ethical issues particular to clinical practice and those relating to research in general practice. It is quite appropriate that both should be part of a continuum. Nevertheless, there are significant difficulties confronting primary care research, and this essay will address these from the perspective of a general practice researcher who has been involved from the beginning with the Australian General Practice Evaluation Program—a research and evaluation program funded by the Department of Human Services and Health.

The ethical dimension has always been seen as an essential element in clinical practice from the time of Hippocrates, the first known writer to have placed on record an ethical standard for the medical profession. A number of changes in society have in the past twenty years prompted a renewed interest and debate about medical matters and this debate has occurred in both the professional and lay press. The most important influencing factors have been improved technology in medicine, with an increased doctor and patient awareness and expectation and, related to this, an increasing concern by patients for what might be called 'patient rights' but are really matters relating to the ethical principle of autonomy (but not to that principle alone).

Clinical decision making in general practice illustrates very well the 'microethical' dilemmas discussed by Paul Komesaroff in this volume. In addition, the ongoing nature of the care provided to individuals within family and community settings makes the issue of communication, and the research associated with it, an essential element of concern, as outlined in its social context by Howard Waitzkin in the previous essay. It illustrates how difficult it is to explore new paradigms in medicine which are regarded with suspicion and sometimes frank hostility by medical peers in other disciplines.

THE DOCTOR-PATIENT RELATIONSHIP

While there is broad agreement (at least within the profession) concerning confidentiality of medical information, this remains only one of several important issues, chief of which is the concern of patients for autonomy. Here there are no clear guidelines for decision making—no simple theoretical model encompasses the richness and variability of the physician's role in the intricacies of clinical encounters.

Christie and Hoffmaster (1986: 64) explore the 'normal' boundaries of the family physician's role and argue that there are no clear limits.

> The conflict between patient autonomy and patient welfare, then, could be a dispute about the moral responsibility of various means to the achievement of an end, not the end itself. Respecting autonomy, in other words, might not preclude a physician from becoming involved with patient welfare. It merely sets limits, moral limits in this case, on the methods a physician may use to promote patient welfare.

However, patients ought to possess the knowledge, authority and power to make decisions about their own care. Beauchamp and Childress (1983: 59) define autonomy as 'the form of personal liberty of action where the individual determines his or her own course of action in accordance with a plan chosen by himself or herself'. But the therapeutic benefit of the doctor–patient relationship (which is supported by measurement of the placebo effect) derives from the *control* of the physician—that is, the ethical boundary has been moved to allow the doctor to breach the autonomy of the patient. The illness role is always a dependency role to a greater or lesser extent. Moral principles remain, then, as a guideline of behaviour, and where apparent conflicts arise and practical solutions are arrived at in the setting of clinical reality, then flexibility of thinking and reasoning are needed. Despite the intuitive appeal of such moral reasoning, competence in this, as in other clinical skills, must be taught at the bedside by precept and example and should form a significant strand of modern medical education. The argument that juries mostly make 'right' moral judgments cannot be extrapolated to clinical care. There is often for the clinician a conflict of duty and justice in the care of complex cases. Patients must be protected from themselves and the system itself, where it is too easy to get caught in an expensive 'merry-go-round' of so-called expert care. The general practitioner must remain at all times the advocate of the patient in the supervision of his or her care.

241

Limiting life-sustaining treatment ('living and letting die')

The increasing desire of patients to be involved in decisions about their care, and of the terminally ill to be cared for at home, together with the availability of technology to 'suspend' death, has led to the formulations of decisions about 'brain death' by the World Medical Association and much argument about tragic individual cases like that of Karen Quinlan in the US. The general practitioner should logically be involved in these decisions, especially where they occur in hospitals. Who better, after the family, to make an informed statement about the patient's quality of life?

The allocation of resources

The ethical principle of justice in the allocation of resources has recently been the subject of reports from expert committees (for example, Black *et al*, 1982; NHMRC, 1990). With the increasing availability of technology such as organ transplantation and complex organ imaging, the setting of guidelines for the profession, and politicians, will become more difficult. The debate—at times acrimonious even within the profession—will become intense. For the general practitioner, who must maintain an increasing level of competence balanced with an awareness of current issues in cognisance of the principle of beneficence for his or her patients, the position becomes complex indeed. How can a service like aerial retrieval of patients in an isolated rural area like western Queensland compare with 'new hips for old' or with resources spent on lowering cholesterol levels largely in middle class males who might benefit in small proportion to cost?

General practice research: an emerging discipline

The ethical issues in clinical care as outlined form a background to any consideration about general practice research, and are shared by other clinical disciplines. There are some problems which are particular to general practice, however, which I will now discuss in some detail.

A number of ethical problems relating to this issue have been brought into sharp focus for me and the other members of a committee responsible for advising the Australian Department of Human Services and Health about the administration and distribution of a $A4.7 million General Practice Evaluation Program. This program began in 1990 in response to a Senate committee of inquiry's criticisms of the lack of data in Australia about general practice. That committee initiated a program to measure proposed changes and thereby make judgments of 'good' or 'less good' in terms regarding the effect of these changes on the quality of care (and, by inference, on value for money) (Doessel, 1990).

The committee came quickly upon a number of serious problems in the development of this program. First, there was little or no infrastructure available for general practice researchers. It is clearly unethical to allow research to proceed in the absence of infrastructure. University departments are desperately short of staff—a situation which has improved very little in twenty years. The nature of general practice, with its heterogeneity and wide geographical dispersal, made the practices themselves unsuitable as a focus for research on any scale. (That is not to deny the body of good work done by a small number of highly motivated people.) The potential for collaborative clinical research in general practice remains to be realised. General practitioners have been guided in the past by clinical acumen (which research has shown is not always reliable) or by guidelines and protocols handed down in a rather paternalistic fashion by specialists and hospital clinics. Some of the latter have been quite inappropriate, since the case-mix of patients which are managed by general practitioners is significantly different.

The second problem is related to the first and forms part of the infrastructure deficit—the lack of qualified peers in the discipline. This has made it very difficult for the committee to assess the value of projects submitted for funding by the process of external review. This will also be a problem when, with further development of the program, the projects are prepared for reporting in the literature. It is already difficult in Australia and elsewhere to get good studies done in general practice settings reported in the available journals. There is an ethical imperative to publicise results, and this may be a serious problem for us in the near future.

The third dilemma we encountered on the committee relates to the interplay, in funding decisions, between considerations of method and relevance to practice. The dilemma of trying to encourage new researchers with relatively unformed ideas and thus add to the infrastructure of research for the discipline is matched against the ethical concerns of inappropriate use of funds by young researchers, no matter how worthy of encouragement. A further dilemma occurred when such projects had also to be seen by institutional ethics committees, thereby leading to duplication of effort and resources. One project, whose topic related to a sensitive behavioural area, was rejected by the institutional ethics committee which reviewed it. This committee's reports were distinctly unhelpful and caused unacceptable delays in the study.

The fourth, and perhaps the most relevant, is the problem of which methodologies are appropriate for general practice research. As an emerging discipline, it needs a new intellectual paradigm (Kuhn, 1970). The tools of hospital-based clinical medicine, namely epidemiology and statistics, are only part of the answer. The science and art of the anthropologist, behaviouralist and sociologist are at least as important here. It is unethical

243

to use inappropriate methods to attempt to answer the important questions which relate to the management of patients in general practice.

The General Practice Evaluation Program Committee has, in the past four years, embarked on an ambitious series of strategies to attempt to address the infrastructure dilemma by holding workshops for researchers on methodology, and setting up a feedback mechanism for referees, some of whom have had to 'learn on the job'. We are also funding a training strategy for both masters and PhD students. Unless we are able to develop an infrastructure as well as a research program, there is a significant risk that the value of our output will be diminished.

We can be judged as unethical in our approach if we cannot keep all these issues together in our deliberations for the future of this and other research programs for general practice.

REFERENCES

Beauchamp, T.L. and Childress, J.F., 1983, *Principles of Biomedical Ethics*, 2nd Edition, New York: Oxford University Press.

Black, D.A.K., Morris, J.N., Smith, C., *et al*, 1982, *Inequities in Health: the Black report*, Harmondsworth: Penguin.

Christie, R.J. and Hoffmaster, C.B., 1986, *Ethical Issues in Family Medicine*, New York: Oxford University Press.

Doessel, D.P. (ed.), 1990, *Towards Evaluation in General Practice: a workshop on vocational registration*, Canberra: Department of Community Services and Health.

Kuhn, T.S. 1970, *The Structure of Scientific Revolutions*, 2nd Edition, Chicago: University of Chicago Press.

National Health and Medical Research Council, 1990, *Discussion Paper on Ethics and Resource Allocation in Health Care: Report on the Health Care Committees Working Party*, Canberra: Australian Government Publishing Service.

CONCLUSION

CHOOSING THE ETHICAL RESEARCH PATH

Jeanne Daly

The contributors to this volume have presented a range of ways of doing good, scientific and ethical research. When a researcher faces a research task, there is often no self-evident way of proceeding. The particular research problem has to be considered in selecting the best research method. In addition, the social context in which the research is going to be carried out has to be scrutinised to ensure that any potential harm is minimised. Each research process raises its own specific problems. As a result, universal guidelines are not always useful and may, in some cases, distort the research agenda. The responsible researcher can therefore be seen as engaging in a quest for Truth through a confusing terrain in which standard guidelines are of dubious benefit.

THE QUEST OF THE RESPONSIBLE RESEARCHER

In the seventeenth century, John Bunyan wrote a book called *The Pilgrim's Progress*. It is an allegorical tale of the search for the Celestial City by Christian and, later, Christiana, a man and woman armed with Christian values. This book is part of a long tradition in religious texts in which the experience of travellers tests a set of values which aim to guide them to the good life. In this century we are more concerned with secular values, but the religious imagery of the quest persists. The analogy I wish to draw is that the path to scientific Truth, like the path to the Celestial City, is beset by a multitude of obstacles. Travellers can draw on established texts for guidance, but they will also require responses to what they find along the way:

This book it chalketh out before thine eyes

The man that seeks the everlasting prize
It shows you whence he comes, whither he goes,
What he leaves undone, also what he does:
It also shows you how he runs and runs,
Till he unto the Gate of Glory comes.
   It shows too who sets out for life amain,
As if the everlasting crown they would attain:
Here also you may see the reason why
They lose their labour, and like fools do die.
   This book will make a traveller of thee,
If by its counsel thou wilt ruled be . . .

Christian and Christiana are reluctant travellers at first. Christiana is discouraged from ever setting out by Timorous. Temptations and wrong paths abound. Worldly-Wiseman urges travellers to settle in the village Morality, tended by Legality, who turns out to be a cheat, and his son Civility, a hypocrite. Hopeful leads straight into the hands of Giant Despair, and there are the temptations of Vanity Fair to be resisted. Evangelist urges trust in the literal text of the Bible; Good Will and Faithful help—but the path to Truth is not an easy one.

On her quest, Christiana meets Valour-for-Truth, to whom obstacles appear as 'mere nothings'. He is secure in his goals and, in illustrations, he is usually depicted as holding aloft a flaming sword. If we substitute 'scientist' for 'pilgrim', he might well seem a role model for the questing researcher who is confident in methodological guides:

Who would true valour see
Let him come hither;
One here will constant be,
Come wind, come weather.
There's no discouragement,
Shall make him once relent,
His first avowed intent,
To be a pilgrim.

Hobgoblin nor foul fiend,
Can daunt his spirit:
He knows, he at the end,
Shall life inherit.
Then fancies fly away,
He'll fear not what men say,
He'll labour night and day,
To be a pilgrim.

To social scientists working in the health field, some of our colleagues from the 'basic' sciences seem to operate from just such a position of confidence based on their trust in their scientific method and in the ultimate benefits of their science to mankind. It is worth noting here that, although Valour-for-Truth is seen as praiseworthy, he is wounded in a battle with Wild-head, Inconsiderate and Pragmatic. The modern history of scientific research might lead us to add Fraud and Deceit to the list of temptations scientists face! The problem of the scientific analogues of Valour-for-Truth, we might argue, is that they rely too heavily on their swords, their traditional scientific procedures, for cutting their way through obstacles.

Many researchers across the spectrum of health research find that they have to approach their research task with more diffidence. The danger they face in calling into question the route chosen by Valour-for-Truth is that of being labelled as hobgoblins. This is where ethics committees are of benefit to research and the researcher—they provide a formal means of focusing the attention of researchers on the fine moral detail of the research task. On the other hand, it is the task of the researcher to engage in the quest for a responsible, ethical research process. If ethics review committees act as if there is only one rigidly defined Path to Truth (especially if this definition is based on rigid principles contained in a set of guidelines), they may be sending an over-confident researcher off on a wrong track, with the quest itself abandoned.

In research terms, we may be able to capture Truth using traditional, familiar methods but we would do well to recognise that we may need a wider, perhaps more subtle collection of tools:

> You see the way the fisherman doth take
> To catch the fish, what engines doth he make?
> Behold! how he engageth all his wits
> Also his snares, lines, angles, hooks and nets.
> Yet fish there be, that neither hook, nor line,
> Nor snare, nor net, nor engine can make thine;
> They must be groped for, and be tickled too,
> Or they will not be catched, what e'er you do.
>   How doth the fowler seek to catch his game?
> By divers means, all which one cannot name.
> His guns, his nets, his lime twigs, light and bell:
> He creeps, he goes, he stands; yea, who can tell
> Of all his postures? Yet there's none of these
> Will make him master of what fowls he please.

Many health researchers therefore travel a different scientific path from Valour-for-Truth. They are more like the fowler and the fisherman. Following Bunyan, they recognise a diversity of tools and paths, including both the bold and the more diffident. In more concrete terms, we need to recognise the value of positivist research techniques as well as methods that are low-key, tentative in their assumptions, more based on understanding than on control, more dependent on human than on technological skills. Sometimes it is *necessary* to speak to people instead of drawing their blood; social contexts sometimes have to be *studied* instead of being excluded as confounding variables.

To return to Bunyan's allegorical tale, the definition of guidelines for good research is no less complicated than devising guidelines for the good life.

> What danger is the pilgrim in,
> How many are his foes,
> How many are the ways to sin,
> No living mortal knows.

No path to good research will be without numerous delusions and seductions. Given these pitfalls for the unwary, guidance may be needed along our way. Since we do not necessarily all tread the same path, the assumptions which underlie this guidance, and the aim of its rules and regulations, are bound to be the source of misunderstanding, even conflict. Finally, all researchers, whatever their persuasion or chosen path, should be prepared to debate the way they go about their task without rancour or recrimination.

John Bunyan wrote *The Pilgrim's Progress* in prison, where he was sent for his support of the Puritan view of religion. We are in the fortunate situation of being able to debate and disagree with research rules and regulations without risking such extreme sanctions.

REFERENCES

Bunyan, J., 1987, *The Pilgrim's Progress*, London: Penguin Books.

INDEX